Contemporary Britain

Second Edition

John McCormick

palgrave
macmillan

First edition 2003
Second edition published 2007 by
PALGRAVE MACMILLAN
Houndmills, Basingstoke, Hampshire RG21 6XS and
175 Fifth Avenue, New York, N.Y. 10010
Companies and representatives throughout the world

PALGRAVE MACMILLAN is the global academic imprint of
the Palgrave Macmillan division of St. Martin's Press, LLC and of
Palgrave Macmillan Ltd. Macmillan® is a registered trademark in
the United States, United Kingdom and other countries. Palgrave is a
registered trademark in the European Union and other countries.

ISBN-13: 978–0–2300–0213–5   hardback
ISBN-10: 0–2300–0213–7   hardback
ISBN-13: 978–0–2300–0214–2   paperback
ISBN-10: 0–2300–0214–5   paperback

This book is printed on paper suitable for recycling and made from
fully managed and sustained forest sources.

A catalogue record for this book is available from the British Library.

A catalog record for this book is available from the Library of Congress.

10 9 8 7 6 5 4 3 2 1
16 15 14 13 12 11 10 09 08 07

Printed and bound in China

Contents

List of Illustrations, Maps, Figures, Tables and Boxes

Illustrations

Preface and Acknowledgements

This is a book about Britain, written for anyone looking for a brief and accessible guide to this remarkable country. Like others in the *Contemporary States and Societies* series, it makes no assumptions about prior knowledge: it provides the key facts and figures that are needed to place Britain in context with other countries – especially its European neighbours – but it also ties the facts together with explanatory analysis. It is deliberately short and concise, and makes no claims to being comprehensive. If it can help its readers better appreciate the key themes and concepts in British political, social and economic life, dispel some of the myths that too often interfere with an understanding of the country and its people, and offer suggestions for further research, it will have succeeded in its mission.

I am a political scientist, but I have tried to make sure that all the key dimensions of life in Britain are covered, from history to geography, economics, society, culture, and politics. My background and credentials will shed light on the approach, and on my arguments and conclusions. I was born in Britain and am still a British citizen, but I have spent most of my life living somewhere else. I was brought up in Kenya, went to boarding school in Britain, attended university in South Africa, and then lived in London from the winter of discontent in early 1979 to the height of Thatcherism in 1986. Since then I have lived in the United States, although I return to Britain at least once every year, most recently spent the second half of 2005 on sabbatical at the University of Sussex, and still closely follow developments in Britain. I see Britain both from near and from far, and because I come and go I am more conscious of the changes that have come to Britain than if I lived there full-time. My approach is also inevitably coloured by my experiences in the United States, by the fact that I specialize in comparative politics, and by my interest in the European Union. All of this gives me a peculiar (idiosyncratic?) perspective on my home country.

The first edition of this book was published in 2003, and was bought by readers in many countries around the world, especially in Europe and North America. It is always good to know that a book has struck a chord, and I hope this second edition will be as useful as the first. As well as taking account of new scholarship published since 2003, it has been thoroughly updated and amended to take account of the fallout from the 2003 invasion of Iraq, the enlargement of the European Union in 2004–07, the 2005 general election, and Tony Blair's departure in 2007. The arguments have been refined, new data has been inserted (most of it from the Office of National Statistics), new boxes and tables have been added, and every chapter has been lengthened by about 10 per cent.

It was my publisher Steven Kennedy who first suggested that I write the book, and he has helped guide its development with his usual good humour and fine judgement, so it is to him that I owe my primary gratitude. My thanks also to an anonymous reviewer who looked over and commented on Chapter 3, and to Stephen Wenham and Brian Morrison for their fine work on the production. This second edition is heavily influenced by my 2005 sabbatical, which gave me a chance to experience the new Britain for six months. My wife Leanne made the transition easily, and probably learned more than she had ever anticipated about the British education system and the National Health Service. And my sons Ian and Stuart enjoyed my ongoing attempts to acculturate them into the ways of their other homeland. To all three, this second edition is dedicated with much love.

JOHN MCCORMICK

The author and publishers are grateful to the following for permission to use copyright material: Panos Pictures for Illustrations 3.1, 3.3, 5.1, 5.4, 6.2, 8.1; PA Photos for Illustrations 1.2, 1.3, 1.4, 3.2, 4.1, 4.3, 5.3, 6.3, 7.2, 7.3, 8.2, 8.3; Leanne McCormick for Illustration 7.1. Illustrations 1.1, 2.1, 2.2, 2.3, 2.4, 4.2, 5.2, 6.1 are by the author. Every effort has been made to trace all copyright-holders of third-party materials included in this work, but if any have been inadvertently overlooked the publishers will be pleased to make the necessary arrangement at the first opportunity.

List of Abbreviations

BBC	British Broadcasting Corporation
CAP	Common Agricultural Policy
EEC	European Economic Community
EFTA	European Free Trade Association
EU	European Union
GDP	gross domestic product
IRA	Irish Republican Army
ITV	Independent Television
MP	Member of Parliament
NATO	North Atlantic Treaty Organization
NHS	National Health Service
OECD	Organization for Economic Cooperation and Development
PR	proportional representation
RUC	Royal Ulster Constabulary
SDP	Social Democratic Party
SNP	Scottish National Party
TUC	Trades Union Congress
VAT	value added tax

Notes: For convenience, the terms 'Britain' and 'British' are used throughout, even though the book is about the United Kingdom. Currency conversions are made at the rate of €1.50 and $1.90 to the pound, the prevailing figures in mid-2006.

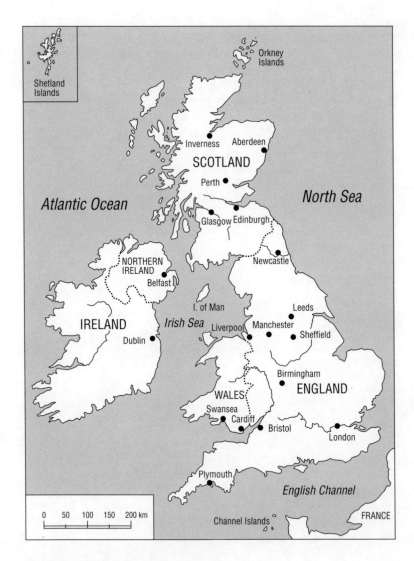

Map 0.1   Political features of the UK

Introduction

Britain is one of the most influential countries in world history. Out of that small cluster of islands off the northwest coast of the European continent came three developments that literally changed the world: the industrial revolution, the parliamentary system of government, and the English language. It is impossible to talk of economic change without referring back to the inventions that spawned the industrial revolution, and the impact of the writings of Adam Smith and John Maynard Keynes on our ideas about capitalism. It is impossible to talk of political change without referring back to the origins of the British democratic model, and the impact of the writings of Thomas Hobbes, John Locke, John Stuart Mill, and others. And it would be difficult for the citizens of different countries to exchange their views without the help of English, which has become the international language of business, communications, diplomacy and – increasingly – everyday conversation.

For these reasons alone, Britain is an important subject of study. But there are other motives as well: life is all about change, and few societies have seen such dramatic changes in the last 200 years as Britain. It has one of the oldest continuously functioning political systems in the world, yet the character of that system has been altered in response to philosophical and popular pressures. It once had the world's biggest economy, yet has found itself having to adapt to a post-imperial economic environment coloured by competition from the United States, Japan and its bigger European neighbours. It has a long history of social stability, yet British society has undergone a fundamental reordering in the last two generations. The signs of change continue to be found everywhere:

- in the growing racial, religious, national and cultural diversity of British society
- in the redefinition of the class system that for so long determined how Britons related to each another, but which has been diluted by

1

improved education, the rise of the middle class, the growth of the consumer society, and by new levels of affluence and social mobility

- in demographic shifts as the British live longer, as the idea of the family is redefined, and as Britons move away from the old assumptions of the welfare state towards a stakeholder society in which benefits are determined by the extent to which individuals have played by the rules
- in the altered balance of power among government institutions as the executive becomes more powerful and Europe becomes more influential
- in the changing relationship between local and national government, and in the rebirth of Scottish, Welsh, Irish and even English nationalism, which has redefined the meaning of 'Britain' and 'Britishness'
- in the new attitudes of voters towards government, in the questions raised about the nature of the electoral system and the balance among the major political parties, and in the rise of alternative channels through which citizens can express their views on politics
- in dramatic developments in communications technology, with satellite, cable and digital options changing the character of television, and the internet revolutionizing the way that people communicate
- in shifts in the direction of economic policy, from the interventionist approaches of the postwar years to the free-market approaches introduced in the 1980s by the Thatcher government, and perpetuated by her successors
- in the redefinition of Britain's place in the world as it has moved from being a global and imperial power to a regional and European power, and as it asks itself questions about whether its future lies with the European Union, the Atlantic Alliance, or both.

In the chapters that follow, the causes of these changes will be examined, and an attempt made to understand the effects on contemporary Britain. Along the way, the book makes two core arguments. First, it rejects claims of the decline of Britain as overstated. Since the 1960s and 1970s, there has been a bandwagon effect among academics, journalists, political leaders, who often bemoan the loss of Britain's pre-eminent economic position in the world, complain that the British political system has failed to meet the needs of the citizens

Table 0.1   Quick facts about Britain

Official name:	United Kingdom of Great Britain and Northern Ireland
Capital:	London
Area:	244,103 sq km (94,249 square miles)
Population:	60.2 million
Population density:	246 per sq km (650 per square mile)
Population growth rate:	0.6%
Languages:	Overwhelmingly English, with some regional languages (Welsh, Gaelic)
Religions:	Predominantly Christian (mainly Anglican, Catholic and Presbyterian), with growing Muslim and Hindu minorities
GDP (2004):	$2,124 billion (€1,570 billion, £1,067 billion)
Per capita GNP:	$33,630 (€24,852, £16,900)
Distribution of GNP:	70% services, 29% industry, 1% agriculture
Urban population:	89%
Literacy:	99%
Infant mortality:	6 per 1,000 live births
Life expectancy:	78.5 years
Government type:	Parliamentary democracy with a constitutional monarchy
Administration:	Unitary
Executive:	Prime Minister and Cabinet
Legislature:	Bicameral Houses of Parliament; House of Lords (currently undergoing structural reform) and House of Commons (646 members). Lords are appointed; MPs are elected for renewable terms of a maximum of five years
Party structure:	Multiparty, with two dominant parties (Labour and Conservative) and several smaller parties
Judiciary:	House of Lords is highest court of appeal until Supreme Court is created in 2008
Head of state:	Queen Elizabeth II (1952–)
Government:	Labour Party (1997–)

of a modern democracy, and find evidence of decline in everything from lowered educational standards to inefficient public services, challenges to law and order, threats to the environment, and even the failure of British sports teams to win international competitions. Studies of postwar Britain are littered with words such as *angst*, *melancholy* and *discontent*.

Adjustments were certainly needed following world war and the end of empire. Where Britain was once the world's dominant military and imperial power, the world's richest country, the biggest creditor nation in the world, and the self-appointed standard-bearer for Western culture and civilization, it inevitably had to self-reflect as conditions changed. But what the doomsayers usually failed to point out was that most of the change was relative rather than absolute. The British today – in the famous phrase of Prime Minister Harold Macmillan – have never had it so good. The British economy is one of the biggest and freest in the world, its government and bureaucracy are more responsive, and society is thriving: the British live longer and healthier lives, they have more access to education than ever before, they are on average much wealthier, their environment is cleaner, and their individual rights are better protected than at any time in their history. Of course there are problems and imperfections, and there always will be, but this is just as true of any other wealthy liberal democracy.

The second core argument is that the British must wake up to the reality that they are Europeans, and that Britain's future lies with the European Union. Britain was slow to appreciate the possibilities of European integration, was late joining what was then the European Economic Community, has dragged its feet over adopting the euro, and has developed a reputation – not always deserved – as a reluctant European. The sentimental British attachment to the United States continues to cast its spell, in spite of a growing chorus of questions about just how much Britain benefits from the 'special relationship'. Britain, argues Hugo Young (1999), has struggled for two generations 'to reconcile the past she could not forget with the future she could not avoid'. Like it or not, Britain is politically, economically, and socially bound to Europe. In a speech in London in October 2006, European Commission president José Manuel Barosso asked Britain if it wanted 'to drive from the centre or sulk from the periphery', and if it wanted 'to shape a positive agenda, which reflects its own agenda, or be dragged along as a reluctant partner'. It is time for Britain to leave behind its past, to understand where its future lies, and to show some positive leadership on Europe.

These and other arguments are explored in the chapters that follow. Chapter 1 provides the historical background. Beginning with the early invasions from the continent, it surveys the rise and fall of feudalism, the rise of the United Kingdom, political and economic changes, and the rise and fall of the Empire. It focuses in particular on postwar history, looking at key political, economic, social and cultural developments, notably the impact of Thatcherism, of membership of the European Union, and of the policies of the Blair administration.

Chapter 2 deals with the geography and resources of Britain – both natural and human. The first half discusses the geography, the natural resources, and the environment of Britain, and the second half looks at the people of Britain, focusing on recent demographic changes, and on the impact of immigration, nationalism, regionalism and race.

Chapter 3 looks at the British social system, beginning with a discussion about the evolution of the class system, then looking at the changing structure of the family. It examines the welfare system, the structure and state of British education, and ends with a review of the performance of the criminal justice system in maintaining law and order.

Chapter 4 examines the British system of government and its major institutions: the monarchy, the Prime Minister and Cabinet, Parliament, the judiciary, the bureaucracy, and local government. It explains how they relate to each other, assesses their relative influence over the political process, and offers a critical review of the nature of British democracy.

Chapter 5 looks at politics and civil society in Britain, beginning with a discussion of the main features of British political culture, then looking at how Britons engage in politics through elections, political parties, interest groups and the media.

Chapter 6 turns to the structure and performance of the British economy. It begins with an overview of the structure of the economy, then assesses economic developments since 1945, contrasting the boom years of the 1950s with the crises of the 1970s, examining the changes wrought by Thatcherism, and assessing the renewed economic successes of the 1990s. It then looks also at the place of Britain in the international system and at the economic implications of Europe.

Chapter 7 provides a survey of British culture, beginning with a general outline and an analysis of the meaning of 'Britishness'. It then examines the state of the arts in Britain, with an emphasis on theatre, film, television and popular music. It looks at how the British spend their spare time, and ends with an examination of the role of sports and religion in national life.

Chapter 8 looks at Britain's changing place in the world. It examines key relationships, including those with the Commonwealth,

within the Atlantic Alliance, and with the European Union, and
argues that the first is weak, the second is deeply troubled, and the
third is where Britain's future lies. It finishes with an assessment of
the changing status of the British military.

1
The Historical Context

The history of Britain – like the history of most European countries – is one of layers upon layers of change, and of new forces mixing with old to create new identities. For a small country, Britain's history is surprisingly complex: in order to understand its modern boundaries, its social system, its tangled relationship with the rest of Europe, and its place in the world, we need to dig down through nearly 2,000 years of history. The story of Britain encapsulates elaborate social change, ongoing political struggles, internal imperialism, external imperialism, and economic revolutions. Like every other European society, it has seen its boundaries altered, has been pulled into repeated European war, and has witnessed constant political change. But almost uniquely within Europe, Britain is an island state, and this has impacted both its view of itself and its view of the world. And – again almost uniquely – change in Britain has been driven more by evolution than by revolution. The British have been able to avoid sudden departures and changes of course, which is part of the reason why so many of them have found the changes that have come since 1945 so hard to digest.

Through all the complexity, there are five themes that hold the story together. First, there has been the ebb and flow of the relationship between the members of the United Kingdom: England, Scotland, Wales and Northern Ireland. It is today ebbing once again as powers are devolved from London to regional assemblies, and questions are raised about the meaning of 'Britishness'. Second, relations with the European mainland have always played a critical role in the development of Britain, whether through the effects of alliances and royal marriages, or through threatened or actual invasions, or through the impact of economic relations and cultural

7

exchanges. Perhaps at no time have those relations been as critical as they are today, as Britain struggles to pin down the terms of its place within the European Union. Third, the nature of the British system of government has changed as the balance of power among the major institutions has evolved. The adjustments continue today as the powers of the Prime Minister are redefined, as the role of Parliament changes, and as the electoral system is restructured. Fourth, Britain's economic fortunes have waxed and waned, from a time when it stood astride the world, to postwar crisis and allegations of decline, to reinvigoration as the state has retreated from the marketplace. Finally, Britain's place in the world has changed, from being first a European and then a global power, and since the 1960s having to come to terms with its place in the European Union.

This chapter provides a brief survey of British history. Beginning with the Roman era, it works through the Saxon, Viking and Norman invasions; the rise and fall of feudalism; the break with the Catholic Church; the changing relationship among England, Scotland, Wales and Ireland; the emergence of the parliamentary system; the rise of the British Empire; the agricultural and industrial revolutions; and the pressures leading up to two world wars. The chapter then looks in more detail at developments since 1945, including the construction of the welfare state, the end of empire, the cultural changes of the 1960s, the economic problems of the 1970s, the advent and effects of Thatcherism, the impact of membership of the European Union, Britain's changing view of itself, and its changing relationship with the world. Change has always been a factor in Britain, but the speed of that change has increased since 1945. The British have had to make core political, economic and social adjustments, and the destination to which they today find themselves travelling remains unclear.

The Emergence of the British State

When the Romans under Julius Caesar first arrived in Britain in 55–54 BC, they found it peopled by Celts who had arrived there between 800 and 200 BC, the latest in a long line of immigrants from Northern Europe and the Iberian peninsula. The Celts – ancestors of the Irish, Scots and Welsh of today – were less a race than a disparate group of peoples who shared a language, religious patterns, and social norms. When the Romans came again in AD 43 (this time to stay), they occupied most of what is now England, Wales and southern Scotland, pushing the Celts west and north. England developed a distinctive social and political system – it had roads, planned towns, a centralized economy, a thriving commercial system, and for 300 years was mainly at peace. Signs of the Roman occupation are still evident, from the stretches of straight road that can be found in parts of England, to many place names, including London (Londinium during Roman times) and any of the cities with the Latin termination for camp (*castra*), such as Winchester, Lancaster and Worcester.

The departure of the Romans at the beginning of the fifth century left behind a political vacuum into which later moved several more waves of invaders, notably Germanic tribes such as the Angles and the Saxons, who arrived in about 500–700. While the Irish Celts were converted to Christianity in the early fifth century by St Patrick, the arrival in 597 of the monk Augustine – on a mission from the Pope in Rome – brought a different form of Christianity to England: at a conference of bishops in 664 (the Synod of Whitby), it was decided to adopt the Roman rather than the Celtic form.

In the eighth century the first Viking and Danish raids took place, turning into a full-blown invasion by the mid-ninth century, an attempt to drive out the native population and to settle permanently, a goal that was only prevented by the resistance of King Alfred of Wessex. By the time of the last successful invasion of Britain – by William, Duke of Normandy, in 1066 – the British Isles had become divided into two zones, one predominantly Celtic and the other predominantly Anglo-Saxon (see Davies, 2003). Although England was now united under the Normans, the cultural and religious divisions persisted, England being distinguished from the Celtic regions by the development of a more stable and centralized system of government. At the same time, England and France were bound together under the Angevins, whose rule peaked between 1150 and 1220, and whose lands stretched from the Scottish border to the Pyrenees (Gillingham, 2001).

Like the rest of Europe, England was a feudal society. Sovereign power lay in the hands of the monarch, who owned the land managed by aristocrats, who in turn bought access to that land with military service and used landless peasants to do the work. Monarchs also claimed to rule by divine right, arguing that they were answerable only to God, exercised religious power on earth, and might even have been gods themselves. But the powers of the monarch began their long decline in 1215 when the despotic King John was forced by his barons – with the support of the Church – to sign the contract known as Magna Carta. Under its terms he was obliged to consult with his aristocrats before levying taxes, and to agree that he could not arbitrarily arrest or seize property from his subjects. Magna Carta did little more than confirm the privileges of the Church and the barons, but it was the first critical step in the redistribution of political power in Britain.

A second step was taken in 1265 when the Norman baron Simon de Montfort – exploiting the political weaknesses of King Henry III (1216–72) – convened the first British Parliament. It was unelected and met only sporadically, but it included both commoners and aristocrats, monarchs came to rely on it for political support, and it provided an alternative focus of political power. Magna Carta and the creation of Parliament by no means moved power into the hands of the ordinary person, but they marked the beginning of the long and complex process by which democracy came to Britain.

Meanwhile, the supremacy of England over the British Isles was established as wars and attrition led to the incorporation of its Celtic neighbours, and as nationalism superseded feudalism as the driving force in politics. The Normans conquered Wales in 1285 but did not fare so well in Scotland – they invaded in 1296, meeting resistance first from William Wallace, and then from Robert Bruce who routed the invaders at the Battle of Bannockburn in 1314. The Normans now looked to expand outside the British Isles, setting off the Hundred Years' War against France in 1337. Revenue from estates was not enough to pay for the war, so the king – Edward III – looked to Parliament for help. It began meeting more regularly and the House of Commons began sitting separately from the barons. The war started well, with notable victories at Crécy and Poitiers, but then the Black Death in 1348–49 halved the population of England. Another victory over the French at Agincourt in 1415 marked the end of the war for the English, who now became diverted by their own Wars of the Roses (1455–85), in which two factions – the Lancastrians and the Yorkists – fought for control of the throne. The Lancastrians prevailed at the Battle of Bosworth in 1485, and King Henry VII became the first member of the Tudor dynasty.

To the ethnic, cultural and linguistic divisions of Britain, religious differences were added when King Henry VIII – aiming to curb the power of the church – dissolved England's ties with the Roman Catholic Church in 1534 and created the Church of England. The break with the Catholic Church was followed by a series of Acts of

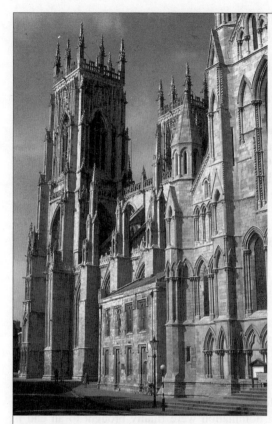

York Minster in northern England, symbolic of the impact of the church on the historical development of Britain, and on the evolution of a distinctive English architectural style. York is the seat of one of the two archbishoprics of the Church of England.

Illustration 1.1 York Minster

Parliament in 1536–42 by which Wales was formally integrated with England. The reign of Elizabeth I (1558–1603) saw England developing new power, prosperity and cultural wealth. Sir Francis Drake set off on his voyages of discovery around the world, William Shakespeare and Christopher Marlowe wrote their plays, Ben Jonson and John Donne wrote their poems, and Thomas Morley and William Byrd wrote their music. When Elizabeth's successor James I came to the throne, Scotland and England shared a common monarch, and in 1707 a political union took place, creating Great Britain. Meanwhile, Ireland was being steadily and violently subjugated, beginning with attacks in the thirteenth century and eventually making it to all intents and purposes part of the British state by the late eighteenth century.

The dominant influence in British politics continued to be the struggle for power between the monarchy and Parliament, which boiled over in 1642 with the outbreak of a civil war. This led to the execution in 1649 of King Charles I, and the declaration of a brief republic (1649–60) under the military dictatorship of Oliver Cromwell (see Morrill, 1990, and Gaunt, 2000). The monarchy was restored in 1660, but when King James II (1685–88) tried to win back the divine right of monarchs, and to rule without Parliament, he was forced to flee the country in the Glorious Revolution. His place was taken by William of Orange, who – as William III – became Britain's first constitutional monarch. In 1689 a Bill of Rights was drawn up which confirmed the supremacy of Parliament over the monarch.

The definition of 'England' was also tightened by its success in fighting off invasion, and by its critical interventions in struggles for power on the European continent, which altered the course of English, British and European history. There had been the defeat of the Spanish Armada in 1588, the defeat of an Irish-French army at the Battle of the Boyne in 1690, and the English intervention in the War of the Spanish Succession (1701–14), in which France and Austria vied for the Spanish empire: the Duke of Marlborough waged ten campaigns, won every battle he fought, and – at Blenheim in 1704 – ended 40 years of French military dominance on the continent. Attempted uprisings in Scotland in 1715 and 1745 failed, and Britain later made decisive interventions in the war against Napoleon. The French navy was defeated in 1805 at Trafalgar, and Napoleon's aspirations for European domination were finally brought to an end in 1815 at the Battle of Waterloo.

With its military and political power growing, Britain also underwent a social and economic revolution (see Horrox and Ormrod, 2006). Organized agriculture had taken root with the Saxons, who cleared forests, introduced new methods of farming, and established the open-field system that was to remain in place until the late eighteenth century. The enclosure movement – begun in Tudor times – saw landowners gradually consolidating their property, clearing wasteland, reducing common pasture and woodland, and denying peasants access to land. The peasantry began to shrink as small landowners were squeezed out by large estates. In 1800, the vast majority of the British population was poor and lived off the land, while barely 10 per cent lived in towns and cities. But this was all to change with the rise of industry, which led to the expansion of towns and cities and the creation of factories, such that by 1900 the population had not only tripled in size – to about 38 million – but had also become more urbanized. Less than a quarter of the population lived in the rural areas, and more than 40 per cent lived in large towns and cities, usually in overcrowded and unsanitary conditions. By 1900 industrial workers outnumbered rural workers by nine to one.

At the heart of the economic changes were developments in the coal-mining industry, where improvements in extraction methods had allowed a 300 per cent increase in production during the eighteenth century alone. Manufacturing industries grew, and Britain became part of the trading system that brought together communities across Europe, and encouraged immigration, emigration, and the transfer of new technologies. New and more efficient processes for smelting iron and making steel were developed by Abraham Darby and others, which sparked the beginning of the industrial revolution (see More, 2000, and King and Timmins, 2001). Weaving and spinning were improved by the flying shuttle (invented by John Kay in 1733), the spinning jenny (James Hargreaves, 1765), and the water frame (Richard Arkwright, 1767). The steam engine was invented by James Watt (1769), George Stephenson developed the first railway engine (1829), industry was mechanized, and large-scale business enterprises emerged.

These technological changes brought about improvements in transport. Major roads, previously badly maintained by local parishes, were taken over by private companies, and engineers such as Robert Macadam and Thomas Telford developed new methods of building roads with harder surfaces and better drainage. The introduction of the railway made it possible for people and goods to be transported more quickly and in greater quantities, and huge new fortunes were made by entrepreneurs. Commerce and markets grew, and Britain was forged into the world's first and most powerful industrial state. By the mid-nineteenth century it had become the 'workshop of the world', producing two-thirds of the world's coal, half its steel, half its cotton goods, and virtually all its machine tools.

With its industry growing, Britain's priority was to find new markets and sources of raw materials, and to build on its competitive advantage over its European rivals, particularly Spain, France and the Netherlands. After centuries during which Europeans had immigrated into Britain, the British began to emigrate to Europe and further afield. England's acquisitive impulses dated back to the earliest attempts to subjugate the Scots, the Welsh and the Irish, and to the expansion of English control over parts of France during the reigns of

Henry II (1154–89), Edward II (1307–27) and Henry V (1413–22). In 1583 the first English colony in the new world was established at Newfoundland, and the settlement of North America began with the foundation in 1607 of Virginia. So was born what was eventually to grow into the British Empire (see Box 1.1).

Meanwhile, changes came to the political system as the shifting balance of powers between the monarch and Parliament continued. George I (1714–27) had little interest in politics, so Parliament became more influential, and when Robert Walpole became the King's First Minister in 1721, he had so much power and independence that he was later acclaimed as Britain's first Prime Minister although it was under William Pitt the Younger (1783–1801, 1804–06) that the office really took form (see Hague, 2004). Parliament was still dominated by aristocrats representing the so-called 'rotten boroughs': mainly rural areas, many of which had only a handful of voters, and in some of which a seat in Parliament could be bought. The House of Lords was made up of unelected aristocrats, while the House of Commons was elected by only a small fraction of the population, in contests that were subject to bribery, fraud and intimidation.

Members of Parliament were not paid, so the Commons came to be dominated by wealthy merchants and landowners. The new middle class of industrialists and entrepreneurs railed against this, and the pressure for change grew. The Great Reform Act of 1832 was followed by more changes during the later nineteenth and early twentieth centuries, which had the effect of transforming Parliament:

- Corrupt electoral districts were eliminated.
- The vote was extended to the wealthy and upper middle class.
- Secret voting was introduced.
- Mass-membership political parties emerged.
- Single-member parliamentary districts were created.
- The aristocratic House of Lords lost most of its remaining powers.
- The vote was extended to women.

With the introduction of pensions and national health and unemployment insurance in 1908–11, government spending grew, and so did the need to generate revenue. At first much came from duties on selected agricultural imports, but increasingly it came from direct taxes, particularly on income. Then came the Great War (1914–18), the first step in a massive transformation of government, society, the

Box 1.1   The British Empire

Britain's global impact rests mainly on the legacy of the British Empire. Tracing its roots to the tradition of mercantilism and seafaring that emerged in the late fifteenth century, Britain's global aspirations saw their first significant expression in the re-conquest of Ireland, in the first settlements in North America, and in trade with the Asian subcontinent.

The defeat of the French at Quebec in 1759 preceded the Peace of Paris in 1763 by which France ceded Canada and all its territory west of the original 13 English colonies to Britain (Anderson, 2000). Robert Clive's victory at the Battle of Plassey in 1759 gave Britain direct or indirect control over much of India, and in 1770 Captain James Cook landed at Botany Bay on the newly discovered east coast of Australia. The key to Britain's power was its navy, which dominated its European challengers, and – in order to be maintained – required the development of a network of supply stations around the world. The loss of the 13 American colonies in 1781 may have dampened enthusiasm for colonialism, and may have brought an end to what is sometimes described as the 'first British Empire', but a new focus on other parts of the world led to the development of the 'second British Empire', which was eventually to include Canada, Australia, New Zealand, parts of western Africa, most of southern and eastern Africa, parts of the Middle East, many Caribbean and Pacific islands, parts of Southeast Asia, and – of course – India, the 'jewel in the crown' of the empire, over which Queen Victoria was declared Empress in 1877. At its height during the late nineteenth century, the empire included about a quarter of the world's population.

Empire meant not only political influence for Britain, but also economic power. Britain required that all trade with its colonies be conducted using British ships, and that the colonies could buy manufactured goods only from Britain. Thus, goods imported into Britain were often re-exported to the continent at a profit, and British ports began doing considerable trade with their colonial counterparts. When the Great Exhibition was held in London in 1851, it confirmed that Britain led the world in almost every field of human endeavour (for details, see Roberts and Roberts, 2002, Chapter 23).

Two world wars were to combine in the twentieth century with revised opinions about imperialism and agitation in many British colonies for greater self-determination or independence to bring an end to empire: between 1945 and 1965 it was largely dismantled, and generally in an orderly fashion (see Douglas, 2002). But the influence of empire continues to linger in the British psyche: at least part of the concern that Britons have with the place of their country in the world is driven by conscious or subconscious comparisons with the heyday of British global power. Analysts remain divided over the historical legacy of empire (see Ferguson, 2002, for example).

economy, and of Britain's place in the global system. The cream of a generation of young Britons died in one of the most brutal and mismanaged conflicts in the history of warfare: more than 800,000 were killed or went missing, and 1.4 million were injured. After the war, competing political ideologies grew in the face of disillusion-ment with the old options (see Marwick, 2000, Chapter 2), women finally won the right to vote, and labour disputes became more common, peaking with the General Strike of 1926.

Nationalist movements had meanwhile begun to emerge in Ireland, India and other parts of the empire. Events in Ireland had the most immediate impact, beginning with calls in the 1880s for home rule. These were accepted in 1914, but were delayed by the outbreak of war. Impatient revolutionaries staged the Easter Rebellion of 1916, which failed, and might have had no lasting impact were it not for the aggressive British response, beginning with the execution of 15 rebel leaders. A struggle for independence broke out in 1918, leading to a peace treaty in December 1921 under which Ireland was partitioned the following year; the 26 southern (and predominantly Catholic) counties became the independent Irish Free State, while the six north-ern (and predominantly Protestant) counties remained part of the United Kingdom. (Ireland left the Commonwealth in 1949 and became a republic.)

The economic slump that followed the Wall Street crash of October 1929 brought widespread unemployment, and emphasized the impact of growing economic competition from Japan, Germany and other rising powers. The United States and the Soviet Union began to emerge as economic and military superpowers, a transition that was confirmed by the Second World War. Britain entered the war in September 1939 as the world's biggest creditor nation, but emerged six years later as one of the world's biggest debtor nations. Its wartime record was heroic: it stood virtually alone in the fight against Nazi Germany between 1939 and 1941, fought off prepara-tions for a German invasion during the Battle of Britain in 1940, withstood the bombing of its major cities, scored the first major defeat over German forces at El Alamein in the North African desert in October 1942, and then played the leading role alongside the United States in invading the continent in June 1944 and finally defeating the Germans. But the rigours of war left its economy devastated, its political influence diminished, its export earnings and merchant shipping fleet halved, and many of its colonies agitating for independence.

Table 1.1   Some key dates in British history

1066	Norman Conquest
1215	Magna Carta signed
1265	Parliament founded
1534	Creation of the Church of England
1536–42	Union with Wales
1642–49	Civil war leads to the deposition of the monarchy
1649–60	Cromwell's republic ends with restoration of the monarchy
1707	Union with Scotland
1801	Legislative union with Ireland
1832	Great Reform Act
1914–18	First World War
1918	Women over age 30 given the right to vote
1922	Irish independence
1928	All women given the right to vote
1939–45	Second World War
1947	Independence of India and Pakistan
1952	Queen Elizabeth succeeds to the throne
1957–70	Independence of most of Britain's colonies
1973	Britain joins the European Economic Community
1979	Margaret Thatcher wins first of three elections
1982	War with Argentina over the Falklands (Malvinas)
1991	British forces take part in Gulf War
1994	Opening of Channel Tunnel connecting Britain and France
1996	Crisis over mad cow disease reaches its peak
1997	(May) Tony Blair elected Prime Minister; (July) Hong Kong is returned to China; (August) death of Diana, Princess of Wales; (September) referendums in Scotland and Wales approve regional assemblies
1998	(April) Northern Ireland peace agreement approved by public referendum
1999	(March–April) Britain joins NATO attacks on Serbia; (May) first elections to Scottish and Welsh assemblies; (November) Northern Ireland government meets
2001	(February) outbreak of foot-and-mouth disease; (September) nearly 70 Britons killed in terrorist attacks in New York; (November) British troops sent to Afghanistan in support of US military attacks on Taliban
2002	(June) Queen Elizabeth celebrates golden jubilee
2003	(March) Britain takes part in US-led invasion of Iraq
2005	(May) Tony Blair elected to a third term; (July) London awarded the 2012 Olympics; 52 people killed in terrorist bombings in central London
2007	Gordon Brown succeeds Tony Blair as Prime Minister

Postwar Adjustment, 1945–79

Within weeks of the end of the war in Europe in May 1945, voters went to the polls in a general election at which the character of postwar Britain would be decided. It was widely assumed that Winston Churchill – Prime Minister since 1940 in a government of national unity, and the hero of Britain's wartime resistance – would be rewarded by being elected to lead a new government of his own. But quite the opposite happened: there was a convincing mandate for the socialist Labour Party, which was elected into power in its own right for the first time, winning 393 seats in Parliament to the 213 won by the Conservatives.

What brought the change? Many explanations were offered, including criticism of the leadership of the prewar Conservative Party, which had been the largest party in Parliament for 18 years and held a majority for 16 years. During a time of poverty, unemployment, and great social and economic inequalities, it had shown its lack of sympathy for working people by breaking strikes, fighting with trade unions, and paying too little attention to education. Furthermore, the government of Neville Chamberlain (1937–40) had tried to appease the Nazis and had waited too long to begin preparing Britain for the war. When war came, the experience had brought the British closer together, obliging them to share the sacrifices of conscription, rationing and austerity, blurring class differences, and convincing many that government intervention could be helpful and useful. Finally, Labour politicians had served the country well during the war, managing home affairs and removing doubts that socialists could govern effectively and fairly (Roberts and Roberts, 2002: 809).

The new Labour government set out to put into practice its vision of a new society and a 'land fit for heroes'. Much of its thinking was prompted by the findings of a 1942 government report authored by William Beveridge, an advisor to Winston Churchill. Warning of the dangers of want, ignorance and poverty, Beveridge had recommended the introduction after the war of a universal social security system, a national health service, and policies aimed at preventing mass unemployment. His report was followed in 1944 by an Act of Parliament providing universal free education to age 15. Now, under the leadership of Prime Minister Clement Attlee, the new Labour government embarked on a programme based on three foundations:

- Completion of the welfare state. Various welfare provisions had existed long before the war but Labour greatly expanded the reach of government assistance. The National Insurance Act of 1946 provided pensions for the retired, payments to the ill and the unemployed, and grants to mothers and widows. Two years later, the National Health Service was created, providing free medical and dental care for all. The government also responded to the shortage in housing brought on by wartime destruction: existing houses were repaired, new houses were built, and prefabricated temporary housing was provided to ease the shortage.
- The development of a planned economy that would prevent depressions and end unemployment. Adopting the philosophy of economist John Maynard Keynes (1883–1946), Labour directed economic activity using monetary and fiscal controls. It altered interest rates to control investment flows, ran budget deficits to pay for its programmes, discouraged consumption by taxing luxuries and controlling imports, and took action to deal with Britain's financial crisis, including the imposition of austerity measures.
- Expanded public ownership of key services. The government nationalized about one-fifth of British industry, including the coal, gas, electricity, iron and steel industries, the railways, the Bank of England, civil aviation, and the road transport system.

The immediate postwar years were ones of continued austerity as the country tried to recover from the war, to stabilize its economy, and to build homes and create new jobs for its citizens. Hopes for a rapid return to a peacetime quality of living were dashed, and criticisms of Labour began to grow: nationalized industries were seen as inefficient and the welfare state as too expensive. At the 1951 general election, slightly more people voted for Labour than for the Conservatives, but the structure of the electoral system (see Chapter 5) meant that the Conservatives were returned to power with a small majority, under the leadership of Winston Churchill (Butler, 1999). However, he left intact most of the changes made by Labour, and British politics in the 1950s was driven by a consensus that whether the Conservatives or Labour were in power, they would maintain the welfare system and a mixed economy with a view to sustaining full employment. (Critics of the consensus thesis argue that there was more disagreement over policy than most analysts suggest (see, for example, Kerr, 1999).)

Another of the legacies of the postwar Labour government was the end of empire. Before the war, Britain had been able to maintain and justify the military commitment that was a necessary part of the maintenance of its colonies and other possessions. But it found the economic costs of empire increasingly difficult to bear; the 1931 Statute of Westminster recognized the independence of the dominions (Australia, Canada, Ireland, Newfoundland, New Zealand and South Africa), and the future of India had been the subject of much parliamentary debate in 1932–35 (Tanner, 2002: 63–4). After the war there was growing pressure for decolonization from the new United Nations, from a segment of the Labour government, and from nationalist movements within many British colonies. The biggest step was taken in August 1947 when independence came to India, which opted to split itself into a predominantly Hindu republic of India and a predominantly Muslim republic of Pakistan, itself divided into two separate blocks of territory. In 1948, independence came to Burma and Ceylon, and the British mandate over Palestine – which had begun in 1918 – ended with the creation of Israel. Negotiations opened that would lead to the independence of most of Britain's remaining African and Asian colonies; the Suez crisis (Box 1.2) shook British confidence; the Gold Coast (now Ghana) became independent in March 1957; and in February 1960 Prime Minister Harold Macmillan made his famous 'wind of change' speech, acknowledging that the days of British colonialism in Africa were numbered.

Meanwhile, the domestic economy was recovering, and Britain began to enjoy the same kind of economic affluence then coming to much of the industrialized world. Wartime rationing ended, workers' wages increased, agricultural production grew by 160 per cent between 1945 and 1957, Britain's share of the world export market returned to prewar levels (nearly 25 per cent of world exports), mass consumption took off as middle-class Britons bought new cars and consumer goods, industrial output and gross domestic product grew, and inflation and unemployment remained low; the British, claimed Harold Macmillan, had 'never had it so good'. But while the British economy prospered and grew, it did not grow as quickly as those of many other industrialized countries, notably the United States, Japan and Germany. Britain now found its global influence beginning to wane. The change can be blamed most obviously on the end of empire, but it was also exacerbated by the costs of the war, handicaps posed to industrial relations by class divisions, an education system that was prejudiced against business as a career, low levels of mobil-

Box 1.2   Watershed at Suez, 1956

The turning point in Britain's role as a world power came in 1956 on the banks of the Suez Canal. Built in 1856–69 by the British and the French (using Egyptian labour), the canal had become a conduit for British contacts and trade with India and the Pacific. Egypt became increasingly resentful about continued British control over the canal after the Second World War, especially after the 1952 coup that brought Gamal Abdel Nasser to power. Seeking to build a dam on the Nile at Aswan, Nasser was promised aid from the United States, Britain and the World Bank. When he also bought arms from the Soviet bloc, the offer of aid was withdrawn, and Nasser responded by nationalizing the canal in July 1956. Political and public opinion in Britain was outraged, and Conservative Prime Minister Anthony Eden felt that – if unanswered – the nationalization would represent an end to British influence in Asia and Africa. Britain responded by colluding with France and Israel to win the canal back.

In October 1956, when Israel launched an arranged attack on Egypt, Britain and France insisted that both sides withdraw to a distance of 10 miles each side of the canal. When they did not, Egyptian airfields were bombed and British and French paratroopers were dropped into the canal zone. The Eisenhower administration in the United States – just a week away from an election, and keen to criticize the Soviets for putting down a democracy movement in Hungary – led the international opposition to the attack, thereby emphasizing the differences that had emerged between the Americans and the British regarding the new international order. The United States was hostile to the idea of colonialism, and was eager to see Britain tie itself more closely to its European neighbours. The British, by contrast, still refused to see themselves as Europeans and saw their main interests lying outside Europe, notably in the white dominions: Australia, Canada and New Zealand.

A ceasefire was quickly arranged, the last British troops left the canal zone in December, and in January 1957 Eden resigned, ostensibly on medical grounds, but reputedly at the insistence of Eisenhower. Britain's international prestige suffered, public opinion began to question Britain's role in the world, the process of decolonization moved into high gear, and the focus of British interests shifted from the empire to Europe (for details, see Louis and Owens, 1989). In his 1977 obituary in *The Times*, Eden was described as 'the last Prime Minister to believe Britain was a great power and the first to confront a crisis which proved she was not'.

ity within the labour force, inadequate investments in industry and in research and development, and high levels of government involvement in production and employment (Jones and Kavanagh, 2003: 197–9).

Where Britain had once been a global actor, it now began to be drawn into its relationship with its European neighbours. During and after the war, Winston Churchill had made a number of suggestions in favour of regional integration, noting in a speech at the University of Zurich in 1946 his belief in the need for a 'United States of Europe'. He made clear, however, that this initiative should revolve around France and West Germany, and that Britain was 'with Europe but not of it. We are interested and associated, but not absorbed' (Zurcher, 1958: 6). This view was widely supported by the British Establishment, so that when six continental nations led by France and West Germany created an experimental European Coal and Steel Community in 1952, Britain opted not to join. It also opted not to join the European Economic Community (EEC) launched in January 1958, instead creating its own looser model of cooperation in the form of the European Free Trade Association (EFTA), founded in May 1960.

Even as the European Free Trade Association was under discussion, however, it was clear that the European Economic Community was working, bringing down barriers to trade among its six member states and encouraging them to cooperate in an ever greater variety of policy areas. The impact of Suez had also finally hit home, shaking Britain's status as an independent great power. In 1961 the Macmillan government lodged Britain's first application to join the EEC, along with Denmark, Ireland and Norway. This was dismissed out of hand by President Charles de Gaulle of France, who saw Britain as a rival for leadership in the Community, resented the way in which he had been kept out of the wartime Anglo–American alliance, and felt that British membership would give the United States too much influence in Europe (Dimbleby and Reynolds, 1989: 258–9). Britain applied again in 1967, and was vetoed by de Gaulle for similar reasons. Following the French leader's resignation in 1969, Britain applied for a third time, was accepted, and negotiations on the terms of membership opened. On 1 January 1973 Britain finally joined the EEC, along with Denmark and Ireland (for more details, see George, 1992; Buller, 1999; McCormick, 2005, Chapter 3).

Meanwhile, Britain's empire had been all but dismantled. Malaysia and Singapore became independent in 1957, Nigeria and Cyprus in

1960, Kuwait and Tanzania in 1961, Jamaica and Trinidad in 1962, Kenya in 1963, Malta and Zambia in 1964, Barbados and Guyana in 1966, Mauritius and Swaziland in 1968, Fiji in 1970, and the Bahamas in 1973. The one holdout in Africa was Rhodesia, whose white minority unilaterally declared independence in November 1965, and was to be first ostracized and then battered by a vicious guerrilla war before becoming legally independent in 1980 as Zimbabwe. By the mid-1970s, little was left of the empire beyond Hong Kong, the Falklands, Gibraltar and a few Caribbean and Indian Ocean islands. Where Britain had once committed its army and navy almost all over the world, it was now a second-ranking power with limited military interests. It was a key actor in the North Atlantic Treaty Organization (NATO), to be sure, had an independent nuclear deterrent, and was one of the five members of the UN Security Council with veto power. However, Cold War tensions between the United States and the USSR dominated international relations, and the British Empire had been replaced by the Commonwealth, whose interests were more cultural and economic than political.

One of the legacies of empire was the immigration into Britain of citizens from its ex-colonies (see Winder, 2004). Initially, these had come mainly from the white dominions of Australia, New Zealand and Canada, but a labour shortage in the 1950s encouraged an influx of immigrants from the Caribbean and from India and Pakistan. The government passed a number of Immigration Acts between 1962 and 1971 aimed at restricting immigration, but a new wave of mainly Asian immigrants from Kenya and Uganda arrived at the turn of the 1970s as they were expelled by the governments of those two countries. In 1951, there had been just 75,000 non-whites in Britain, or about 0.2 per cent of the population. By the early 1980s, the number of non-whites in Britain had jumped to more than 2 million, or about 4 per cent of the population, and racial tensions had begun to mount (see Chapter 2).

More cultural change came in the 1960s. Reacting to what they saw as the conformist and conservative 1950s, and fed by new injections of American culture, the easy availability of birth control, and concerns about social and political problems, young people questioned old attitudes, reflected in their love of rock-and-roll, new fashions, the sexual revolution, and support for mass movements whose target were mainly the Establishment: opposition to nuclear weapons, to gender discrimination, to the war in Vietnam, and to threats to the environment. The musical revolution was led by The Beatles, The

Rolling Stones, The Who, The Kinks, Cream and other musicians who took the music charts on both sides of the Atlantic by storm. The fashion revolution was led by designers such as Mary Quant and Biba, the introduction of the mini-skirt, and the images associated with Carnaby Street and Swinging London (Levy, 2002). Cinema captured the spirit of the new Britain as Sean Connery's James Bond exuded panache and sophistication, Michael Caine's Alfie glorified anti-heroes, and Lynn Redgrave's Georgy Girl emphasized changing sexual mores. England won the football World Cup in 1966 and *Sergeant Pepper's Lonely Hearts Club Band* shook the music world in 1967 – Britain's empire may have gone, but now it dominated Western popular culture.

Domestic developments of another kind exploded in Northern Ireland in 1969. The province had governed itself since 1922, largely forgotten by national government. The Protestant majority, concerned about its place in the province, had maintained a policy of discrimination towards the Catholic minority on housing, jobs and political rights, ensured in particular by its control of the police, the Royal Ulster Constabulary (RUC). In 1968, a movement campaigning for equality for Catholics had been aggressively opposed by the RUC, which also broke up a civil rights march from Belfast to Londonderry in January 1969. Violence and rioting followed, the British Army was sent in to restore order in August 1969, and from there the problems escalated. Internment without trial was introduced by the British government, terrorist groups representing the Protestant and Catholic causes brought death and destruction, while soldiers, members of the RUC, and ordinary citizens were killed and injured in street violence and bombings. Direct rule from London was imposed in March 1972.

Meanwhile, the economic growth of the 1950s began to falter, and commentators and political leaders began to talk of a 'British disease' that had come to afflict the country. The Right blamed 'creeping socialism' in the form of growing welfare, powerful and recalcitrant labour unions, high rates of taxation, and the large public sector. The Left questioned this interpretation, asking why – if welfare was to blame – other countries with extensive welfare and high tax rates (such as France and Sweden) did not have similar problems. Their explanations focused less on workers and more on management, whom they blamed for failing to adjust to the postwar world in which new competition was being posed by the United States and a resurgent West Germany and Japan. They also pointed to a class system that prevented management and workers from developing a constructive joint effort, and that gave more value to inherited 'old money' than to 'new money' earned by hard work and entrepreneurial innovation. Confrontation became more common than cooperation in relations between managers and workers, leading to bitterness, low productivity, and a sense of 'Us versus Them'.

Meanwhile, the fabric of Britain came under new pressure as Scottish and Welsh nationalism went through a rebirth. The Welsh nationalist party Plaid Cymru won its first-ever seat in Parliament at a 1966 by-election, and saw its share of the vote grow, winning two seats at the February 1974 election. In the case of Scotland, the neglect of central government combined with declining support for the Labour Party and the development of North Sea oil (large reserves of oil and natural gas had been discovered in the early 1970s) to give a boost to the Scottish National Party (SNP). Founded in 1928, it had never won more than about 1 per cent of the vote in general elections. In 1967, it won its first seat in Parliament, and its share of the Scottish vote grew from 11.4 per cent in 1970 (when it won two seats in Parliament) to 21.0 per cent in February 1974 (when it won seven seats). The Labour government responded with plans to devolve power to Scotland and Wales, and referendums were held in both countries in March 1970, a favourable vote of 40 per cent or more being required to proceed. Only 33 per cent were in favour in Scotland, and only 12 per cent in Wales, so devolution was temporarily shelved.

A new low point in Britain's economic fortunes came at the end of the 1970s. Against a background of high unemployment, 16 per cent inflation, and a record budget deficit, the Labour government of Harold Wilson was obliged in 1976 to ask the International Monetary Fund for a loan to help offset a run on the pound and to help Britain service its debts. Then, during the 'winter of discontent' in 1978–79, public-sector workers went on strike across Britain, almost shutting the country down. Clearly it was time for a new approach both to economic policy and to government. In 1979, there was a general election, which resulted in the return to power of the Conservative Party, led since 1975 by Margaret Thatcher.

The Thatcher Revolution, 1979–90

Alone among twentieth-century British Prime Ministers, Margaret Thatcher's name has been applied to a set of political ideas and a style of administration. Thatcher believed she had identified the critical elements of the 'British disease', and set out to give Britain the hard medicine that she believed must be applied if postwar economic problems were to be addressed. Above all, she felt, this meant an end to consensus politics and an abandonment of compromise, bargaining and the search for policies acceptable to the majority (Clarke, 1996: 367–79). In its place, Thatcher wanted a new kind of politics, variously labelled adversarial, confrontational or conviction politics.

The philosophy of Thatcherism revolved around a belief in the guidance of one's own passionately held beliefs, in markets, monetarism and authoritative government, and in the development of a strong state and a free economy (Kavanagh, 1987: 2). Marquand argues that Thatcherism had four basic dimensions: 'a sort of British Gaullism' born out of a growing sense of despair with Britain's difficulties, economic liberalism, traditional Toryism (including patriotism and a pride in tradition), and a style of politics that was both populist and charismatic (Marquand, 1988: 160–4). Among other things, Thatcherism meant rolling back the state, privatizing businesses and industries owned and operated by the government, reducing trade union power, promoting family values in order to ensure a 'higher' moral level in society, and a strong British role in international affairs.

The impact of Thatcherism on Britain is debatable. Her supporters argue that she sparked the changes needed to reverse Britain's relative economic decline by freeing up the marketplace, cutting the power of unions, reducing dependence on welfare, and promoting a stakeholder culture in which more Britons became involved in creating their own wealth and opportunities. For her detractors, she heightened class tensions, failed to meet the needs of the underclass, and allowed too many people to slip through the safety net of welfare. She also widened the gap between the 'haves' and the 'have-nots'; the number of British millionaires grew as a result of her tenure, but so did poverty and homelessness, and many felt that Britain became a less caring society.

Thatcher was also criticized for her views on Europe, where she was frequently at odds with other European Community leaders. Europe played a critical new role in domestic politics in Britain during her tenure, not least because of the signing in 1986 of the Single European Act, designed to complete the final steps in the creation of a European market free of borders, within which there was free movement of people, money, goods and services. Europe was

Margaret Thatcher,. Prime Minister from 1979 to 1990. Her place in history remains controversial: some argue that she addressed many of the problems that contributed to Britain's postwar economic woes, and helped revitalize Britain's international standing, while others argue that she was divisive and too dismissive of those unable to help themselves.

Illustration 1.2   Margaret Thatcher

also growing, with membership expanding to three poorer countries: Greece, Spain and Portugal. Finally, work had begun on the Channel Tunnel, which promised to remove an important psychological barrier between Britain and the continent (it was opened in 1994). Despite these developments, Thatcher dragged her feet on Europe, most famously demanding (and receiving) a reduction in Britain's contributions to the Community budget.

Thatcher won three elections (1979, 1983 and 1987), but by the late 1980s had become widely unpopular, both within her party and with the broader electorate. Her insistence on seeking advice from outside the Cabinet combined with differences over policy to lead to resignations by key ministers in her government, emphasizing her weakness. Her attempt in 1989–90 to replace progressive local taxes (rates) with a poll tax to which rich and poor alike would be subject proved highly unpopular. Finally, a squabble between pro- and anti-European Conservatives (the latter led by Thatcher) revealed that her policies on Europe were becoming too divisive. In 1990, after a party leadership vote which she won, but not convincingly, Thatcher resigned the leadership and the Prime Ministership, and was replaced by John Major. He won his own mandate at the 1992 general election, but in-fighting continued among the Conservatives, mainly over Europe, and the opposition Labour Party in 1994 elected a new leader – Tony Blair – who was intent on reforming the party.

Membership of the European Union combined with the effects of Thatcherism to bring great change to Britain. It was visible in the renewal of cities, in the rise of a new entrepreneurial spirit that was transforming the attitudes of business and industry, and in the growth of the middle class and the consumer society. The average Briton today is healthier, better-educated and more affluent than before, and there is a new spirit of liveliness and optimism, at least among the younger generations. Many even argue that Britain is being Americanized – not only has its economy rediscovered something of the competitive nature that made it so strong in the nineteenth century, but many aspects of politics (notably election campaigns) have taken on a more aggressive American character. But in one area there are few signs of Americanization: Britain's cost of living has increased dramatically, boosted mainly by a surge in property prices (see Chapter 6).

Blair and Beyond

The legacy of Thatcherism was reflected in the policies pursued after its May 1997 election victory by the Labour government of Tony Blair. Taking political analysts by surprise, the rejuvenated Labour Party swept the internally divided Conservative Party out of office after 18 years in power, winning a remarkable 177-seat majority in Parliament. Under Tony Blair, 'New' Labour in opposition had abandoned many of its more socialist ideas, and had adopted key elements of the Thatcher programme. Blair came into office underlining the importance of the free market, and emphasizing the need to improve education, rebuild the National Health Service, invest more heavily in Britain's human capital, build a society less dependent on government, take a tough stance on crime, and work in a more constructive fashion with Britain's EU partners. Blair also made much of his view that Britain should be 'repackaged' as a society that had deep roots in history and culture, but which was also forward-looking and economically dynamic. For his policies and style he won wide public support, polls in 1998 revealing that he was the most popular of all postwar British Prime Ministers.

During its first term in office (1997–2001), the Blair administration made far-reaching changes to the institutions of government:

- Sweeping reforms were made to the upper chamber of Parliament, the House of Lords, long criticized for being anachronistic and undemocratic. The right of hereditary aristocrats to sit in the House ended in 1999, and a commission was appointed to develop plans for the future of the chamber.
- Following referendums in 1997, regional assemblies were created for Wales and Scotland, completing the process of devolution first discussed in the 1970s. Elected mayors were also created for several major cities, including London.
- Proportional representation (PR) was introduced for the 1998–99 elections to the regional assemblies, and for the 1999 elections to the European Parliament, the assumption being that PR might also eventually be introduced for the general election.
- The Bank of England was given independence in 1997.

Coincidentally, the first Blair administration also saw a new and critical focus on the place of the monarchy in British national life. In an attempt to make it more open and relevant, Queen Elizabeth – beginning in the late 1960s – had allowed greater media access to the life of her family. This became something of a feeding frenzy in the 1980s and 1990s as the failed marriages of her three eldest children – Charles, Anne and Andrew – attracted the attention of the tabloid press and its readers. In particular, the rather dry style of the royal family had been challenged by the fashionable and socially conscious Princess Diana, who in 1981 had married Prince Charles, the heir to the throne. In August 1997, Princess Diana – by now divorced from Charles – was killed in a car accident in Paris, and the remarkable public outpouring of grief in Britain stood in stark contrast to the reserved response of the Queen, who for several days failed to make a public statement or to sanction an official royal response. This single event seemed to represent a broader need for the monarchy to modernize and to catch up with a new set of public expectations about its status and role.

Meanwhile, there were new developments in Northern Ireland. The conflict had worsened during the 1980s, with sectarian killings, and bombings both in Northern Ireland and on the British mainland; by the mid-1990s more than 3,500 people had died. It strained government resources, incurred additional costs for the military, and tarnished Britain's reputation as a champion of civil rights and liberties: trial without jury was allowed, as was arrest for seven days without charge, and a ban was imposed on broadcasting interviews with terrorists. An attempt was made on the life of Margaret Thatcher at the Conservative Party annual conference in Brighton in October 1984, and a mortar attack was made on the London residence of the Prime Minister in 1991.

An Anglo–Irish agreement was drawn up in 1985 pledging the British and Irish governments to work towards a solution that would recognize differences between the Catholic and Protestant communities in the province. In 1993, the Downing Street Declaration committed the government to hold talks with any groups that renounced violence, and negotiations began in 1995. They continued under the Blair government, which underwrote negotiations between the warring factions chaired by former US Senator George Mitchell. These led to the Good Friday Agreement of April 1998 which brought a ceasefire between the warring sides, founded a regional assembly for Northern Ireland in which Protestants and Catholics shared power, and created cross-border councils that would bring members of the new assembly together with members of the British and Irish parliaments. After a delay involving a dispute over whether or not the Irish Republican Army (IRA) would turn in its weapons, the new Northern Ireland regional government eventually met for the first time in November 1999. Unfortunately, ongoing disputes over disarming combined with disagreements over power-sharing to lead several times to the suspension of the Northern Ireland government. When a new power-sharing government took office in May 2007, and five years of direct rule from London ended, new hope was born for the troubled province.

Meanwhile, Europe continued to pose challenges and opportunities. A critical issue was Britain's position on the single European currency, the euro (see Box 6.2). In January–February 2002, 12 of the 15 EU member states replaced their national currencies with the euro, the only holdouts being Denmark, Sweden and Britain. Majority public opinion in Britain was (and remains) hostile to the abolition of the pound, but Tony Blair himself was in favour, his government set its own series of economic tests for joining the euro (see Chapter 6),

Illustration 1.3 Anti-war demonstration

A demonstration in London against the war in Iraq. Not only was Britain's part in the war controversial, but it undermined the political standing of Tony Blair, raised questions about the merits of the Anglo–American special relationship, and heightened tensions within Britain between Muslims and non-Muslims.

and he promised to put the issue to a public referendum. But with the passing years this became increasingly unlikely, and there today remains little short-term prospect of Britain joining the euro.

On foreign policy, the Blair administration proved more willing to commit British troops to service overseas than were any of its Labour predecessors. Britain played an active role in the NATO attack on Serbia in 1999, in response to a programme of ethnic cleansing directed by the Milošević regime against Albanians living in the province of Kosovo. Following the terrorist attacks of September 2001 on targets in New York and Washington DC, Blair was quick to come to the support of the Bush administration, and British troops played a key role in mopping-up and peacekeeping operations in Afghanistan following the US-led attacks on the Taliban regime in late 2001 and early 2002. But then Blair went against public and political feeling in Britain and the EU in 2002–03 by refusing to oppose the plans of the Bush administration to remove Saddam Hussein from power in Iraq. Public opposition to the war was widespread, criticism of Blair administration policy deepened, an anti-war demonstration in London in February 2003 turned into the largest such public protest in British history, and Blair became stuck in a morass of charges that his government had lied about the reasons behind British support for the March 2003 invasion (see Cox and Oliver, 2006: 178–84). Cultural and political tensions led to bloodshed in July 2005 when four suicide bombers killed themselves in central London, taking the lives of 52 people.

Blair also found his government under attack for its failure to stem the decline in the quality of public services. Waiting lists for patients wanting operations under the National Health Service grew, several headline-making and deadly accidents underlined the declining state of Britain's railways, and concerns were raised about the state of the British educational system. But the economy was doing well, the Conservatives did not offer a popular alternative, and Blair was returned to office in the June 2001 election with his majority barely reduced. The gloss of victory was tarnished by a fall in voter turnout (from 71 per cent in 1997 to just over 59 per cent in 2001), and the result was seen as much as a reflection of voter disillusionment with the still-divided Conservative Party as of support for Labour. Blair was returned to a third term in office in May 2005, but with a reduced majority and against a background of clearly declining enthusiasm for his leadership. Iraq had dealt the first blow, but his government was also affected by charges of sleaze, with accusations that Blair had awarded peerages in the House of Lords in return for donations to the Labour Party. By 2006 Blair was widely unpopular, his public approval rate running as low as 27–30 per cent, an all-time low. He had announced that the 2005 election would be his last; during 2006, pressure grew for him to say when he would be stepping down; he eventually left office in 2007, surrounded by questions about his legacy.

Britain today is once again in a state of flux. In the last decade it has seen fundamental changes in its system of government and in the character of its politics, its economy is much improved since the dark days of the 1970s and 1980s, both government and the public sector have become more responsive to the needs of consumers and citizens, Britain plays a more assertive role in the international arena, and – whether the British like it or not – the definition of 'Britain' is being reviewed as the relationship between England, Scotland, Wales and Northern Ireland changes, and as its place in the European Union evolves. The Blair era is over, but what this will mean for the Labour

Illustration 1.4   Gordon Brown

Gordon Brown, who – after serving successfully as Britain's Chancellor of
the Exchequer (finance minister) and waiting in the wings for more than a
decade – finally succeeded Tony Blair as Prime Minister in June 2007.

grip on power, or whether there is an opportunity for opposition
parties to make their mark, remains to be seen. But the distinctions
among those parties have become hard to find as they all cluster
around the middle ground of British politics, where the centre of
gravity now seems to lie. And fundamental questions continue to
plague Britain's international role: how long can it continue to
provide support for unpopular US foreign policies, and how long can
it continue to resist the lure of Europe?

2

Land and People

Like most of its European neighbours, Britain is a small, crowded country. Its residents live in close proximity to one another, the physical dimensions of everything from homes to shops, offices, roads and parking spaces are small, and the landscape everywhere bears the imprint of human activity. It is difficult for Britons to escape permanent human habitation, whether in the form of sprawling cities, small villages or isolated farmhouses. Similarly, it is impossible to ignore the changes made by humans; the conversion of land to agriculture has combined with the removal of forests and the use of hedgerows as plot dividers to create a landscape that is almost unique and instantly recognizable: winding roads, immaculately maintained fields, patches of woodland, compact towns and villages, landscaped parks, and public footpaths.

This is a society where a large population has had to make the best possible use of limited resources. Britain has rich agricultural land, and meets most of its own basic food needs. It has a wealth of energy resources, from the coal that drove the industrial revolution to the oil and natural gas that meet its needs today. But growing population has put increased pressure on those resources, and the changes wrought first by agriculture and then by industry have taken their toll on the environment, first with the air and water pollution that were once such grim features of Britain's cities, then with the threats posed to nature and wildlife by more 'efficient' agriculture. Some might argue that the British have also been moulded by the climate of their country, with its mild temperatures and mythically persistent rain. Climate has certainly helped make Britons a phlegmatic people, provides a recurring topic of conversation, and has driven many to leave for sunnier and drier parts of the world.

The people of Britain have also been influenced by important social divisions, the most fundamental of which stem from the cultural, historical, political and linguistic differences that distinguish the English, the Scottish, the Welsh and the Irish from each other. This is still a 'united' kingdom, but nationalist movements against English domination first took Ireland out of the union, then brought violence and civil strife to Northern Ireland, and then encouraged movements for greater local control – and even for independence – in Wales and Scotland. The redefinition of the term 'British' has been further complicated by waves of non-white immigration since the Second World War, which pushed the issue of race up the political and social agenda, and more recently by new arrivals from the continent of Europe.

This chapter looks at the land and people of Britain. The first half examines topography, climate and key natural resources, and looks at the state of the British environment, the threats it faces and the policy responses it has prompted. While there have been advances in some areas, there are concerns about changes in energy needs and continuing threats to natural resources and nature, and new debates about the welfare of rural areas. The second half of the chapter looks at recent demographic trends in Britain, with a focus on some of the remarkable changes that have taken place in patterns of migration, on the relationship between regionalism and national identity, and at some troubling trends in the area of race relations. Notable among these have been questions about multiculturalism arising out of a new debate about the place of Muslims in British national life.

The Geography of Britain

The most notable geographical facts about the UK are (a) it is small, (b) it is an island state, and (c) its dimensions are moderate in almost every way: there are no extremes of distance, size, height, length, climate, or variety of animal life and vegetation. It has no great mountain chains, no great rivers or estuaries, no large lakes, and no sweeping forests. Its highest mountain (Ben Nevis in Scotland) is less than one-sixth the height of Mt Everest and less than one-third the height of Mont Blanc, Europe's highest mountain. Its largest lake (Lough Neagh in Northern Ireland) could fit into Lake Superior more than 215 times, and its longest river (the Severn in England) is barely one-twentieth the length of the Nile, and barely one-eighth the length of the Danube, Europe's longest river. It has just 420 animal species and 1,400 flowering plant species, few of which are unique to the British Isles.

At the same time, though, Britain is notable for the variety of its landscapes, which are the product of a combination of geological and climatic change over time, and of centuries of human activity. Its geological history has seen the British landmass pushed from the southern hemisphere to the northern, and its landscape types have included tropical rain forests, deserts, freezing ice caps, high mountains and mudflats. The last great natural influence on its geology came with the Ice Age, which ended 375,000 years ago, and during which ice sheets and glaciers covered all but what are now the most extreme southern reaches of England. The result is that Britain today has – for its size – one of the richest and most diverse sets of geological features of any country in the world: examples of most of the different types of rock, soils, minerals and land forms found elsewhere in the world can be found somewhere in the British Isles.

During the Ice Age, Britain was connected to the European mainland, but the melting of the icecaps caused sea levels to rise, creating the island of Great Britain and many of its neighbouring smaller islands, such as the Isle of Wight off the southern coast of England, Anglesey off the northern coast of Wales, the Isle of Man in the Irish Sea, and the islands of Arran, Islay, Mull, Skye and the Hebrides off the west coat of Scotland. Britain is now divided from the continent by the North Sea, and by the English Channel, which is just 35 km (22 miles) wide at its narrowest point. Britain and Ireland for their part are divided by the Irish Sea, which is 21 km (13 miles) across at its narrowest point. The only land boundary that the UK has with another country is the 488-km (303-mile) border with Ireland.

The landscape continues to change even today. The long-term effects of the end of the Ice Age mean that Scotland is slowly rising, while southern England is slowly sinking and the sea is moving up its estuaries; at one of its lowest points in the Fens of East Anglia, wetlands prevail. The weather and the sea continue to exert their effects on the land, with wind and rain breaking down exposed rocks, rivers eroding the land and carrying debris downstream, and the action of wind and the oceans breaking up coastal rocks and headlands. Added to these changes have been the effects of humans on the landscape, almost every accessible square metre of which has been remodelled by human activity. Physically (see Map 2.1), Britain today can be broadly divided into highland and lowland regions. The

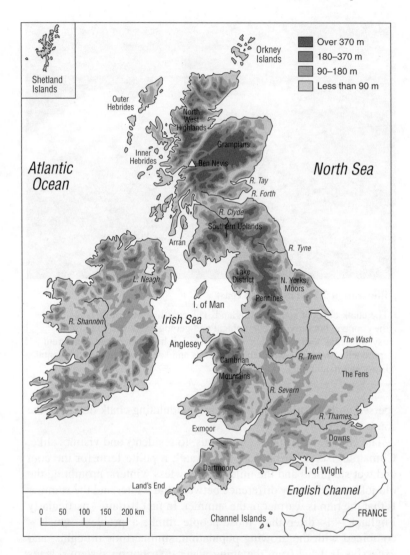

Map 2.1   Physical features of the British Isles

highest land is found in the south west (Dartmoor and Exmoor), and the Pennine mountains of north-central England; the Cambrian mountains of Wales; the central areas of Northern Ireland; and the southern uplands, Grampian mountains, and north-west highlands of Scotland. The rest of Britain consists of plains and lowlands inter-

Illustration 2.1   The British coast

The chalk cliffs of southern England. The coastline of Britain helps define the country, not only in geographical and geological terms, but also in psychological terms. Because it is an island, it has always had a different approach to relations with other countries and societies than its continental European neighbours.

spersed with moorland and the gently undulating chalk downs of the south east.

The climate of Britain is notorious, to residents and visitors alike. Climatologists describe it as 'moderate', a polite term for the cool and wet summers and the mild and snowless winters, prompting the old joke that the only difference between the winter and the summer is that the rain is warmer in the summer. In fact Britain – particularly England – is drier than most people think, a problem which – combined with the growing population, summertime droughts, and excessive leakage from the aging water distribution system – leads to increasingly frequent bans on the use of hosepipes to water gardens or wash cars. And the experience of recent years suggests that climate change is helping make British summers warmer; in both 2005 and 2006 there were long spells of hot weather with little rain, leaving large parts of Britain dry and parched. And 2006 turned out to have the highest average temperatures since records began in 1914.

The most telling influences on Britain's climate are surrounding seas (which act as a temperature buffer that keeps coastal areas cool when inland areas are warm, and vice versa), the intersection between cool air moving down from the North Pole and warm air moving up from the tropics, and the Gulf Stream, which carries warmer water from the tropics to the Arctic, and has a moderating effect on Britain's weather, making it much warmer than areas at similar latitudes in Asia or North America. January temperatures are generally in the range of 3–5°C (37–41°F) and July temperatures are in the range 11–16°C (52–61°F). Rainfall is usually well distributed throughout the year, and tends to be soft and steady rather than sharp and heavy, with few major storms. One of the results is the characteristic lush greenery of the British landscape, which usually lasts throughout the summer and the winter. Another result is that the British are often caught wrong-footed by more extreme weather, such as hot summers or heavy snow in winter. Whatever the conditions, weather is one of the standard topics of conversation among Britons (Fort, 2006).

Natural Resources

Britain may not be well-endowed in land, and may have lost most of its natural forest cover to agriculture, but it has a wealth of commercial energy resources: it is one of the most fuel-rich countries in the EU, with significant supplies of coal, natural gas and oil, is rich in fisheries, has much rich and productive agricultural land, and is self-sufficient in almost every foodstuff that can be grown in its climate.

Coal was one of the foundations of the industrial revolution. It was the presence of vast coal resources in the midlands and the north of England, and the south of Wales, that offered the opportunity for the generation of steam power, which in turn allowed for the exploitation of seams of coal that had previously been out of reach. More recently, coal has been at the heart of the redefinition of Britain's political and economic priorities, the struggle between government and miners' unions being a defining part of the changes wrought by Thatcherism (Taylor, 2005). While coal is still an important source of energy, it now accounts for just 16 per cent of British energy consumption, down from 30 per cent in 1990; most is used to generate electricity at steam-powered generation plants. Coal has been superseded by three other sources of energy: natural gas, oil, and nuclear power. For

Box 2.1   Britain or the UK: What's in a name?

Something that routinely confuses and puzzles people – even sometimes the British themselves – is the correct name of the country. The
problem stems from the fact that the United Kingdom is four countries
in one: a union of England, Scotland, Wales and Northern Ireland. Each
has its own separate identity, its own history and culture, its own
'national' sports teams, and – in the case of Scotland – its own separate
legal and educational system.

Formally, the full name is the United Kingdom of Great Britain and
Northern Ireland. Great Britain consists of England, Scotland and
Wales, while Northern Ireland is physically separate but is part of the
union with Great Britain. However, while the term 'United Kingdom'
is used at government conferences and in diplomatic dealings, in everyday conversation most Britons use the terms 'Britain' and 'British' as
shorthand, even though it is technically incorrect to refer to all four
countries together as anything but the United Kingdom. If this is a
forgivable sin, it is more unforgivable to use the term 'England' when
referring to the United Kingdom, as (for example) many Americans
persist in doing. It would be the same as describing all Americans as
'Texans' or all Germans as 'Bavarians'.

The complications do not end there. The Isle of Man in the Irish Sea,
and the Channel Islands to the south of England – consisting of Jersey,
Guernsey and neighbouring smaller islands – are usually assumed to be
part of the UK. Their inhabitants speak English, and their ways of life
are almost indistinguishable from those of people on the mainland. Yet
the islands are not part of the United Kingdom, nor are they even
members of the European Union. Instead they are dependencies of the
British Crown. They each have their own legislatures and system of law
(the Tynwald on the Isle of Man is the oldest continuously functioning
legislature in the world), and the British government is responsible for
their foreign and defence policies. The free movement of services and
people that applies to the EU does not apply to the islands, making it
difficult for someone living in mainland Britain to move permanently
to one of the islands.

decades Britain has been self-sufficient in electricity generation, but
the planned closure of nuclear and coal-fired power stations has led
to projections that it could only be 80 per cent self-sufficient within a
decade. Pressure has grown for greater investment in renewable
sources of energy (such as solar, wind and geothermal power), but the
Blair government caused a stir in 2006 by launching a 50-year energy
plan which embraced nuclear power as a key energy source and
argued the need for new stations; most of Britain's existing 23 nuclear

power stations, which provide about 20 per cent of electricity needs, are due to be closed by 2023.

Since oil was discovered in the North Sea in the 1960s, with production picking up momentum during the 1970s and 1980s, Britain has been a major oil producer. This has increased government income, reduced Britain's dependence on imported oil, and transformed the economic prospects of many coastal communities. But British North Sea oil output has declined steadily since 1999, and Britain during 2006 became a net importer of oil, helping push its trade deficit to a new record of nearly £6 billion (€9 billion/$11 billion). Oil will still be drawn from the North Sea for several more years, but production levels will continue their steady decline, and there will be diminishing profits and returns as smaller and more expensive oil fields are exploited. This will mean less income for government, and oil will become an increasingly important security issue. The news is better for natural gas, which is Britain's biggest source of primary energy, accounting for 40 per cent of needs. Britain is the world's fourth biggest producer, and supplies from offshore gas fields are expected to allow Britain to continue being self-sufficient well into the century.

As an island nation, Britain is well-endowed with fisheries; it is one of the EU's largest fishing nations, and it meets about half of its own domestic demand. The size of the fishing fleet has fallen by nearly one-third in the last ten years, and employment in the fishing industry by a quarter, but total landings by quantity and value have remained steady, as has household consumption. But life has changed for fishing communities. First, fish catches dropped substantially as a result of overfishing and of changes in the breeding patterns of fish. Then fishing quotas were imposed under the EU's Common Fisheries Policy, new technology improved the efficiency of catching fish, and access to waters outside the 20-km (12-mile) limit was opened up to fishing boats from other EU countries. The impact of these changes has been most obvious in Britain's traditional fishing communities, where fewer people work in fishing, and new jobs in other fields have not always been created to take up the slack.

Agriculture in Britain has long been among the most technologically innovative and productive in the world (see Soffe, 2003). Technical advances have allowed British farmers to exploit the limited land area of Britain to produce as much as is physically possible from a country with its climate. Farmland takes up just over three-quarters of the land area of Britain (much higher than the figure for

Illustration 2.2   Didcot Power Station

Energy has recently moved up the political agenda in Britain. Coal- and gas-fired power stations – like this one at Didcot in Oxfordshire, opened in 1968 – play a key role in electricity supply, but their contribution is declining, leading to questions about future sources of British energy.

the EU as a whole, which is just 42 per cent), and there are about 235,000 farm units, ranging in size from large industrial operations to small family farms. Barely 2 per cent of the workforce is employed in agriculture, and it contributes just 1 per cent of Britain's gross domestic product (figures which are similar to those in other European countries), but Britain's farmers provide two-thirds of the country's food needs, with much left over for export.

Half of Britain's farms concentrate on dairy farming, and on raising beef cattle and sheep; most of the beef and sheep farms are in the northern, western and south-western parts of the country, and they account for about one-third of Britain's agricultural output. The other half focus on poultry and egg production (in which Britain is almost self-sufficient) and on raising arable crops such as wheat, barley, oats and vegetables; crop farms are found particularly in eastern and central-southern England. The agricultural industry has been heavily impacted by the EU's controversial Common Agricultural Policy (CAP), which sets minimum guaranteed prices for food products. While the CAP has helped promote

European agricultural production, standardized the quality of that production, and increased productivity and efficiency, it also swallows up nearly half the EU's annual budget, has promoted overproduction, encourages farmers to rely more on chemical fertilizers and pesticides, and has upset the EU's major trading partners (even those which, like the United States, have their own system of subsidies to farmers).

British agriculture in recent years has been hit by two crises that have brought economic hardship to farmers, many of whom have gone out of business. The first was the advent of mad cow disease (BSE, or Bovine Spongiform Encephalopathy). First identified in the mid-1980s, it led to controls on the use of cattle organs in animal feed in 1990. When the government announced a link between BSE and a human equivalent in 1996, the EU imposed a worldwide two-year ban on exports of all British beef. According to one assessment (Packer, 2006), the government response to the crisis was little more than a combination of informed guesswork and sheer good fortune. The second crisis was the outbreak in February 2001 of foot-and-mouth disease, which began in northern England and quickly spread to other parts of the country. Over the next seven months, in order to contain the disease, more than 3 million sheep, nearly 600,000 cattle, and nearly 140,000 pigs were slaughtered.

The combined effects of BSE and foot-and-mouth disease meant significant hardship for Britain's rural areas. Ironically, though, the crises may actually have long-term benefits for the countryside, because they have emphasized the links between agriculture and other parts of the rural economy, such as tourism. There is also more sympathy for those working and living in rural areas, and lobbying organizations with an interest in rural issues have become more active, leading – as Michael Woods (2005) puts it – to 'the strange awakening of rural Britain'. Many were mobilized by the decision of the Blair government to outlaw fox-hunting with dogs in 2005 (hounds can still be used to chase and flush out foxes, which can still be shot, or killed by birds of prey – they cannot be killed by foxhounds). Long a controversial pastime, criticized as much for its mistreatment of foxes as for its elitism, fox-hunting was defended by its supporters as both an important tradition and a key source of jobs in rural areas. One of the results of concerns about rural issues was the creation of the Countryside Alliance, a lobbying organization that has drawn new public attention to those issues.

The Environment

The state of the British environment has been determined by three major forces: Britain's long history of human settlement, the density of its human population, and the long-term effects of the industrial revolution. These have combined to make sure that every part of the country has been directly or indirectly impacted by human development, and that there is no true wilderness left in Britain. In many ways, the British countryside is nothing more than a large man-made park, most of which is actively farmed and remodelled. Nature and agriculture have long had to coexist, with nature usually coming off worst. Industry and population growth have also combined to produce a society heavily impacted by the fallout from the use of fossil fuels, the growth of road vehicle traffic, and the spread of housing. Britain was once notorious for its urban smogs, and indeed the term 'smog' was coined to describe the combination of smoke and fog that once polluted the air over major cities, notably London (Brimblecombe, 1989). Air and water in Britain are cleaner today than at any time since the rise of industry, but most of Britain's major environmental problems – like those of all post-industrial societies – still stem from the use of fossil fuels (petrol, oil, coal, and natural gas).

The natural vegetation of the British Isles is deciduous woodland. Except for heaths and moors, most of Britain was once covered by forests dominated by oak, ash, beech, elm and – along the banks of rivers – water-loving species such as alder and willow. The first forest clearances were carried out by Neolithic man beginning about 6,000 years ago, since when there has been an almost continuous process of change (Rackham, 2004). In the Middle Ages, forests still occupied about one-third of the land area, but today only about 7 per cent of land is covered by forest, and less than one-third of what remains consists of ancient woodlands and broadleaf forests. Visitors to Sherwood Forest, the New Forest and the Forest of Dean will find only the vestiges of once great natural forests. Postwar government policies have allowed landowners to make more money from converting woodland to cornfields or to commercial conifer plantations, and an outbreak of Dutch elm disease in the 1960s and 1970s brought more change; by the 1990s there were few mature elms left in Britain (or in most of northern Europe). The result is that Britain today has less forest cover per square kilometre than any other country in Europe except Ireland. It has only been during the last

20–30 years that there has been broader public awareness and concern about the loss of forests.

Wildlife and natural habitat in Britain is now found only in those areas not immediately impacted by human activity, or in isolated pockets surrounded by farmland or in the heart of cities. Agricultural intensification during and after the Second World War combined with the spread of cities and the creation of new towns to bring marked changes to the landscape. Wetland, moorland, heathland and down-land were 'reclaimed', hedgerows and woodland were cleared to make way for bigger fields that were easier to plough and to crop, and increasing quantities of chemical fertilizer were applied to the land. The resulting increase in agricultural yields has been remarkable, but the natural environment has suffered proportionately:

- While the population and size of Britain's major urban areas has fallen, the number and size of towns has grown, as has the population of rural areas. One result has been the steady conversion of agricultural land (or greenfield sites) to new development. Meanwhile, much old industrial land in cities (or brownfield sites) has been left derelict. Brownfield sites are more difficult to develop because they may be contaminated, and because the owners of these sites often have inflated ideas about the value of the land.
- Nearly one-fifth of Britain's plant species and many of its animal species are threatened, mainly by loss of habitat: the draining of wetlands, the removal of hedgerows and forests, the expansion of development, and the use of chemicals in agriculture.

On the positive side of the ledger, the area of protected land has increased substantially since the Second World War. Britain has a network of 14 national parks, including the Lake District and the Yorkshire Dales in northern England, Exmoor and Dartmoor in the south-west, Snowdonia in Wales, and the Cairngorms in Scotland. There are also 42 Areas of Outstanding Natural Beauty, 40 National Scenic Areas in Scotland, 17 forest parks, more than 200 country parks, protected coastlines, designated areas of special scientific value, and greenbelts around cities where building is strictly controlled. Together, they cover more than 20 per cent of the land area of Britain. Levels of protection vary, however, and many of these areas are protected as much for recreation as for conservation. And unlike national parks in other parts of the world, where

Illustration 2.3   Exmoor, England

British agriculture is both productive and technologically innovative, and
has also helped give the British landscape its characteristic look of small
fields divided by hedgerows. Even national parks – such as Exmoor in
south-west England, shown here – are still actively farmed.

permanent human habitation is not allowed, British national parks
were already settled and farmed, and continue that way, albeit with
restrictions.

Meanwhile, there is both good news and bad news on the relationship between transport and the environment (Banister, 1998). The
good news is that Britain's air is cleaner today than it has been since
pre-industrial times. The Victorian era saw the pollutive effects of
heavy industry reach their peak, with the Black Country of the west
midlands being particularly notorious, and inspiring this description
by Charles Dickens in *The Old Curiosity Shop* (1841):

> On every side, as far as the eye could see into the heavy distance,
> tall chimneys, crowding on each other … poured out their plague
> of smoke, obscured the light, and made foul the melancholy air. On
> mounds of ashes by the wayside, sheltered only by a few rough
> boards, or rotten pent-house roofs, strange engines spun and
> writhed like tortured creatures … making the ground tremble with
> their agonies.

Britain finally began to take the first small steps to clean its air in the 1950s, but it took many more years of being known as 'the dirty man of Europe', and being criticized by Scandinavian governments for its major role in the production of acid pollution, before real progress was made during the 1980s and 1990s to clean its air, and even then it was prompted mainly by the requirements of European Union law (for details, see McCormick, 1997: Chapter 5). The result is that nitrogen oxide emissions, most of which come from road traffic, were down in 2002 by one-third on 1989 levels, and are projected to fall another 70 per cent by 2015. Meanwhile, sulphur dioxide emissions, coming mainly from power stations, have been reduced by 80 per cent since 1970, and carbon monoxide emissions have been halved in the same period. Finally, emissions of carbon dioxide – the primary constituent in climate change – fell by nearly 15 per cent between 1990 and 2004 (although they have climbed slightly since, thanks to increased oil and gas consumption).

The bad news is that road traffic is worsening, threatening the quality of the air and encroaching on the land as new roads and all their subsidiary services are built. There are 29 million vehicles on British roads, the highest volume per kilometre of any EU country except Italy and Portugal. Despite the fact that only 48 per cent of homes have the regular use of one car, travel by road vehicle has doubled in the last 30 years. More traffic causes more congestion, which is worsened by the constant need to maintain roads to meet the needs of that traffic. New roads have been built – such as the M25 motorway surrounding London – but they have added to the problem by encouraging more people to travel by road. Meanwhile, the quality of public transport has declined. In 2003, London introduced a system under which drivers in central London had to pay a daily congestion charge, but while this proved successful and has been extended into western London, the broader problems of road transport in Britain only promise to become worse.

As with all other EU member states, environmental policy standards in Britain are now driven more by the requirements of European law than by those of British law (see Lowe and Ward, 1998; Jordan, 2002). The EU has been an active and productive source of new regulations and standards on environmental quality, and Britain's goals are now mainly the same as those of the rest of the EU. European policy has been focused mainly on improving the quality of water and air, reducing the production of waste, improving the management of chemicals and pesticides, conserving energy, and managing forests and fisheries (see McCormick, 2001). Sustainable development – meaning the exploitation of resources at rates that do not negatively impact the environment – has become the core goal in Britain as in the rest of the EU.

The People of Britain

Like most of its European neighbours, Britain is a crowded country. In mid-2005, the population was estimated to be about 60.2 million, which was roughly the same as that of France, but living on a land area half the size of France. Population density runs at nearly 250 people per sq km (650 people per sq mile), although there is wider regional variation: more than 380 people per sq km (990 per sq mile) in England and just 65 per sq km (170 per sq mile) in Scotland. The most densely populated parts of the country are in and around London, the environs of Birmingham and Coventry in the Midlands, a crescent in the old industrial areas from Liverpool to Manchester and Sheffield, and small clusters around Newcastle, Glasgow, Cardiff and Belfast. The most sparsely populated regions are south-west and northern England, Wales, and most of Scotland.

England is the dominant partner in the United Kingdom, not just by land area (54 per cent of the total), but also by population and by demographic change. Nearly 84 per cent of the British population lives in England, which has also had the greatest population increase over the past century (64 per cent, compared to just 14 per cent in Scotland), and that population is expected to continue to grow for many years while that of Scotland has already started to decline. Most of the major cities of the UK are in England, including London, Birmingham, Manchester and Liverpool, and – like cities everywhere – it is to these that people migrate in search of jobs, wealth and opportunity.

Typically for a post-industrial society, the rate of population increase in Britain has been declining, and currently stands at just 0.6 per cent annually. At this rate, the population is expected to peak in about 2040 at nearly 66 million before beginning to decline. This sets Britain apart from most other European countries – notably Germany, France, Spain and Italy – where growth rates are smaller and population numbers are already declining. An increasingly important determinant in British population numbers has been the change in rates of

Illustration 2.4   Terraced houses

Britain is both highly urbanized – with nearly 90 per cent of its people living in towns and cities – and densely populated. These terraced and detached homes in the town of Lewes in East Sussex are typical of dwellings in many small British towns.

migration. Natural change – the difference between births and deaths – accounted in the first half of the twentieth century for nearly all the increases in Britain's population, running in the range of 250–500,000 people annually. By the end of the century, the rate of natural change had fallen to just 60–100,000 people per year, while migration rates had changed from a net outflow of 60–100,000 (in other words, more people were leaving Britain than arriving) to a net inflow of 130–160,000 people per year. The net inflow in 2004 reached a record high of 223,000.

These changing patterns have had a significant impact on the diversity of Britain. Until the Second World War, Britain was a predominantly white country – most immigrants over the centuries had come from continental Europe, and later from the white dominions of the Old Commonwealth: Australia, Canada, New Zealand and South Africa. Also, the number of emigrants was much greater than the number of immigrants. But since 1945 – and particularly in the last two decades – there have been four significant developments:

- People are leaving Britain in ever greater numbers. There was a 50 per cent increase in the number of emigrants between 1994 and 2004, with 360,000 people leaving the country in 2004. Where emigrants once left mainly for the white dominions and the United States, the greatest numbers of those leaving Britain today (about 40 per cent) are moving to other EU member states. Recent polls have shown a sharp increase in the number of Britons who have considered emigration, the most common reasons given being the search for a better quality of life (a notion that is all but impossible to quantify), dislike of British weather, and concerns about the rising cost of living.

- Immigration from the New Commonwealth, notably the Indian subcontinent (India, Pakistan, Bangladesh) and the Caribbean, has grown. As a result, the number of non-whites living in Britain (Northern Ireland excluded) has grown from about 75–100,000 (0.2 per cent of the population) in 1945 to about 4.7 million (7.9 per cent of the population) today.

- Migration to and from other EU member states has grown. The average annual inflow of people from other EU states during the 1990s grew from 71,000 to 89,000, and the number of Britons moving to other EU countries grew in tandem. Unlike old-style migration, where people moved because of economic necessity, or because of a general need to improve the quality of their lives, recent migration flows have included work-related factors (companies moving workers to foreign offices) or 'lifestyle choices'; many Britons, for example, have retired to France, Spain, or Portugal. The arrival in Britain of workers from Eastern Europe has grown since EU enlargement in 2004, such that the image of the Polish plumber has achieved almost mythical proportions in Britain, as in other parts of the EU. Immigrants from the ten new member states of the EU made up an estimated 80 per cent of the increase in net inflows to Britain in 2003–04.

- There have been changes in the number of people seeking asylum in Britain. Thanks to some of the loosest laws on asylum in the EU, Britain since the 1990s has proved an irresistible lure to asylum-seekers from a growing variety of countries. Annual applications rose from 33,000 in 1992 to more than 80,000 in 2002, placing Britain second only to Germany in the EU in terms of the number received. Since then, a tightening of regulations – including an increase in the number of removals of failed applicants – has brought numbers down to less than 30,000 annually. Most recent asylum-seekers have come from the former Yugoslavia, Iraq, Iran, Afghanistan, China, Somalia and Zimbabwe, adding to the social diversity of Britain.

The British have also become increasingly mobile within Britain. It was once typical for people to be born, to live, to work and to die in the same city, town or village, which would likely have been where their parents and grandparents before them had lived. The pace of mobility changed with the industrial revolution, when thousands were drawn over time to mining towns and to the factories being built in the rapidly growing urban centres of Scotland, south Wales, and the English midlands (for details, see Rubinstein, 1998, Chapter 16).

During the twentieth century, social mobility increased, prompted by improvements in transport and a revulsion against life in the city. The most notable general trends in recent decades have been (a) the move away from the old centres of heavy industry in northern England, Scotland and Wales towards jobs in light industry and services in southern England and the midlands, and (b) the move away from the old city centres to the suburbs and to neighbouring towns, with a resulting increase in the number of people commuting to work. The biggest net movement has been out of London: driven off by congestion, worsening traffic problems, the high cost of property, and rising rents, many people have moved to cheaper, quieter and cleaner towns in the areas surrounding London. The population of the capital has continued to grow however, thanks mainly to the inflow of people moving to London from outside Britain, especially from other EU member states.

As with all post-industrial societies, the population of Britain is becoming older as birth rates decline and people live longer. In 1901, just over a third of Britons were aged under 16, while 10 per cent were aged older than 55; in 2004, the respective figures were 19 per cent and 23 per cent. Nearly one-quarter of adults are of pensionable age (60 for women, 65 for men), which represents an increase of 18 per cent since 1971. In this respect, Britain fits with trends across the European Union and in other industrialized countries outside Europe. There will be important political and economic ramifications:

- There will be increased pressure on the health-care system as people live longer, as more must be spent on the provision of health care, and as the demand for doctors and nurses continues to grow.
- The workplace is being affected as the number of retirees who opt to continue to work for financial reasons continues to grow.

- Younger people will bear an increased burden of the social security system as fewer working-age Britons make contributions into the system and more retired Britons make withdrawals.
- The political power of the elderly will grow: there are greater numbers of older people, and voter turnout in this age group is high (80–87 per cent for those aged 55 and above as compared to 50–60 per cent for those aged 35 and below). Concerns about the welfare of the elderly (or 'pensioners' as they are known in Britain) have long been a hot-button issue, but despite the existence of many organizations representing the interests of the elderly, such as the National Pensioners Convention, Help the Aged, and Age Concern, they have not yet become an effective lobbying movement. This is likely to change as the population of Britain becomes older.

Nationalism and Regionalism

The relationship among the four partners in the United Kingdom has not always been an easy one, with ongoing memories about the way in which England subjugated the three others, concerns about the cultural, economic and political dominance of England, and efforts to protect and rebuild minority cultural identity. Despite the existence of a 'United' Kingdom, regionalism is a factor in national politics, leading even to minority support in Scotland and Wales for complete independence.

Wales lost its independence in 1285 and was united with England in 1536–42, as a result of which its early political institutions and processes developed along English lines, and the two countries today have the same legal and administrative systems. Scotland was different: the Scottish and English crowns were united in 1603, but political union did not come until 1707, and even then the two countries retained many separate features, including different religions, different legal codes, and separate educational structures. As for Ireland, the partition that came in 1922 with the creation of the Irish Free State left behind Northern Ireland, which has since been governed mainly as a semi-autonomous state, with its own civil service, its own political parties, and (except when direct rule from London was imposed in 1972–99) its own Parliament (now the Northern Ireland Assembly) at Stormont.

What are the differences among the four countries?

• Each has its own flag,* its own culture, and its own writers and artists. Each country even has its own sports teams, so that while English, Scottish, Welsh and Northern Irish athletes at the Olympics wear the colours of Great Britain, there are separate national football and rugby teams (although the national rugby teams occasionally combine with Ireland under the colours of the British and Irish Lions).

• Scotland, Wales and Northern Ireland have their own regional political parties: the Scottish National Party (SNP), Plaid Cymru in Wales, and a cluster of Northern Irish parties. All have representation both in the national British Parliament and in the new regional assemblies.

• Class and regional differences overlap, a result of the development of industry in the eighteenth and nineteenth centuries in Scotland, Wales and the north of England. These regions saw the rise of the new industrial class of manual labourers, and have since suffered the worst effects of industrial decline and economic adjustment. So while England has a per capita GDP slightly above the average for the UK, the figures for Scotland, Wales and Northern Ireland are all lower than average (see Table 2.1).

• Scotland and Northern Ireland have legal and educational systems that are separate from those used in England and Wales, and the Church of Scotland – created in 1560 – is also separate from the Church of England (see Chapter 7).

• Wales is officially bilingual. About 20 per cent of the population of Wales (that is, about 500,000 people) speak Welsh, which has had equal status with English since 1993, and Wales also has its own Welsh-language radio and TV stations. By contrast, only about 8 per cent of the people of Northern Ireland speak or write Irish Gaelic, and a bare 50,000 people in Scotland – about 1 per cent of the population – speak Scots Gaelic; forecasts have been made of its imminent extinction.

The strength of the relationship among the four countries has ebbed and flowed, but talk of the potential break-up of the United Kingdom is exaggerated, the pressures having been reduced since the 1960s by

---

* The old flag of Northern Ireland – a red hand inside a white star on a red cross – has strong connections with the Protestant community, and is no longer official but is still occasionally flown. The official flag of Northern Ireland is the Union Flag of the United Kingdom.

Table 2.1   The four nations compared

	Land area '000 sq km	Population		Per capita GDP (UK = 100)
		Million	*Density per sq km*	
England	130.4 (54%)	50.4 (84%)	384	102
Scotland	78.8 (33%)	5.1 (9%)	65	96
Wales	20.8 (9%)	3.0 (5%)	139	81
N. Ireland	14.1 (6%)	1.7 (3%)	121	77
Total	244.1	60.2		

Source: Office for National Statistics (2006). Figures are for mid-2005.

devolution (the transfer of selected powers from the national government in London to regional governments). This is an idea that traces its origins in political discourse back to the 1880s (Bogdanor, 2001), but it has moved up the agenda in recent decades (O'Neill, 2004). The Conservative Party was traditionally opposed to the idea, seeing it as the thin end of a wedge that would eventually lead to full independence, at least for Scotland. Meanwhile, the Labour Party had for many years promised constitutional reforms leading to devolution, and – upon coming to power in 1997 – the Blair administration moved quickly to hold referendums in Scotland and Wales on a proposal to create regional assemblies. Nearly 75 per cent of Scots voted in favour, while a bare majority of the Welsh (50.3 per cent) were in favour. The result was the creation in 1998 of assemblies for Scotland and Wales, followed in 1999 by the re-establishment of an assembly for Northern Ireland (see Chapter 4 for more details).

While the Scottish independence movement has not gone away, polling data on its strength is inconclusive: recent surveys have found between one-third and one-half of Scots in favour, depending on how the question is worded. Whatever the balance of opinion, there is resentment against the national government in London, strongest in the poorer parts of Scotland and Wales. The priorities of voters are reflected in the support given to regional political parties at regional and national elections, which has been mixed. At the regional assembly elections in 2003, the Scottish National Party won 23 per cent of the vote while Plaid Cymru won 20 per cent of the vote. Support for both parties at the 2005 general election was less than expected, suggesting strong continued support in Scotland and Wales for national political parties, along with an undercurrent of support for the idea of local issues being taken care of by local parties. Nationalists took heart from improved results in the 2007 regional elections, but how much the vote was a reflection of disenchantment with Labour was hard to say.

The creation of regional assemblies has led to an interesting anomaly, known as the West Lothian question. Speaking during a 1977 House of Commons debate over devolution, the MP for the Scottish district of West Lothian – Tam Dalyell – asked how long English Members of Parliament (MPs) (and constituencies) would tolerate MPs from Scotland, Wales and Northern Ireland having a say over British political decisions when English MPs had much less say over affairs in Scotland, Wales and Northern Ireland. It was largely a theoretical question until the creation of the regional assemblies, which resulted in greater self-government for the regions. So not only do Scottish, Welsh, and Northern Ireland MPs now more obviously have a say over English affairs, when the reverse is not true, but they also have less say over affairs in their home regions. Some have argued that all matters discussed by the House of Commons ultimately impact the whole country, but others are not so sure.

It is also important to appreciate that regionalism is not simply about national frontiers, but that Scotland, Wales and Northern Ireland are divided within themselves. The Scots have different religions, and there are cultural rivalries between highlanders and lowlanders, and between Glasgow and Edinburgh. The Welsh are divided economically between the old industrial centres and coal-mining communities of the south and the agricultural regions of the north, and between those who speak Welsh and those who do not. Meanwhile, Northern Ireland suffers a variety of religious, economic and cultural divisions, and is split between those who support continued union with Britain and those who do not.

England, too, has its own regionalism, with a recent rise in sympathy for the idea of a distinctive English national identity (Kumar, 2003). Surprisingly for so small a country, there are distinctive regional identities that set the English apart from each other. The values, attitudes and priorities of people who live in London and its suburbs are different from those who live in the rural and small-town environment of the 'home counties' around London, in the farmlands and the tourist meccas of the south-west, in the old industrial areas of the midlands and the north, and in the dales of Yorkshire and the mountains and lakes of Cumbria. Most unusual of all is the enclave

Box 2.2   The dominant role of London

Not all capital cities play a major role in national affairs, because power is often dissipated and shared among multiple urban areas. Washington DC may be the capital of the United States, for example, but it is a relatively provincial city: New York has a population 15 times greater, Los Angeles a population seven times greater, and they are more nationally significant.

The situation is quite different in Britain, where London plays the foremost role in almost every aspect of British life, so much so that Britain is not only dominated by England, but in many respects is also dominated by London. More than one-third of the British population lives in and around London, and as well as being the seat of national government, it is also the national hub for the following:

- *Communications*: it is the home of all the major national newspapers and radio and TV stations.
- *Finance*: it is the home of the Bank of England, the London Stock Exchange, and most of the major banks and financial corporations.
- *Transport*: the rail and motorway systems centre on London, which is also served by Britain's three biggest airports, Heathrow, Gatwick and Stansted.
- *Culture*: London has some of the world's finest theatre, opera, ballet, and symphony orchestras, and is home to recording studios and major rock concert venues.
- *Sports*: the national football stadium is at Wembley in north London, and the capital is also home to Wimbledon for tennis, Twickenham for rugby, and Lord's and The Oval for cricket.

Inner London – including the shopping and cultural districts of the West End, and the financial district of the City of London – is the wealthiest region in the European Union. For statistical purposes, the EU is divided into 268 regions; taking 100 as the average per capita gross domestic product for those regions, the poorer parts of the EU have a per capita GDP in the range of 25–35, while the figure for inner London is 303 (figures from Eurostat, the EU statistical service). Unfortunately, inner London is also one of the most expensive places to live in the world, topping comparative tables for the cost of renting and buying property, for eating out at restaurants, and for going out to the theatre or the cinema.

of Cornwall on the south-western tip of England: the Cornish are related to the Celts of Ireland, Wales and Scotland, have a distinctive culture, and – although very few now speak it – have their own language.

Nationalism has had its most destructive effects in Northern Ireland. The province was created in in 1922, when Ireland won its independence and was partitioned: while the 26 southern and largely Catholic counties were reconfigured as the Irish Free State, the six northern counties had Protestant majorities (tracing their roots back to the arrival in the seventeenth century of Scottish Presbyterians) and opted to remain part of the United Kingdom. Protestants discriminated against Catholics in the province, marginalizing them in schools, jobs, the police and local government. In 1968, Northern Irish Catholics held demonstrations in support of improved civil rights, to which the Protestant-dominated local police responded with force. British troops, dispatched to the province to maintain peace, were quickly accused by Catholics of taking the side of the Protestants.

Over the following 30 years, about 3,500 people died and many thousands more were injured in the conflict, which saw the rise of political parties representing the different communities, and of paramilitary groups that used terrorism as a means to achieving their political ends. While the Ulster Unionists and the Ulster Defence Force (UDF), among others, promoted the Protestant cause, Sinn Fein and the Irish Republican Army (IRA) promoted the Catholic cause. Assassinations, bigotry and tribalism became the tragic norm, and every attempt to bring peace to Northern Ireland failed. Most Catholics identified with the nationalist cause, demanding a reunification of Ireland, while most Protestants remained loyalists or unionists, insisting that the province remain part of the UK. Successive British governments meanwhile found themselves caught in between, pleasing neither side, and occasionally making the situation worse.

A troubled peace now reigns in the province. The Blair government underwrote negotiations between the warring factions, generating the Good Friday Agreement of April 1998, which owed much to the personal and diplomatic skills of Tony Blair (Aughey, 2001). It brought about a ceasefire between the warring sides, set up a regional assembly for Northern Ireland in which Protestants and Catholics shared power, and created cross-border councils that would bring members of the new assembly together with members of the British and Irish parliaments. The new Northern Ireland regional government finally met for the first time in November 1999, and – despite its suspension in October 2002 following an unwillingness by unionists to share power with Sinn Fein – the advent of a new power-sharing government in May 2007 offered hope for the future.

Immigration and Race

Racial diversity is a relatively recent issue in Britain, despite many centuries of immigration. As recently as the beginning of the nineteenth century, there was virtually uncontrolled movement of people throughout Europe, and passports and immigration controls were all but unknown. However, only the wealthy could afford to travel, and since they were not seen as an actual or potential drain on national economies, neither were they seen as posing any kind of threat. This began to change with the advent in the late 1800s of the era of mass emigration, prompting governments to begin restricting movement. The first significant immigration control imposed by Britain came with the Aliens Act of 1905, directed mainly at limiting the immigration of Jews from Eastern Europe. There were still relatively few foreigners living in Britain before the Second World War, and most of them were white, so the issue of race barely registered on political, cultural or economic radars. It was certainly far less a source of social tensions than class.

Under a 1948 law, citizens of the Empire and Commonwealth were considered British subjects with the right of entry to Britain. This elicited little controversy because most immigrants were still white. But labour shortages in the 1950s encouraged employers to recruit workers from the New Commonwealth (especially the Caribbean) to work in public transport, in the National Health Service, and in northern factories. Race now became an issue. The law was changed in 1962 to require that Commonwealth immigrants had work permits, and was further tightened in 1968 when East African Asians holding British passports lost their automatic right to live in Britain, a move that was widely (and rightly) condemned as racial discrimination (Clarke, 1996: 326). The growth of the non-white community led to an increase in racial tensions, and to the infamous warning by Conservative politician Enoch Powell in a 1968 speech of the threats posed by immigration to the 'British way of life', and the prospect of the streets running with 'rivers of blood'.

The debate continued in the late 1960s with the arrival of British citizens of Indian and Pakistani extraction from Kenya, who were joined in 1971 by more Indians and Pakistanis expelled from Uganda by the notorious military dictator, Idi Amin. The law was changed again to limit the right to enter or stay to those who had been born in Britain or whose parents or grandparents were of British origin, and as a result there were by the late 1970s only 75,000 immigrants entering the country each year, a number that was smaller than the number of emigrants leaving each year. By the early 1980s, the number had fallen to 54,000 annually, of whom just over half were from New Commonwealth countries.

Additional laws in the 1960s and 1970s made it illegal to discriminate against anyone on the basis of race, and set up a Race Relations Board (replaced in 1976 by the Commission for Racial Equality) to which anyone could appeal who felt that they had been the target of discrimination. Many non-white immigrants initially had difficulty being integrated into British society, and lived in economically depressed inner-city areas. Tensions peaked during the spring and summer of 1981, when violent clashes broke out between police and minorities in the Brixton and Southall districts of London, the Toxteth district of Liverpool, and in Manchester, but it is debatable whether or not these were race riots. The violence was directed against property and the police, and the rioters were both black and white. Racial prejudice was a factor in the violence, it is true, but so were economic recession, job losses, the decline of inner cities, and concerns about crime. A government enquiry into the violence (the Scarman enquiry of 1981) was critical of policing methods, and resulted in a substantial reformation of police–community relations.

Today, nearly 5 million people – or nearly 8 per cent of the population of Britain – belong to an ethnic minority (see Figure 2.1), and a growing proportion of the non-white population consists of people born and raised in Britain, and who have been more fully assimilated into British society than their immigrant parents. Minority cultures have in many respects become a part of mainstream British culture, there is more social mobility for non-whites, and non-whites have become more prominent in British popular culture and professional sports (tellingly, the 1966 England World Cup football squad had not a single non-white player, whereas the 2006 squad had nine). But racism has not gone away, as reflected in cases of racial harassment and a number of controversies in recent years involving the police and non-whites in London, where 20 per cent of the population is from an ethnic minority. The issue of race was at the heart of a particularly notorious incident in April 1993, when a black teenager named Stephen Lawrence was beaten to death by a group of white teenagers in south-east London. Failures in the policy enquiry that followed led to charges of systematic corruption and institutionalized racism in the police force, and to the passage of 1998 legislation introducing new assault, harassment and public-order offences, applying higher penal-

Figure 2.1   Ethnic minorities in Britain

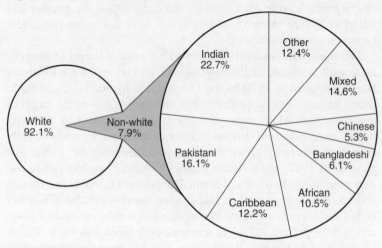

Source: Office for National Statistics, www.statistics.gov.uk. Figures based on 2001 census.

ties in the case of those that are racially aggravated. No-one has been convicted of the crime.

Immigration has become a touchstone political issue again in recent years with the arrival in Britain of new immigrants from Eastern Europe and the Middle East, drawn by the lure of Britain's strong economy. The proportion of foreign-born residents of Britain grew from just over 4 per cent in 1951 to 8.3 per cent in 2001, most new arrivals coming from the Indian subcontinent, the Caribbean, and other parts of Europe (see Figure 2.2). Britain has a smaller proportion of foreign-born residents than the US, Germany, France, or Australia, and yet opinion polls find that immigration has become a major issue of public concern, with a large majority of Britons calling for annual limits.

Political leaders approach the issue cautiously, worried about creating a backlash that would strengthen support for far-Right anti-immigration political parties, as the issue has done in Austria, France, Germany and the Netherlands. They are also concerned about a backlash from minorities themselves, who suffer economic inequalities, have an unemployment rate that is three times that of whites, and still often live in run-down suburbs. Non-whites have not yet built their own movement for political change, instead mainly preferring to work within the established Labour Party.

Figure 2.2   Major countries of origin of foreign-born legal residents

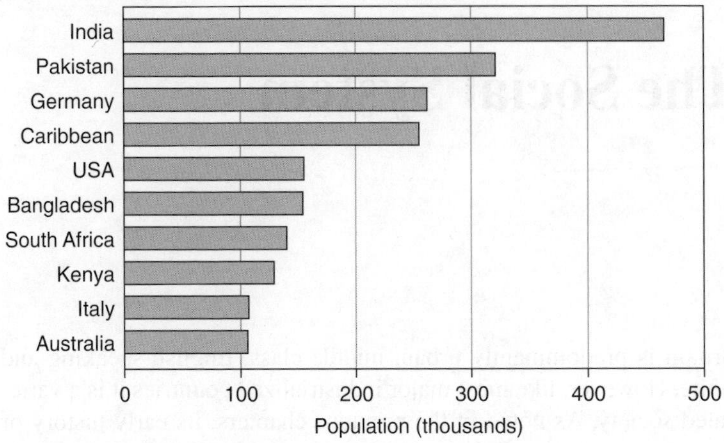

Source: Figures from 2001 census, excluding citizens of Ireland.

An issue of rising concern has been the status of British Muslims, whose place in national life has taken on a new significance with the rise of international terrorism (see Lewis, 2002; Modood, 2005). Three of the four men who carried out the July 2005 London bombings were British-born and bred, leading to concerns about a new brand of home-grown terrorism. By 2006, there were warnings that al-Qaeda posed a serious threat to Britain, with concerns that the volume of travel and personal contacts between Britain and Pakistan in particular had created close connections that increased the likelihood of attacks on the British mainland (Corera, 2006). Unfortunately the attention paid to extremists has impacted attitudes toward Muslims in general. Matters were not helped in October 2006 when former British foreign secretary Jack Straw commented that relations between communities were made more difficult when Muslim women wore veils. This sparked a debate in which troubling questions were raised about just how well Britain's brand of multiculturalism was working.

3

The Social System

Britain is predominantly urban, middle-class, English-speaking and white. However, like most major industrialized countries it is a variegated society. As noted in the previous chapters, its early history of invasions from the continent has combined with England's incorporation of its neighbours and more recent waves of immigration from the Commonwealth and other parts of the European Union to create important cultural and religious diversity. There are economic divisions, too, which began with feudalism, were only partly addressed by the industrial revolution, and live on in a society divided by class and opportunity; the welfare state and the expansion of educational opportunities have so far failed to create a level playing field. These divisions in turn have had an impact on the distribution and expression of political and economic power.

British society is both fascinating and complex. Obelkevich and Catterall (1994: 1) put it best:

> British society is a complicated affair, full of loose ends and bits that don't fit. This may be a good thing for the people who live in it, but it is a source of frustration for those who study it and try to understand it. Every attempt to sum it up in a simple formula – as a 'class society' or whatever – has proved to have so many exceptions and qualifications that it was more trouble than it was worth. The first thing to understand about British society is that there are no short-cuts, no master keys.

The structure of society, the ways in which people relate to one another, the kinds of opportunities available to Britons, and the quality of their lives when measured by personal safety and by access to health care and education have all undergone much change since the Second World War, and particularly since the era of Margaret Thatcher and her programme of rolling back the frontiers of the state. But it is unclear what this has meant, or what kind of society it has created. There has been a redistribution of opportunity and a blurring of class distinctions, but on top of the predictable social divisions of the prewar era have been added new postwar layers of ethnic, religious and national diversity.

This chapter sets out to paint a social portrait of Britain. It begins with an assessment of the class system, which some feel is still strong but others argue is on its way out; either way, it impacts the way Britons relate to each other. It then looks at the changing structure of the family, and the effects of the trend towards smaller families, changing rates of marriage and divorce, and the growing number of children born outside marriage. It examines the welfare system, the structure of social security, and the state of the National Health Service, which is both widely cherished and often criticized, but which has undergone significant reform in recent years. It looks also at the education system, elements of which are renowned around the world, but yet which still fails to provide some Britons with even the most basic skills. Once again, though, much change has come to the system, although the jury is still out on whether these changes will be beneficial. The chapter ends with a discussion of the performance of the criminal justice system in maintaining law and order, and with a discussion about the public debate over incivility and anti-social behaviour.

Social Class

Not surprisingly for a society that evolved out of feudalism and still has an aristocracy, Britain has a class system. There are many who question its significance, and there are others who might not use the term 'class' but still make much of the social divisions that characterize Britain. Tony Blair was among the latter; several key elements of Blairite policy (notably education and welfare) were based on the argument that there are inequalities of opportunity in Britain, and that the removal of the barriers to social advancement must be a central element of the actions of government. The distinctions that set one class apart from another have declined, to be sure, most notably with the rise of the postwar middle class. However, enough remain for many Britons – consciously or subconsciously – to continue to relate to each other on the basis of such distinctions (see Roberts, 2001, and Mount, 2004). Whatever the arguments about class differences, the British remain fascinated with the debate and with discussing the social and economic distinctions that divide them.

During the feudal era the class system revolved around relationships with land and the monarchy: the lords managed the land, while the peasants worked the land, and were obligated to the lords in almost every way. Political and economic power was focused in the hands of a landed elite. Even during the industrial revolution, which saw the rise of urban entrepreneurs who often accumulated huge fortunes, 'new money' made by hard work and personal endeavour was still seen as worth less than inherited 'old money', and class distinctions continued to be driven more by heritage, occupation and social values than by relative monetary worth. You could be a money-less minor aristocrat, but you were still socially superior to a wealthy factory owner. Meanwhile, the class system became more complicated. Instead of a landed aristocracy and a peasantry, a distinction now had to be made between the urban working class and the rural peasantry.

Where the class system was once divided simply into upper, middle and working class, it is today more complex, and the narrowing of wealth and income differentials has made it more difficult to make generalizations about class (Jones and Kavanagh, 2003: 12–14). There is still a pyramid of social layers recognized by the government, ranging from managerial and professional occupations to lower supervisory, semi-routine and routine workers, to the long-term unemployed (see Table 3.1). However, the balance of power and opportunity among classes has changed, the core development of the last 50 years being the rise of the middle class: about 60–65 per cent of Britons today consider themselves middle-class (non-manual and managerial), up from about 20 per cent in 1914. Meanwhile, about 30 per cent consider themselves working-class (skilled and unskilled manual workers), a significant drop from 1914 when the figure was closer to 80 per cent.

Class differences remain, it has been argued, because Britain has not experienced the kinds of revolutions, wars or periods of mass immigration that brought greater social mobility to other European states (Budge *et al.*, 2000: 37). Although most Britons will deny it, many still see each other through the lenses of economic status, family background and lifestyle. Many of the determinants of class

Table 3.1   Social class in Britain

---

1 Higher managerial and professional
   1.1 Employers and managers in larger organizations (company
      directors, senior bureaucrats, senior military officers, etc.)
   1.2 Higher professionals (doctors, lawyers, clergy, teachers, etc.)
2 Lower managerial and professional (nurses, journalists, actors,
   musicians, lower military and police ranks, etc.)
3 Intermediate occupations (clerks, secretaries, etc.)
4 Small employers and own-account workers (farmers, taxi drivers,
   painters and decorators, etc.)
5 Lower supervisory and technical occupations (printers, plumbers,
   butchers, etc.)
6 Semi-routine occupations (shop assistants, bus drivers, cooks, etc.)
7 Routine occupations (labourers, waiters, refuse collectors, etc.)
8 People who have never had paid work, and long-term unemployed

---

The numbering system is that used by the UK government.

are not easily observable or quantifiable, and are based as much as anything on what one person instinctively feels about another. But other determinants are more obvious, and include education, the jobs that people do, their social habits, the communities in which people live, and even the newspapers they read – broadsheets such as *The Times* and the *Guardian* are identified with the upper and middle class, while tabloids such as the *Sun* and the *Daily Mirror* are identi-fied with the working class.

For many Britons, accent is the most obvious (if simplistic) deter-minant of class, and there is still some truth to the sentiment expressed more than 80 years ago by the playwright George Bernard Shaw in *Pygmalion*: 'It is impossible for an Englishman to open his mouth without making some other Englishman hate or despise him'. At the same time, accents are misleading, and as a badge of cultural, social and class identity they have been on the decline (Mugglestone, 2003). The benchmark for much of the early and middle twentieth century was Received Pronunciation (RP), otherwise known as Oxford or BBC English; this is the kind of accent with which members of the royal family speak. No more than 5 per cent of the population ever had such an accent (a proportion that has been halved in recent years), but RP was the benchmark against which all other accents were measured. It was widely – if undeservedly – interpreted as a badge of education, authority and trustworthiness. Meanwhile, almost anyone speaking with a regional accent was assumed to be working or lower middle class. Thus the accents of Devon and Yorkshire were associated with the rural working class, and the scouse accent of Liverpool or the cockney accent of London were associated with the urban working class.

The BBC perpetuated the distinction, for many years, employing only announcers with an RP accent. But the BBC has also done much to undermine the dominance of RP since the 1980s, employing announcers with regional accents, particularly on local radio and TV stations. Accents are still something of a social straitjacket, however, and anyone who speaks with an accent that does not correspond with his or her social credentials is immediately regarded as suspect. In a telling incident in 1999, Prime Minister Tony Blair – who is soundly middle-class – appeared on a television chat show hosted by a singer and comedian named Des O'Connor. Blair began the interview speaking in the clipped middle England tones for which he is known, but as he relaxed he began to adopt so-called Estuary English, an accent named for areas of south-eastern England, including suburbs and towns lying along the Thames estuary, where words are often shortened and key vowels are dropped. There was much comment in the national media the next day about the significance of this, with Blair being accused of hiding his middle-class heritage.

Social mobility – the ability to move from one class to another with a change of generation – has accelerated since the 1960s, reflecting new access to education, a growth in the proportion of Britons in managerial and professional jobs, a decrease in the number of people employed in manual labour, the effects of the welfare system, and a weakening of the class system. The rich tend to remain rich, it is true, and the gap between the rich and the poor is substantial (see Box 3.1). Studies also suggest that there is less social mobility in Britain, France, Germany and the United States than is generally supposed, or than there is in Australia, Japan or Sweden (*The Economist*, 6 April 2002: 47). However, the British middle class is bigger and more stable than in the past. Where children would typically follow the occupational path (and the social status) of their parents, it has become more usual for offspring to move up the occupational ladder, and for those who have been able to create new wealth or status for themselves to change their class identity. This has been possible in part because welfare and improved education have helped reduce the chances of downward mobility. There has also been a decline in the value once accorded to inherited wealth – in today's more egalitarian and meritocratic Britain, 'new money' attracts more admiration.

The emergence of the consumer society has also made a difference. The idea of 'going without' and of avoiding conspicuous consumption – a hangover from prewar years when most Britons were too poor to own their own homes or to furnish them with more than the basic necessities – was extended by postwar austerity and rationing. Even the boom of the 1950s reached relatively few people, and certainly the British were a pale shadow of middle-class Americans when it came to being more adventurous with their leisure time, or acquiring material possessions. It was only in the early 1970s that low-cost travel allowed more people to spend their holidays in Spain or Greece or Morocco rather than seaside English resorts. It was only in the 1980s that consumption began to move into high gear, and the British spent more money installing central heating and double-glazing in their homes, buying new cars, TVs, and other electrical appliances, and going on holiday to the United States, Africa, or the Far East and Australia.

The British class system has also been impacted by several other developments:

- Changes in occupational structure. The number of jobs in labour-intensive heavy industry has fallen, to be replaced by jobs in more automated and lighter industry, and particularly by jobs in the service sector. This has altered the balance of population numbers between the working and middle classes.
- A substantial increase in private home ownership. In 1900, just 10 per cent of Britons owned their own homes, but today the figure is more than 70 per cent. A breakthrough came in the 1980s with the decision by the Thatcher government to sell off council houses (state-owned housing stock) to their tenants, creating over a million new owner-occupier families almost overnight. The value of homes has grown dramatically, going through booms in the mid-1980s, the early 1990s, and again in 2000–03, increasing the net worth of homeowners and blurring the distinctions between different social classes.
- The rise of the upper middle class. Increases in incomes and benefits and improvements in working conditions for managerial and professional staff have increased the buying power, financial options and political influence of the upper middle class, even going so far as to create a 'super class' of senior professionals and managers with new power, who are increasingly separated from the rest of society by money, education, values, residence and lifestyle (Adonis and Pollard, 1997).

Box 3.1   Poverty and affluence

Poverty is a troubling issue in every industrialized country, in part because of the debates over how it should be defined, and in part because of the large numbers of people who are apparently still 'poor' in the midst of growing wealth. In Britain, as in most other comparable countries, the overall quality of people's lives has improved dramatically since the Second World War. People have higher incomes, better job security, more access to education and health care, and more of them own homes and cars. However, not all is well:

● If the government definition is accepted (people living in households with less than 60 per cent of the median national income, after housing costs), then about 16 per cent of the population (nearly 10 million people) is poor. This is down from the mid-1980s peak of 21 per cent, but is still one of the highest rates in the EU.

● As in most wealthy societies, there is a large income gap between the rich and the poor. Despite the doubling of real household disposable income since 1971, the income gap in Britain grew rapidly in the late 1980s, fell slightly in the early 1990s, rose again in the late 1990s, and has fallen again since 2000. The average annual income of the top 20 per cent of households in 2004–05 was just over £66,000 (€99,000/$125,000), or 16 times the average income of the lowest 20 per cent.

● Single-parent families and retired people are overrepresented in lower income groups, as are households with children. At the bottom of the scale, about 150,000 people are homeless according to official government figures, although unofficial estimates suggest that the figure may actually be twice as high.

● The remarkably high cost of living in Britain means that even high incomes do not go as far as they do in other liberal democracies. There are regional variations, to be sure, but London has been ranked in several recent studies as one of the three most expensive cities in the world, and the high costs of accommodation, travel, and eating out take their toll throughout the country.

Meanwhile, affluence has become more visible in the last generation as the net worth of the upper middle class has expanded. The amount of money that people had left to save or spend after taxes and other deductions (adjusted for inflation) more than doubled between 1971 and 2004. This was made possible by lower income and estate taxes, increases in the value of homes, and profits from shares and other investments. The wealthiest 10 per cent of the adult population now owns 56 per cent of household marketable wealth. Symbolic of the change has been the growth of business for home improvement stores, and the growth in the number of individual shareholders, up from 8 per cent of households in 1980 to 20 per cent in 1987 to 26 per cent in 2003.

The changing nature of the class system can be seen in the changing relationship between class and political activity. While the Labour Party was for many decades the champion of the working class, and the Conservative Party attracted more support from the middle class, the link between class and voting has declined. The share of the middle-class vote for the Conservatives has fallen from 80 per cent to 60 per cent since the early 1970s, while the share of the working-class vote for Labour has fallen from 60 per cent to 50 per cent. Labour under Tony Blair realized that economic changes meant that it could no longer rely on the working-class vote, so the policies of 'New' Labour were more geared to middle-class needs. In the 1950s, 10 per cent of voters in managerial and professional classes voted Labour and 85 per cent voted Conservative; by 2005, the percentages were 28 and 37 respectively (figures quoted in Leach *et al.*, 2006: 78). Sociological factors are now less of an explanation of voting behaviour than are political factors (see Chapter 5).

The Changing Family

The British have the same worried conversations as do the citizens of most other liberal democracies about the break-up of the nuclear family, the reduced sense of community, and the seeming decay of moral values in the wake of reduced parental guidance. The definition and the place of the family have certainly changed in Britain in recent years, but the process of change has been under way for more than a century. In the 1860s, the live birth rate for married women was 5.7, but by the 1920s, the figure had fallen to 2.2, where it has more or less remained ever since. The nuclear family – a mother, a father and dependent children – was already relatively unusual 30 years ago (accounting for just one-third of British households) and has become even more so today (just under one-quarter of households). So the idea of 'traditional' family values has been a misnomer for decades, and it is really only social pressure – and perhaps the portrayal of families in television dramas, sitcoms and commercials – that keeps the spirit of the nuclear family alive.

There are several explanations for the changing landscape:

- There has been a trend towards smaller families. There was a time when people had more babies because of higher mortality rates, and because children were needed to work the land for the family.

But mortality rates have fallen, children are no longer needed for their labour, there is less social pressure to have children, and – indeed – having a child has become an expensive proposition. To feed, clothe, house, educate and take care of the health of a child is now a major financial commitment. As a result, the average completed family size in Britain has fallen from 3.2 children in 1951 to less than 2.0 today.

- Women are delaying having children. Many more are taking their education further, and many more are looking to establish a career before starting a family. As a result, the mean age at which British women have their first child has risen from 26.2 years in 1972 to 29.1 today. At the same time, the number of women opting not to have any children at all has increased; about one-fifth of women born after 1965 are projected to remain childless.
- There have been changes in attitudes towards marriage. The majority of British men and women still marry, but the proportion has been declining, with more people living together before getting married, and more people simply living together without getting married: about one-sixth of the non-married adult population of England and Wales is estimated to be living together. It is now as common to hear British adults referring to their 'partner' as to their husband or wife.
- There was almost a sevenfold increase in the divorce rate between 1961 and the peak year of 1993, since when the rate has fallen slightly but still remains high. A boost has been given by changes to the law (including the 1969 Divorce Reform Act, which introduced a single ground for divorce: the irretrievable breakdown of a marriage), but more broadly there has been a decline in the social stigma attached to divorce, couples in an unhappy marriage are more likely to break up rather than struggle on as their parents might have done, and women are earning higher wages and better qualifications, and so developing more independence.
- The number of children born outside marriage has increased, the rate in Britain now being among the highest in the industrialized world: nearly 40 per cent of children were born outside marriage in 2000, a 50 per cent increase over the rate in 1990, and a 500 per cent increase over the rate in 1971. Only Iceland, Sweden, Denmark and France have higher rates, while the rate for the United States is about 33 per cent, and the rate for the European Union as a whole is 27 per cent (*The Economist*, 6 July 2002: 49).

- The number of people living alone has grown, up from 18 per cent of households in 1971 to 29 per cent in 2004. One factor in this has been increased life expectancy, contributing to growing numbers of empty-nesters (parents whose children have grown up and left home) and of widows and widowers. However, the biggest growth has been in the number of men under age 65 living alone, which has tripled since 1971 to account now for one in ten households.

The cumulative result of all these changes has been a reduction in the size of the average household over the last 50 years, from 4.6 people to 2.4 people, and projections that it will fall to 2.2 by 2021. The 'unconventional' household has become more common, with important effects on the way people relate to one another, on the structure of communities, on the provision of social services, and on the upbringing of children. The most alarming implications have been for the number of children living in poverty: in 2004–05 nearly 2.5 million children were members of families living below the poverty line. By no means do all of them live in single-parent households, but there is a close link between being a single parent and being poor. The Blair government made a pledge in 1999 to end child poverty within a generation, and although the number of children living in poverty has fallen, the extent of the problem is still unconscionable for a wealthy industrialized society like Britain.

Social Services and Health Care

Like all modern industrialized societies, Britain is a welfare state, or one in which government makes provision under the law for those in need, particularly the elderly, the sick, the poor, the disabled and the indigent. There have been elements of a welfare system in place since the sixteenth century, when a Poor Law provided limited support for those in need, although churches continued to provide most of the services needed to help the poor and the unemployed. With industrialization, the population of Britain grew rapidly, as did the number of people working in cities, which became overcrowded, filthy and polluted. The expanding working class lacked basic amenities such as adequate housing, sanitation, health facilities and utilities such as a clean water supply. Working conditions were often appalling, child labour was common, the poor were exploited and typically denied the vote, and when the government finally did take action in 1834 to provide assistance for the indigent, the solution was to create a network of workhouses where inmates lived in prison-like conditions, separated from their families and working long hours for little reward.

Responding to decades of pressure for social reform (see Bernard Harris, 2004), the Liberal government that was swept into power in 1906 laid the foundations of the modern welfare state by creating state schools, providing a state pension, providing free school meals for children, and creating unemployment benefits. However, it was not until after the Second World War – on the recommendation of the 1942 Beveridge Report (see Chapter 1) – that a comprehensive welfare system was finally developed. Entering office in 1945 on the crest of a wave of reforming zeal, the new Labour government of Clement Attlee oversaw the passage of legislation that created a social security system designed to provide help for the unemployed, widows, and the retired, and a National Health Service that would provide mainly free medical services to anyone not already covered by other programmes (Clarke *et al.*, 2001).

The calculations made about welfare needs in the 1940s were quite different from the realities that have emerged since then. For example, it was assumed that unemployment would mainly be a short-term problem and affect few people, that families would typically be supported by a male breadwinner while wives would stay at home, and that the number of contributors to social insurance would greatly exceed the number of dependants (Mohan, 1999: 135). In fact, Britain has witnessed long-term unemployment, changing patterns of participation in the labour market, smaller families, and increased life expectancy.

Thanks in part to such changes, the social security system has become the single biggest item on the national government budget, accounting between 1995 and 2001 for about 28 per cent of annual government spending. In 2006, the government spent £151 billion (€220/$272 billion) on social security, or nearly £2,600 (€3,800/$4,700) for every man, woman and child. About half of spending goes on retirement pensions, which are paid to anyone who has made a certain number of contributions into the social security system while working. The pensionable age for women is 60, and for men is 65, although starting in 2010 the age for women born after 1950 will be gradually increased to 65. Payments are not substantial (the basic state pension in 2006 was just under £4,400 annually per person (€6,600/$8,400)), but then the system is intended only to act as a safety net to avoid the kind of poverty that particularly afflicted elderly people before the advent of the welfare state. Other items in the social security budget include payments to long-term sick and disabled people (about one-quarter of spending), support to families (including maternity pay and child benefits), unemployment pay, and support for widows and widowers. In all, just over a quarter of the British population receives benefits of some kind.

The second key element in the social services system is the National Health Service (NHS). Created in 1948 by the National Health Service Act, the NHS provides residents of Britain with a health-care system in which almost all services are free, particularly to pregnant women, new mothers, children, the elderly, full-time students, and those on low incomes. The NHS is paid for out of public funds, with all taxpayers, employees and employers paying into the system, and services being provided on the basis of need rather than the ability to pay. The single biggest employer in Western Europe (with a total workforce of about 1 million people), the NHS cost just short of £100 billion in 2005/06 (€145/$180 billion).

Public opinion on the NHS is divided. Few in Britain question the principle of universal free medical care, and there is much pride in the concept of the NHS, but recent polls have found that only about 60–70 per cent of Britons have been satisfied with the service. (Interestingly, the public view is less positive than that of people who have actually used the service, hinting at the myth that tends to surround the NHS.) Complaints typically focus on poor standards, bureaucracy, low pay and long hours for doctors and nurses, the amount of time it sometimes takes for a patient to see a doctor, the waiting time in accident and emergency departments in hospitals, and charges that older patients are sometimes discriminated against. Most controversial of all have been the waiting lists for patients seeking operations: until recently, it could take up to 18 months for someone to receive non-urgent surgery, 9–12 months to receive hip- or knee-replacement surgery, and even several months for cancer patients to start receiving treatment. The number of patients on waiting lists has fallen in recent years, although critics of government policy charge that this has happened only at the cost of patient care as resources have been diverted to meeting targets for waiting lists.

Every British government in recent decades has had to face the issue of reforms to the NHS, the only question being where to focus efforts. Most critics argue that the best response is to spend more

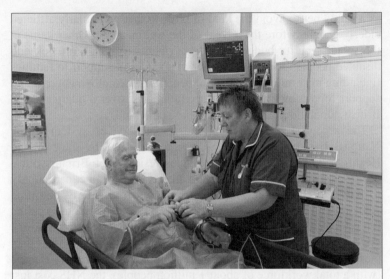

Illustration 3.1   National Health Service

The British live longer and healthier lives than ever before, thanks in part to the availability of universal health care. Concerns about the quality of that health care have been addressed in recent years with reforms to the National Health Service, which provides most of its services at no cost to the patient.

money, and the Blair administration responded accordingly: spending on the NHS increased at an annual rate of 6.4 per cent in the period 1999–2004. Other critics argue that the shortfall of staff is the real problem, citing OECD figures which show that Britain in 2003 had fewer doctors per head of population than most other OECD member states (see Figure 3.1). Some of the methods used to address this issue – such as launching overseas recruitment drives for doctors and nurses, or sending patients to other European countries for treatment – have created their own controversies. In 2000 the Labour government published its NHS Plan, a ten-year programme for the reform of the NHS, which focused on the need to modernize the service, to pay more attention to the needs of patients, to provide a system of rewards for the best-performing hospitals and NHS services, to encourage more students to enrol in medical schools, to recruit more doctors and nurses, and to make significant cuts in waiting times and waiting lists. The result has been a fundamental redefinition of the work of the service, which has become a funder of care, the provision of that care

Figure 3.1 **Numbers of doctors in selected OECD states**

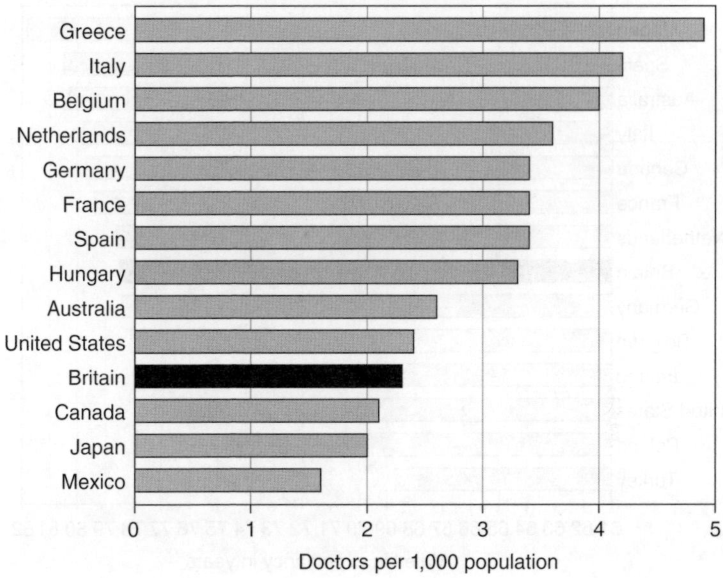

Doctors per 1,000 population

Source: OECD (2006), www.oecd.org. Figures are for 2004.

coming from a variety of sources, including the public sector (Talbot-Smith and Pollock, 2006).

Alongside the NHS, Britons can take out private health insurance and attend private clinics; roughly 10 per cent of the population is covered by private medical insurance taken out with organizations such as the British United Provident Association (BUPA). The Conservative governments of the 1980s and 1990s encouraged the development of the private health-care sector, in part to take pressure off the NHS but also to provide patients with choice, and to promote the most effective use of expensive facilities and treatments. But the private sector still tends to cover only relatively minor treatments, and most long-term, expensive health care is provided by the NHS.

Despite all the debates about the NHS, the indicators typically used to measure quality of life show that the effects of health care have improved significantly in Britain. For example, life expectancy is now more than 78 years, placing Britain above countries that spend more on health care (such as Germany and the United States) (see Figure 3.2). Meanwhile, healthy life expectancy (defined as life

Figure 3.2   **Life expectancy in selected OECD states**

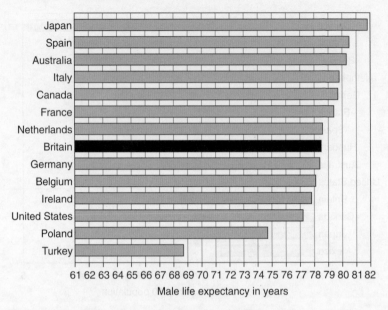

Male life expectancy in years

Source: OECD (2006), www.oecd.org. Figures are for 2003.

expectancy in good general health) has increased by two years for men and women since 1981. Death rates from cancer and coronary heart disease – while still high – have fallen in recent years, the number of people smoking has been nearly halved since the mid-1970s, and there have been marked improvements in the British diet, with a decline in the consumption of red meat and foods containing fat, increased consumption of fruit, and greatly increased public awareness about the chemical content of food (leading to new demand for organic food combined with widespread suspicion of genetically modified products).

While health trends are positive in some areas, in at least two others there is cause for increased concern:

• Britain has one of the most serious drug problems in Europe (see Simpson *et al*., 2006), with drug-related deaths over the last decade holding in the range of 2,000–3,000 per year. Addicts are becoming younger, consumption of hard drugs such as heroin and cocaine is the highest in Europe, and drugs are a central factor in crime:

about two-thirds of all those arrested for mugging, burglary, robbery, shoplifting or car theft test positive for drug use. The rise in the number of drug offences is also one reason why Britain in 2004 had the biggest prison population in its history: more than 73,000 people were incarcerated, a 64 per cent increase on 1993.

- Britain is witnessing the emergence of a public health problem that until recently has mainly been associated with the United States: the rising incidence of obesity. In 1980, just 7 per cent of British adults were classified as obese, but by 2004 the number had increased to 24 per cent, making Britain the fattest country in Europe, and second only to the United States (where one in three adults is obese) in the OECD. The problem is not so much an increase in consumption as a combination of sedentary lifestyles, not enough exercise, genetic predisposition, and the Northern European diet, which is lower in fruit, vegetables and fish than the Mediterranean diet.

There has been a new consensus in Britain since the 1990s that there should be a change away from the attitude that the state must be responsible for providing a safety net, and a move instead towards a 'stakeholder' ethic; this is the idea that while everyone should benefit from membership of society, they should do so only to the extent to which they have played by the rules of society (Finer, 1997). This was a concept adopted enthusiastically by the Blair government, which moved towards a reduction in the reach of the welfare state. Among other things, it encouraged more people to join private health-care schemes and to take responsibility for their own retirement needs rather than relying on social security, and encouraged private funding for education. It also launched a 'welfare to work' scheme in 1998 that was aimed at encouraging the non-employed (such as mothers who choose to stay at home) to move back into the workplace as a means of reducing the welfare bill and tackling the social problems that sometimes come with workless households.

Despite assurances by the Blair administration that its priority was to focus more time and energy on improving the quality of public services, the British public remained largely unconvinced. Polls in the final years of the Blair government found that conditions in the National Health Service were regarded as the dominant issue of concern by nearly half the electorate, and the quality of education by one-third of the electorate, and that nearly half of all Britons believed that the Blair administration had not kept its promises to address problems in these areas. In its first two years in office, the strategy of the Blair administration was to blame such problems on its Conservative predecessors, but this became increasingly unviable, and expectations among voters – and criticism of the Blair administration – began to rise. However, trying to encourage a fundamental change in public attitudes toward the provision of basic services has proven a tall order.

Education

When asked to outline his priorities in the lead-up to the 1997 election, Tony Blair frequently replied that they were 'education, education and education'. The Labour government argued that education was a critical investment in social capital, that improved education offered people the ability to escape social exclusion and to take part in economic activity, and that it was not only good for individuals but for society at large (Alcock, 2000). Conscious that fewer people were being educated in Britain than in many other industrialized countries, Labour promised to cut class sizes, invest in building repairs, give incentives to good teachers, and make education more accessible. The results have been mixed.

On the positive side of the ledger, Britain has spent more on education. In 1999 it was spending just 4.9 per cent of GDP on education, compared to an OECD average of 5.3 per cent. By 2005, it was spending 5.5 per cent of GDP on education, just short of the OECD average of 5.6 per cent. More students are also going on to higher education, and Britain compares well in this area with other OECD states: in 2003, nearly half of school-leavers were going on to university, compared to 33–36 per cent in France and Germany, and an average of 53 per cent for the OECD. But in other areas Britain is not doing quite so well:

- A government-sponsored report published in 1999 found that nearly a quarter of adults were classified in the lowest literacy level (being unable, for example, to use the index in a *Yellow Pages* phone directory), and in the lowest numeracy level (being unable, for example, to calculate the change they would receive from a simple shopping list). Among European countries, only Poland and Ireland had worse records. Sweden had the best record, at 7 per cent in each category.

• A common criticism made against British education is that its quality varies so much, and that national statistics disguise the fact that most of the problems have come in the more troubled state schools, while the better state schools and those in the independent sector have been doing well, with exam results improving in recent years. The number of young people entering higher education during the 1990s grew from one in five to one in three, but instead of promoting social mobility and reducing differences in opportunity for the advantaged and the disadvantaged, nearly 75 per cent of university students still come from the top half of the economic and social spectrum. Labour felt that there was need for change in order to help people find work and stable income sources in a competitive global market, and to break the cycle of welfare dependency (Kendall and Holloway, 2001).

Since 1972, the law has required that British children receive full-time education between the ages of 5 and 16 (in Northern Ireland they are required to start at age 4). About 70 per cent stay on in full-time education beyond 16, obtaining further schooling or going on to higher education (where women outnumber men by 11 to 9). About 20 per cent go into government training programmes, and the balance enters the workplace. Schools are divided into two groups: state schools that are operated by public funds, and independent schools that are privately financed. Education at state schools is free, and about 93 per cent of children in England and Wales take this option. By contrast, education at independent schools is often expensive, and is usually an option only for wealthy families or for children with scholarships or financial aid.

The 1944 Education Act created a tripartite system for England and Wales in which children in the state system attended primary school until age 11, at which point – on the basis of a standardized exam known as the Eleven Plus – the more academically gifted were channelled into grammar schools, while those who failed the exam went to less academic secondary-modern schools. (Technical schools made up the third element in the system, but few were built.) Grammar schools prepared children for national exams that qualified them to go on to higher education or for entry into the professions, while secondary moderns did not. Critics charged that the system was socially divisive, perpetuating class differences and determining life choices for children at too young an age. Beginning in the 1960s, the local education authorities that administered schools were allowed to decide whether they wanted to keep the dual system or to replace it with non-selective comprehensive schools which would provide an education for children of all ability levels and different social backgrounds. Although there are concerns that bright children suffer from being in classes with less able children, comprehensives are now attended by nearly 90 per cent of children in the state system, and there are few grammar schools and secondary moderns left.

Meanwhile, Scotland and Northern Ireland have their own education systems. Schools in Scotland have long been comprehensive, and have a different system of exams from those in England and Wales; only about 5 per cent of Scottish pupils attend private schools. In Northern Ireland, state schools are selective, with about 40 per cent of children attending grammar schools and the rest attending non-grammar schools. State schools are supposed to be open to all religions but tend to be divided into Protestant and Catholic schools, and single-sex education is more common than in England and Wales. State schools in England and Wales use a national curriculum which includes English, maths, science, history, geography, art, music and a modern foreign language. Northern Ireland has its own curriculum, but Scotland does not.

Alongside the state school system Britain has private (or independent) schools, which are both more expensive and more exclusive, and tend to give their students a better-quality education overall (although there are many fine state schools in the system). Confusingly, the private schools are known as 'public' schools, because they were long designed to train pupils for public service, in either the military or the government. As a result they were long run on semi-military lines, with compulsory chapel every day, younger pupils sometimes acting as valets for older pupils, and compulsory involvement in sports and military-style cadet corps. They are mainly boarding schools, although the number of day pupils has increased, and they were once almost exclusively single-sex, although the number of co-educational public schools has increased. Entry is determined by examination and is not restricted by social class or connections, although the ability to win a scholarship or else pay the often high fees is critical. British public schools include such famous establishments as Harrow, Eton, Winchester and Marlborough, and over time have produced many of the leading figures in British political, commercial and military life. Their influence is declining, though, as Britain becomes more egalitarian and meritocratic (see below).

Recent policy developments have brought much change to the state education system. The 1988 Education Reform Act allowed schools to compete with each other for pupils, the idea being that market forces would encourage schools to improve their records. A national curriculum was also introduced, standardized tests were introduced at four levels to assess the progress of students, league tables were published to show the comparative performance of schools, and schools could opt out of local government control (if enough parents agreed), and receive funding direct from national government, thus becoming grant-maintained schools. Labour added to the changes, replacing grant-maintained schools with Foundation Schools (which are run by local authorities but allowed a degree of independence), creating specialist schools that offered specialist subjects in addition to the National Curriculum, and creating city academies (new schools that take over from existing but failing schools, and are independent but within the state system).

Higher education is provided by an extensive network of universities and of more specialized colleges offering, for example, teacher training and other vocational skills. Britain has more than 100 universities, which can be categorized into four types:

- The ancient universities that have existed for centuries, and for a long time were the *only* universities, all of them restricted to men. The oldest English universities include Oxford and Cambridge (founded in the twelfth century), and the oldest Scottish universities include St Andrew's and Glasgow (founded in the fifteenth century), and Edinburgh (sixteenth century).
- The so-called redbrick universities founded mainly in the late nineteenth and early twentieth centuries, including Birmingham, Leicester, Liverpool and Sheffield.
- The universities founded in the 1960s, often in rural areas, and including Bath, Essex, Surrey, Sussex and East Anglia.
- The 'new universities' that were once vocational polytechnics but were given university status in 1992, including Greenwich, Thames Valley, Manchester Metropolitan, and West of England.

Where British universities – and a British university education – were once considered among the best in the world, their status has been undermined in recent decades by a combination of an increase in student numbers and government policy that has been slow to catch up with needs. In 1960, barely 5 per cent of school-leavers went on to university or college, and there were just 200,000 students in higher education. In 2005, the figure was closer to 50 per cent of school-leavers (most of the growth in numbers having come since the late 1980s), and there are today more than 1.2 million students in British universities. Thus, higher education has ceased to be something available only to an elite few. The Blair administration wanted to take this further by ensuring that as many as half of all those in the 18–30 year age range experience some form of higher education, a figure that would put Britain in the same rank as the United States.

Unfortunately, much of this growth took place against a background of falling government spending on higher education. Just as the number of 18–21-year-olds doubled in the period 1989–2000, so spending per student was cut by two-thirds (*The Economist*, 16 November 2002: 52). Even though spending has increased since 2000, as a percentage of GDP it is still less than half what it is in Canada or the United States, ranking Britain alongside France and Germany at about 1.2 per cent. The universities receive support from the government, but they are independent institutions and – particularly since the Thatcher administration – have been expected to depend less on public funding and instead to raise a large percentage of their own financial support. The positive results have included more attention being paid to marketing, fund-raising, and academic performance. At the same time, though, there have been less happy trends:

- A reduction in staff numbers, with the student–lecturer ratio down from 9:1 in 1990 to about 16:1 today
- A reduction in research funding from the government
- A declining share of top-level research output, reflected – for example – in the declining numbers of British scientists winning Nobel prizes (down from 12 in the 1970s to 5 in the 1990s, and 4 in 2000–06)
- The use of a Research Assessment Exercise (RAE) by which the work of every university researcher is assessed in order to decide how much government funding universities will receive. The exercise – which demands considerable time and effort – has been opposed by many, and is criticized in particular for discriminating against good teaching, and for leading to department closures, job losses, and the poaching of productive researchers. It is to be abolished in its current form in 2008

- A deterioration in the quality of buildings and other facilities
- A brain drain as academics have left to work overseas

The question of student fees for university education was the subject of a controversial new law (the 2004 Higher Education Act) that came into effect in the 2006–07 academic year. Before the change, students paid up to £1,250 per year as a contribution to their tuition costs, the amount being based on their parents' income. They could also take out loans to cover the balance of their costs, those loans to be repaid (with interest) after graduation. But with the so-called top-up fees that now apply, universities can charge students anything up to £3,000 per year (Scottish universities charge less). The fees are paid by the Student Loans Company, a government-owned body, and students will then be billed after graduation, and will have to pay back their 'loans' with interest. The law flew in the face of a Labour manifesto promise not to introduce top-up fees, and its critics argue that it will discourage poorer students from going to university out of concern for the debts they will accumulate. There are also concerns that students will be diverted away from technology and science degrees because they take longer to complete and so will involve more debt. And while parents will no longer be faced with having to pay fees, the debt burden will simply be transferred to their children. Regardless of the concerns, almost all universities now charge the full fee.

In spite of the regular claims of 'failure', 'crisis' and 'decline' in British education since 1945, Ken Jones (2003a) argues that levels of achievement and participation have risen, and inequalities have been reduced. Where once it was almost required that anyone wanting to advance to the highest levels of the professions or government should attend the 'best' schools and universities, a private education is no longer as much of an advantage over a state education as it once was. This is reflected in an informal study undertaken by the weekly news magazine *The Economist*. In 1972, it looked at the educational background of the holders of what it defined as the 100 'top jobs' in Britain, which included positions in politics (including the Prime Minister, senior government ministers, and party leaders), business (the heads of major companies), academia, the media, the professions, sports and the arts. It found that 67 per cent of the jobholders had attended a private school and that 52 per cent had attended either Oxford or Cambridge. It carried out the same study in 1992 and found the figures little changed. However, when it replicated the study in 2002, the results were noticeably different: only 46 per cent of

Illustration 3.2   Top-up fees

University students demonstrating in London against the government's plans to introduce top-up fees. Higher education has become available to a much greater proportion of Britons in recent decades, but universities have had to take care of more of their own financing, helping lead recently to increases in tuition costs.

jobholders had attended a private school, and only 35 per cent had attended Oxford or Cambridge (*The Economist*, 7 December 2002: 53–4). If the survey reveals greater educational equality, it reflects little progress on gender equality – only five of the jobs in 2002 were held by women.

Law and Order

Debates about law and public safety in Britain have tended to veer back and forth between conservative concerns about the breakdown of order and allegations of an intergenerational reduction in the quality of life, and liberal arguments that the problem is one of too much control rather than too little. Reiner (2000: 163) argues that 'the British have long been regarded as peculiar in relation to order', the peculiarities shifting with time: in the eighteenth century they were regarded as ungovernable, then in the Victorian era the national

Illustration 3.3   Police

Police officers on duty outside the Labour Party annual conference. The British police have been at the heart of a debate about trends in public order and civility, with opinion divided on whether conditions are improving or worsening.

image 'was one of unflappable self-discipline and orderliness ... symbolized by institutions like the queue, or the imperturbably stiff-upper-lipped gentleman', and in the last generation there have been 'a succession of law-and-order panics' ranging from football hooligans to urban and rural riots, generating agonized discussions about 'vanished virtues'.

Britain is the birthplace of the organized police – the oldest police force in the world is London's Metropolitan Police, created in 1829 by Prime Minister Sir Robert Peel, after whom the police were long known as 'Peelers'. There is no national police force in Britain, but instead there are 52 independent forces based either around major urban centres or around counties and regions. They answer to local police authorities made up of a combination of elected officials, magistrates, and independent members – the authorities in turn appoint a chief constable to run the force, taking responsibility for policy, promotion and discipline.

Statistics and trends in crime are controversial because of the difficulties of developing an accurate measure. According to the figures

Box 3.2   The legal system

The British legal system is based on a combination of criminal and civil law, the former dealing with wrongs affecting the community and the latter with disputes involving two or more parties. No clear distinction is made between the two in England, Wales and Northern Ireland, where courts have jurisdiction in both areas. There is no common national system of law, England and Wales having its own system while Scotland and Northern Ireland have their own systems.

There are four main sources of national law: statutes passed by Parliament, common law in the form of precedents set through decisions made by courts, laws adopted by the European Union and the decisions of the European Court of Justice, and international treaties of which Britain is a signatory. For example, the European Convention on Human Rights – which provides for the right to life, liberty, personal security, privacy, and freedom of thought, speech, religion, assembly and association – was incorporated into British law by the 1998 Human Rights Act. (In Scotland, statutes passed by the Scottish Parliament – the old one that existed before 1707 and its modern counterpart – are an additional source of law.)

The law is enforced by professional judges and part-time unpaid magistrates (or justices of the peace), the former being qualified lawyers and the latter being given enough training to oversee a trial and apply the law. Magistrates' courts deal with about 95 per cent of all criminal cases, all of them less serious; the magistrates typically sit in benches of three members, are advised by trained law clerks, and have limited powers of punishment. Indictable cases such as rape and murder are passed on to higher Crown courts for trial by jury. Parties in a case are usually represented either by barristers (advocates in Scotland) or solicitors; the former practise as individuals and tend to be trial lawyers, while the latter work in partnerships and deal also with general legal matters, such as wills, estates, taxes and the transfer of property.

of crimes reported to the police there were 5.6 million offences in England and Wales in 2005–06. However, the figure was nearly twice as high according to the British Crime Survey, which has been conducted annually since 1982 and which asks representative groups of people about their experiences with crime. Of the cases reported to the police, theft and burglary accounted for 48 per cent, violent crime for 22 per cent, criminal damage for 21 per cent, fraud and forgery for 4 per cent, drug offences for 3 per cent, and sexual offences for less than 1 per cent (although it is sexual offences which are typically underreported). According to the Survey, there have been decreases in almost every form of crime in recent years; after peaking in 1995, overall figures had fallen by 44 per cent by 2005–06, with vehicle thefts down 60 per cent and burglary down 59 per cent. In spite of this, the Survey has found that nearly two-thirds of Britons think that crime rates are rising (Walker *et al.*, 2006).

The British have long prided themselves on being fundamentally decent and cooperative, with a respect both for privacy and for private property. As with all such stereotypes, there is a hefty element of myth in this view, which is driven as much by perception as by reality. Probably as long as civilization has existed, every generation has bemoaned the decline of community, respect, and public safety, and has claimed that things were better when they were young, even if this was not necessarily so: many studies have shown that incivility and anti-social behaviour have been a fact of life in Britain – as in many other countries – for generations, and most Britons seem to have misconceptions about trends in crime. Most of the indications of a decline in the quality of life are driven not so much by an increase in the volume of incivility and anti-social behaviour, but rather by a greater willingness to recognize that the problem exists and to talk about it.

Headline-grabbing events give the impression of a decline in order and discipline, with Britons over the last 30 years reminded of the often violent confrontations between management and striking workers in the 1980s, the unfortunate reputation for hooliganism that British football has won because of the behaviour of a minority of 'fans', race riots in a number of major cities, the troubles caused by 'lager louts' in bars on the continent, the growing number of cases of road rage caused in part by frustration with traffic congestion, and everyday violence and destructive or anti-social behaviour. The impression has been created that such problems are widespread and worsening, but the popular perception may in fact be quite different from the reality, because trends in the crime rate in Britain are (at worst) not dramatically different from those in other industrialized countries, and Britain is in many ways still a paragon of orderliness and good manners.

The decline of civility has been a topic of much recent national debate in Britain, and was addressed by a new law passed in 2003 after the issue had moved up the Labour government agenda. The idea has been to give police and the government the power to punish certain kinds of behaviour, and thereby to tackle Britain's 'yob culture'. The targets include everything from littering and vandalism to dealing with noisy neighbours, reducing truancy, enforcing parental control, evicting anti-social tenants, and punishing people who drink or use drugs in public. Anyone who sees anti-social behaviour can report it to their local police station or council, which can result in the issuance of an anti-social behaviour order (ASBO) that can prevent an offender from repeating the offence, or from returning to a specific area for up to two years.

While the extent of the problem of crime is debatable, as is the appropriate response, there are elements of life in Britain which still support Reiner's notion of 'unflappable self-discipline and orderliness'. In their dealings with one another on a daily basis, most Britons still display courtesy, good manners and consideration (see Fox, 2004, for an entertaining discussion). They may appear stand-offish to Americans (notorious for their willingness to strike up personal conversations with complete strangers), they may appear stolid to Spaniards and Greeks (with their Mediterranean expansiveness), and they may appear controlled to Italians (who appear unable to form and maintain a queue), but they have created a society in which cooperation and order are still more common than confrontation and disorder.

4
Government and the Political System

Britain is the birthplace of the parliamentary system, the most successful and widely adopted of the world's different governing systems. Otherwise known as the Westminster model, after the area of central London where the British Houses of Parliament are situated, the key elements of parliamentary government include the following:

- a fusion of the executive and the legislature
- a symbolic head of state and a political head of government
- an executive made up of a head of government and a Cabinet of ministers
- representative democracy, by which elected officials are held accountable to voters
- responsible government, by which government ministers are held collectively accountable for their decisions and for running their departments
- a multi-party system based around strong party discipline within the legislature

Because Britain has a long history of parliamentary government, has avoided revolutionary change, and has one of the world's oldest remaining monarchies, it is often assumed that its political system is both stable and predictable. Nothing, however, could be further from the truth. Even the most cursory review of British political history shows a system in a constant process of mutation. For centuries, the changes were driven by the struggle for power between the monarchy

89

and Parliament. More recently, they have been driven by debates over the appropriate role of government, by the fluctuating balance of power between Prime Minister and Parliament, and by the expansion of 'government' at the European and local levels, which have reduced the powers of government in London, raising questions about the very notion of 'British' politics (Norman Davies, 2000: 853–86).

The pace and the extent of change were particularly striking during the administrations of Prime Ministers Margaret Thatcher and Tony Blair. If Thatcher altered the style of government, taking a more hands-on approach to leadership and more fully exploiting the implied powers of her office, Blair not only continued to redefine the place and the character of the office of Prime Minister, but also made significant changes to the institutions of government (such as his reforms of the upper chamber of Parliament, the House of Lords) and to the balance of national and local government (notably his government's creation of regional assemblies for Wales, Scotland and Northern Ireland). Meanwhile, the irresistible impact of Europe continues to be a strand that runs through the work of every British administration.

This chapter examines the structure of the British system of government. It begins with a review of constitutional principles, and then looks in turn at the monarchy, the Prime Minister and Cabinet, Parliament, the judiciary, the bureaucracy and local government, explaining their relative roles in the process by which Britain is governed. It identifies the institutions with the most and least influence over the political process, discusses changes in the balance of power among (and within) those institutions, examines the centralization of power in national government and in the office of Prime Minister, and critically assesses the nature of the British model of parliamentary democracy.

Principles of Government

Just as there has been a debate since the Second World War about British economic decline (see Chapter 6), so there has been much talk about the decline of the British state (for example, see English and Kenny, 1999). Critics have accused government of failing to deliver economic growth and the kind of political stability and social cohesion demanded by citizens of a modern democratic, capitalist system. They have also raised concerns about the lack of controls on an ambitious Prime Minister, questioned the relevance of the monarchy and the House of Lords, and worried about an electoral system that misrepresents the balance of support for competing political parties (see Chapter 5), and about the lack of a codified bill of rights for citizens. The term 'decline' has become so fashionable in academic debates about the British political system that questions have been raised about the very legitimacy of that system.

While Britain has certainly witnessed its share of political and social upheavals, so too have many other countries. And in a world where democracy and successful free-market economic policies have taken root in perhaps only a few dozen countries, the Westminster model stands out more for its strengths than its weaknesses. Those strengths have long stood as a model for political development around the world, and the principles of parliamentary government can be found in one form or another in all the world's most stable and economically successful countries, including almost all European states, Japan, Australia, Canada, New Zealand, and the United States. Perhaps the British political system could be more responsive and transparent, but the same could be said for every other democratic political system. Perfection is impossible when you are dealing with human nature, particularly when power is at stake.

The British system has not declined since 1945, but has simply continued to evolve. The effects are most clearly reflected in the gaps between the theory and practice of the Westminster model, which is based on six key principles:

- *Balanced government.* In theory, the powers of the executive – the Prime Minister and Cabinet – are balanced by those of the legislature, to which the executive is accountable. In practice, the balance of power has shifted away from Parliament, just as it has shifted away from legislatures more generally (Norton, 2005: 2–3). The marginalization of Parliament was especially clear during the first two Blair administrations; policy-making power was concentrated in Downing Street, Blair distanced himself from Parliament, and it was only in November 2005, more than eight years after he took office, that his government suffered its first defeat in the House of Commons, when the latter rejected a plan to extend the period for which the police could detain terror suspects without charge from 28 days to 90 days.
- *Parliamentary sovereignty.* In theory, only Parliament has the right to make or unmake laws, and its powers are not limited or

constrained by any other authority. In practice, while sovereignty remains, Parliament has seen its powers reduced by the expansion of European Union law, by the work of the Scottish and Welsh assemblies, by the increased use of public referendums (see below), and by the growth of executive powers. Thus, parliamentary sovereignty has to some extent become executive sovereignty (Smith, 1999: 11).

- *Representative democracy.* In theory, the people rule, while the work of government is carried out by their elected representatives, who stay in office only as long as they have the support of voters in their local districts. Government is directly accountable to the people in what it does. In practice, it has long been debatable – in Britain as in other democracies – just how much elected representatives convey and champion the views of their constituents, even assuming that they can always be sure what their constituents want. Also, turnout at general elections has been falling, suggesting an increased disconnection between voters and their representatives.

- *Responsible government.* In theory, government ministers are responsible to Parliament for running their departments, and make decisions that are then implemented by a neutral bureaucracy. In practice, the actions of ministers are driven more by personality, ideology, obligations to the Prime Minister, and concerns about the next election, and the bureaucracy has more influence over government policy than most people realize.

- *Collective responsibility.* In theory, the Cabinet is responsible as a group to the public and to the Prime Minister for its conduct and for its policies. Ministers may disagree over policy within the Cabinet, but if a minister cannot support the government line, he or she will either be dismissed or be expected to resign. If the government loses a crucial vote in Parliament, or if there is a vote of no confidence in the government, the Cabinet as a whole is expected to resign (Kavanagh, 2000: 50). In practice, Cabinet government has become less important with time, and recent Prime Ministers – notably Margaret Thatcher and Tony Blair – have often made decisions without first checking with the Cabinet, and have relied more on outside advisors.

- *Constitutional monarchy.* This is perhaps the only one of the Westminster principles where theory and practice still coincide. Britain has a monarch, and government is carried out in the name of the monarch (whose permission is technically needed for most key political decisions), but the monarch has little real power. Any

attempt by the Queen to actually exert her theoretical powers –
example, by vetoing a new piece of legislation – would result
uproar and a constitutional crisis.

The Westminster model has traditionally been described as a
pyramid, with the Prime Minister at the top, government ministers in
the middle, and Parliament and the bureaucracy below. But recent
analysis suggests that it makes more sense to see British government
as a complex network of interdependent institutions, where power is
distributed horizontally rather than vertically, and is no longer
concentrated in a limited number of institutions. In this 'core executive' model, the rules are often informal, institutions are less important than culture and values, roles are more important than structures,
and the decision-making system is less hierarchical (for more discussion, see Smith, 1999; Moran, 2005: 115–17).

The Constitution

A constitution is an instrument that outlines the rules by which a
government functions. It lists the principles underlying the process of
government, describes the structure of the major government institutions and their responsibilities, explains the process by which laws
are made, and spells out the rights of citizens and the limits on the
powers of government. The vast majority of countries have constitutions that are codified: there is a single written document in which the
powers of government and the rights of the governed are outlined and
systematized. However, there is another way of looking at constitutions. Instead of simply being a set of principles and rules, they may
be a summary of how a society is politically constituted or how its
legal and political order fits together. Rather than starting with a
formal statement of norms and then looking at how they are applied,
Johnson (1999: 46) argues,

> the constitution is treated as the outcome of shared experiences and
> practices, the result of a common history rather than a founding
> declaration ... It is not so much a set of instructions on how to do
> things as a set of precedents and notes of guidance extracted from
> past experience ... [It] is unlikely to have special rules for its
> amendment, chiefly because it is the outcome of adaptation and
> evolution in response to changing circumstances and needs.

This model of a 'customary constitution' applies to Britain, where – instead of a single, discrete document – government operates on the basis of many different documents and traditions (Leach *et al.*, 2006: 166–7):

- *Common laws.* These are the product of custom and of judgements handed down over time by British courts. Among the most important are those dealing with freedom of speech, the power to make treaties and declare war, and the sovereignty of Parliament.
- *Statute laws.* These are Acts of Parliament which override common law and have the effect of constitutional law. Many of the details of Britain's system of government – including the relative powers of the two houses of Parliament, the expansion of the vote, British membership of the EU, and the creation of regional assemblies – have been established (and can be changed) by the passage of new statutes. Controversially, a host of statutes have – in the wake of the rise of global terrorism – both restricted civil liberties and expanded the powers of the state.
- *European laws.* As a member state of the EU, Britain is subject to all laws adopted by the EU, which are binding on Britain and override British laws in those policy areas where the EU has primary responsibility (or 'competence'). These include trade, agriculture, social issues, consumer protection and the environment, but exclude tax policy, foreign policy, education and criminal justice (policy areas over which the EU does not have jurisdiction, or has only limited or shared jurisdiction).
- *Traditions and conventions.* Many of the actions of government in Britain (and in other democracies) are based on custom and tradition. For example, nothing in the British constitution says that the Prime Minister and Cabinet should come out of the majority party in the House of Commons, or that the Cabinet is bound by collective responsibility; these are simply traditions that have become an accepted part of the political process.
- *Scholarly commentaries.* Many of the principles and practices of British government have come out of commentaries written by constitutional authorities, such as Walter Bagehot (author in 1867 of *The English Constitution*, and one-time editor of the news weekly *The Economist*) and Albert Venn Dicey (author in 1885 of *An Introduction to the Study of the Law of the Constitution*). Dicey was influential in confirming three of the basic features of the British system: the sovereignty of Parliament, the rule of law, and

the importance of conventions and customs (Thomas, 1999: 144–5).

It would be wrong to assume that government is based solely on the rules found in constitutions, even in those countries – such as the United States – where the constitution is regarded as being at the heart of government. Much of what happens in government is driven by other forces, including judicial interpretation, political feasibility, opportunism, loopholes in the law, public opinion, or simply muddling through. But constitutions provide the blueprint against which the theoretical expectations and the practical actions of government can be compared, better understood, and given structure and order.

In contrast to the constitutions of France or Germany, which spell out in detail how government should work, and whose gaps are filled in by the rulings of national constitutional courts, Britain takes a more pragmatic approach to government. As Philip Norton puts it, the rules of British government are determined 'on the basis of what has proved to work rather than on abstract first principles' (Norton, 2001: 57). This approach allows for greater flexibility, and avoids the need for the government to make formal amendments to the constitution. An example of a change introduced by the Blair government, which has now become an accepted part of constitutional practice, is the referendum. These have been used before in Britain, particularly when the government has been divided on an issue (for example, over membership of the European Community in 1975, and over devolution in 1979), but they have been used so often since 1997 that most major constitutional changes are now likely to be put to a referendum (Jones and Kavanagh, 2003: 63). Blair used them on the question of assemblies for Scotland and Wales (1997), on an elected mayor for London and the Northern Ireland peace agreement (1998), on elected mayors for local authorities (2001 and later), on a regional assembly in north-east England (2004), and long promised to use one on the question of whether or not Britain should adopt the euro. It is important to note, though, that a referendum is advisory, and the result is not binding on government (Leach *et al.*, 2006: 173).

Flexibility has its advantages, but critics of the current system in Britain argue that there is too much potential for the abuse of powers by a strong Prime Minister; Blair, for example, was widely criticized for engaging Britain in an illegal war in Iraq, and for supporting anti-terrorism measures that compromised personal freedoms. Actually, such concerns apply also to the American political system, in spite of the pride that Americans have in their written constitution, in the separation of powers, and in the US Supreme Court. In Britain, the effect has been a growth in support for a written constitution, which is now favoured by about 80 per cent of Britons. But the challenge of codifying laws, legal judgements and traditions dating back several hundred years, and of agreeing both the principles and the details, make such an initiative unlikely. Many constitutions in other countries were written as a result of a shift from one system of government to another, a process which focused the minds of the authors. Such a focus would be lacking in the British case. The failure of the proposed European Union constitution – rejected by voters in the Netherlands and France in 2005 – should be a salutary lesson. The attempt by its authors to cover as many eventualities and details as possible, rather than focusing on broad and general principles, resulted in a document that was lengthy, turgid, and open to criticism from many narrow interests.

The Monarchy

Britain is a constitutional monarchy. In contrast to an absolute monarchy (where power lies in the hands of a single ruler) or an aristocratic monarchy (where the ruler governs with the support of aristocrats), the powers of the British monarch are limited by law. The actions of government are carried out in the name of the monarch, who acts as the living embodiment of the state but does little that could be defined as exercising independent judgement over government. Indeed, so marginal has the monarchy now become that textbooks on British politics rarely give it much space. But it cannot be ignored.

Except for a brief spell between 1649 and 1660 when the Cromwellian republic was proclaimed, England has been a monarchy since the ninth-century reign of Alfred the Great (871–99). Like their continental European counterparts, English kings and queens once had a virtual monopoly on political power, but – as noted in Chapter 1 – their control began eroding with Magna Carta in 1215, and the 1689 Bill of Rights finally confirmed the supremacy of Parliament. Today's monarch – Queen Elizabeth II (Box 4.1) – is little more than a ceremonial head of state. She has no clear political role, but is instead expected to be a neutral symbol of the state, the government and the people. It is often said that the British monarch reigns but

does not rule. At the same time, though, the Queen has several vesti-
gial 'reserve powers' that are politically important:

- She can dissolve Parliament and call new elections, although in
practice she does this only when asked by the Prime Minister. She
could theoretically deny the request, but never does.
- Before a bill can become a law, it must be signed by the Queen
(that is, given the Royal Assent). Theoretically she could veto a
piece of legislation, but the last time a monarch did this was in
1707 (Norton, 2001: 308).
- If no one party has an absolute majority of seats in the House of
Commons after an election, the Queen can arbitrate, and – on the
advice of the Prime Minister – name the person she thinks most
likely to be able to form a government. Queen Elizabeth has had to
do this three times. For example, when Conservative Prime
Minister Edward Heath lost his majority after the February 1974
election, and failed to agree a coalition with the Liberal Party,
Labour Party leader Harold Wilson was invited by the Queen to
form the first minority government since 1931.
- Every autumn she presides over the State Opening of Parliament,
giving a speech in which she outlines the government's programme
for the next year. The speech is written by the government, and the
Queen simply reads it aloud, but the event still symbolizes the fact
that government is carried out in her name.
- She meets with the Prime Minister at confidential weekly meetings, during which she has the right – in the words of Walter
Bagehot – 'to be consulted, the right to encourage, and the right to
warn'. She is briefed on the government agenda, and can share her
thoughts on the decisions of government, although there is no
obligation on the Prime Minister to act on her advice.
- The Queen is the Head of the Armed Forces, and it is she alone
who can declare war and peace, although this again can only be
done on the advice of her ministers. There was a time when
monarchs raised and equipped armies, and led them into battle.
King George II in 1743 was the last to do that, but the symbolic
link remains, and all members of the Army, Royal Air Force and
Royal Marines (but not the Royal Navy) must swear an oath of
allegiance to the Queen.
- Above all, the Queen is the embodiment of 'the Crown', a term
which in some respects is akin to 'the state'. The government
works on behalf of the Crown, bureaucrats are servants of the

Crown, judges dispense justice in Crown courts, and government ministers are conferred with the powers of the Crown (Johnson, 1999: 50–1).

The monarchy was long surrounded by an air of mystery, and little was publicly known about the private lives and personalities of members of the royal family (although the rumour-mill was always kept busy). This privacy was seen as an important part of the stability, success and exceptionalism of the monarchy; in the words of Walter Bagehot, it was important not to 'let in daylight upon magic'. All has changed in the last 15–20 years as the private lives of the royal family have become the focus of intense media coverage and public interest all over the world. The relevance of the monarchy to modern Britain has been the topic of intensified debate, and the monarchy has changed in response. That a divorced heir to the throne could become king – once unthinkable – has now been accepted, and attempts have been made to end the ban on the heir marrying a Catholic, to abandon primogeniture (under which a

Illustration 4.1   State Opening of Parliament

The splendour of the State Opening of Parliament, an annual event at which the Queen – before members of both Houses of Parliament – outlines the government's programme for the upcoming year in a speech written for her by the Prime Minister and th PM's advisors.

Box 4.1   The monarch: Queen Elizabeth II

Queen Elizabeth came to the British throne unexpectedly. Her uncle David had been heir to his father George V (1910–36), and would have been crowned King Edward VIII in 1936 had he not decided to abdicate so that he could marry the American divorcée Wallis Simpson. His younger brother Albert instead succeeded to the throne as George VI, and when he died in 1952, he was succeeded by his eldest daughter Elizabeth.

The Queen was optimistically expected to rule over a new Elizabethan age in which Britain's military, technological and cultural achievements would mirror those of the age of Queen Elizabeth I (1558–1603). But while the British economy prospered during the 1950s, and Britain led the way on the development of the jet engine, nuclear power and other new technologies, significant changes were underway that would radically alter Britain's place in the world. It had already begun to dismantle its empire, and decolonization accelerated during the 1950s. The economies of the United States, West Germany, France and later Japan all offered new competition to Britain, which slipped down the league of the world's major economic powers. Racial tensions grew as workers were invited to come from the Caribbean and the Indian subcontinent to meet Britain's labour shortages. Then came the social and cultural revolutions of the 1960s that altered the balance of power, by class, gender and age.

With Britain undergoing social, political and economic change, the reign of Queen Elizabeth took on an entirely different aspect. The role of the monarchy changed as anti-monarchists questioned the place of heredity in a modern democratic state. It was decided to modernize the royal family and to allow greater media and public access to its inner workings, but the revelations were not always positive: the Queen's three eldest children and her own sister underwent messy divorces, and the Queen herself seemed unable always to keep up with popular demands for change in the role of the monarchy.

As an individual, Queen Elizabeth is popular, as reflected in the outpouring of support during her golden jubilee celebrations in June 2002. However, opinion polls suggest that public support for the monarchy has slipped since the mid-1980s from 85–90 per cent to about 75–80 per cent today. The Queen turned 80 in 2006, and while almost no-one expects her to abdicate into retirement, the day approaches when Britain will face the accession of a new monarch. Her eldest son Prince Charles is next in line, but there has been speculation that he might step aside in favour of his eldest son Prince William.

first-born daughter is overtaken in the line of succession by a younger brother), and to cease expecting the monarch to be head of the Church of England. Adaptability has long been integral to the survival of the monarchy, and its recent adjustments have just been the latest in a long series of responses to new styles, expectations, and political realities.

Prime Minister and Cabinet

While the monarch is Britain's head of state, the head of government is the Prime Minister, who provides policy leadership and oversees the implementation of law through a Cabinet of senior ministers. By definition, the Prime Minister is the leader of the political party or coalition with the most seats in the lower chamber of Parliament, the House of Commons. As long as he or she can keep the support of his or her party in Parliament, the Prime Minister has considerable power over deciding which laws will be passed, and which policies adopted.

At first glance, Prime Ministerial powers can seem almost dicta-torial. Critics of Margaret Thatcher complained that she abused the powers of the office (or at least exploited them to a far greater extent than her predecessors), and that she manipulated government by appointing ministers to her Cabinet who were easily controlled. But not long into her third term she had disagreements over Europe with her Foreign Secretary, Geoffrey Howe, and over economic policy with her Chancellor of the Exchequer, Nigel Lawson. Howe was moved to a less important position, then Lawson resigned from the Cabinet, then Howe resigned as well, weakening Thatcher's author-ity. She won the largest number of votes in the normally routine annual party leadership contest in November 1990, but did not have a big enough margin to be declared outright winner. Her credibility undermined, she resigned and was replaced by John Major. She fell because of a complex combination of unpopular policies, disagree-ments with key Cabinet allies, an unwillingness to heed the advice of ministers, and a failure to maintain alliances in the Cabinet to ensure that she had support for her policies (see Smith, 1999: 97–100).

Similarly, critics of Tony Blair complained that he was too much the micro-manager, that he became more like a president than a Prime Minister, and that he moved the centre of power away from Parliament and the Cabinet and into his own office, where he relied on political and media advisors to 'spin' his policies and to manipulate political and public opinion. But – like all Prime Ministers – he ultimately relied for his power and his credibility upon support within the Cabinet and within his political party, and on his standing in the court of public opinion. He may have been able to hold on to power in spite of declining political credibility following the 2003 invasion of Iraq, but his authority was permanently damaged. By 2005–06, his public approval rating had fallen to record lows and repeated calls were being made for his resignation.

As with all government leaders in democracies, Prime Ministers have a combination of formal and informal powers. Formally, they act as the head of government, appoint senior members of government, chair the Cabinet, oversee the security services, lead their parties, choose the date for the general election, report to Parliament in a weekly Question Time, and represent Britain in political dealings with other countries. Informally, they are the driving force in setting the national political agenda, are responsible for managing crises, and set the style and tone of government according to the policies they adopt, the management methods they use, and their appointments to the Cabinet. They can also involve themselves in their favourite policy areas, sometimes overshadowing the relevant secretaries and ministers. For example, Callaghan was interested in education policy, Thatcher in economic and foreign policy, Major in Northern Ireland, and Blair in foreign policy.

There are two core foundations to the authority of a Prime Minister:

- *The power of dissolution.* Prime Ministers decide when to dissolve the House of Commons and call new general elections. These must be held at least once every five years, but they can be called any time within that period, at 3–4 weeks' notice. Unlike leaders in countries where elections are held on a fixed timetable – such as France, Germany, or the United States – Prime Ministers can use elections strategically, perhaps using the threat of calling an election to bring uncooperative Cabinet members or a recalcitrant party into line. If they have the luxury of time, Prime Ministers will call an election when the polls suggest that their party has the best chance of winning. More rarely, a Prime Minister may have to call an election because they have lost a critical parliamentary vote, lost a vote of confidence, lost their majority in Parliament, or lost the support of their party. The last time an election was called because

Table 4.1   British Prime Ministers from Attlee to Blair

Date	Prime Minister	Governing party
July 1945	Clement Attlee	Labour
February 1950	Clement Attlee	Labour
October 1951	Winston Churchill	Conservative
May 1955	Anthony Eden	Conservative
January 1957*	Harold Macmillan	Conservative
October 1959	Harold Macmillan	Conservative
October 1963*	Alec Douglas-Home	Conservative
October 1964	Harold Wilson	Labour
March 1966	Harold Wilson	Labour
June 1970	Edward Heath	Conservative
February 1974	Harold Wilson	Labour
October 1974	Harold Wilson	Labour
April 1976*	James Callaghan	Labour
May 1979	Margaret Thatcher	Conservative
June 1983	Margaret Thatcher	Conservative
June 1987	Margaret Thatcher	Conservative
November 1990*	John Major	Conservative
April 1992	John Major	Conservative
May 1997	Tony Blair	Labour
June 2001	Tony Blair	Labour
May 2005	Tony Blair	Labour
June 2007*	Gordon Brown	Labour

* In these years, leadership of the governing party changed – through health, resignation, or loss of political support – without a general election being held.

of the loss of a vote of confidence was in March 1979, when the Labour government of James Callaghan – which had for two years governed in a pact with the small Liberal Party – lost the support of the Liberals, then lost a parliamentary vote.

- *The power of appointment.* As well as leading their party, Prime Ministers decide the size of the Cabinet, call and chair Cabinet meetings, appoint and remove members of the Cabinet and other senior government officials (about 100 people in all), can reshuffle Cabinets (bringing in new members and either removing existing members or moving them to new posts) and can reorganize government departments. The power of appointment (or patronage) allows the Prime Minister to manipulate and control the Cabinet, alter the personality and character of the government (for example, revitalizing it by bringing in new blood), reward supporters, penalize or undermine the position of opponents, marginalize those who pose a threat to his or her tenure, and cultivate potential successors.

British Prime Ministers are normally experienced national politicians who have worked their way up through the ranks of party and Parliament. They must be members of the House of Commons, and usually serve a lengthy apprenticeship before winning the leadership of their parties. Margaret Thatcher served 16 years as a Member of Parliament (MP) before being elected leader of her party in 1975, and another four years as leader before being elected Prime Minister in 1979. By contrast, John Major and Tony Blair rose to the top relatively quickly, serving as MPs for 11 years and 14 years respectively before becoming Prime Minister.

Prime Ministers govern with the help of the Cabinet, a group of about two dozen men and women who head the major government departments, including the Foreign and Commonwealth Office, the Home Office, the Treasury, and the Department of Trade and Industry. Together, the Prime Minister and the Cabinet constitute Her Majesty's Government: they run their departments, plan the business of Parliament, discuss and attempt to resolve policy differences among departments, oversee and coordinate government policies, and take collective responsibility for the decisions and actions of government (Kavanagh, 2000: 238–9). While a Prime Minister is technically no more than a 'first among equals' in the Cabinet, his or her powers of appointment and agenda-setting mean that loyalty to the leader is a prerequisite for Cabinet members. Once the Cabinet makes a decision, all members are expected to support it in public, whatever their personal feelings may be. If they cannot, they must either resign or – more rarely – may be removed. Cabinet members are all members of Parliament (mainly of the House of Commons), and the Cabinet is an important testing ground for anyone with ambitions to become Prime Minister.

The relationship between Prime Minister and Cabinet – and the role of the Cabinet in the process of government – is very much driven by the personality of the Prime Minister (for more details, see Hennessy, 2001):

• Margaret Thatcher led from the front, was noted for her forcefulness, particularly after her landslide victory at the 1983 general election, and was famous for stretching the powers of her office

Box 4.2   Tony Blair and Gordon Brown

Tony Blair was elected leader of the Labour Party in 1994 at the age of just 40, and moved quickly to abandon some of its more left-wing policies and to bring it closer to the centre of the political spectrum. At the May 1997 election, he decisively ended 18 years of Conservative government with a 177-seat majority in the House of Commons, becoming the third youngest Prime Minister in British history, the first Prime Minister born after the Second World War, and the first truly post-imperial Prime Minister. Many Britons had high hopes for his administration, and his reforming zeal met with wide initial approval. He was able to control left-wingers within his party, worked hard to achieve peace in Northern Ireland, improved Britain's relationship with the European Union, and brought changes to the structure and character of British government. He was elected to a second term in office in June 2001, his majority barely changed – this was the first time that the Labour Party had won two consecutive full terms in office.

Thereafter it was mainly a downhill slide. He lost credit for his decision to support the unpopular 2003 US-led invasion of Iraq, and was later pilloried by the media and public opinion for justifying the invasion with unsubstantiated claims that Saddam Hussein had weapons of mass destruction, and for his support of the widely reviled George W. Bush. He was also criticized for being too slow to improve Britain's public services, and although he was elected to a third term in May 2005, the honeymoon was over: voter turnout was low, the Labour majority fell to 66, and Blair's standing in public opinion polls collapsed. Unwisely, he announced before the election that it would be his last campaign, generating speculation about how long he would stay in office. It was difficult not to contrast the hope and freshness of 1997 with the tiredness and resentment of 2005–06.

Rumour had it that Blair had made an informal pact over dinner one evening in 1994 with Gordon Brown – later Chancellor of the Exchequer – that Blair would be Prime Minister and would then step down in favour of Brown halfway through his second term. The gossip columns now overflowed with speculation about how long Brown was prepared to continue to wait, and how the relationship between the two men was bearing up under the strain. Brown, meanwhile, had married and fathered two children, generating speculation that he was softening up his previously rather dour image in preparation for moving in to the Prime Minister's office. And while he had presided over strong economic news for Britain, there were doubts by late 2006 about how much this would help him succeed in replacing Blair, and about whether he would be able to turn around Labour's fortunes post-Iraq. The questions continued to dog him even after Tony Blair resigned and firmly endorsed him as his successor in June 2007.

almost to their limit. She took key decisions outside the Cabinet, reduced the number of Cabinet meetings, and removed 12 ministers in 11 years.

- John Major was in a weaker position, serving out two years of Thatcher's last term before winning his own mandate in 1992, but even then presiding over a tired and divided party, and often having to react to problems rather than leading the way. He made more use of his Cabinet, allowed a greater variety of opinion, emphasized collegiality and consensus, and intervened less in the affairs of departments.
- Tony Blair imposed strong discipline on his party and his Cabinet, helped by his large parliamentary majority. He delegated discretion to strong ministers prepared to follow the government line, relied less on the Cabinet than on a small inner circle of advisors and aides, and elevated the role of his press and communications staff.

There has been growing debate since the 1960s about the extent to which the office of Prime Minister has become more like that of an executive president (see Crossman, 1963; Benn, 1980; and Foley, 2001, for example). Analogies are made with the presidency of the United States, reflecting the extent to which Prime Ministers have become independent from their Cabinets and from Parliament, and to which election campaigns are dominated by personalities rather than policies. The Prime Minister's office has developed more of a life of its own, with an increasing number of advisors, aides, speechwriters, spin doctors and liaison staff, and the emergence of a staff that looks much like that clustered around the US president in the White House. Meanwhile, the Cabinet has played a less important role in policy-making. Smith (1999, pp. 76–7) notes several reasons for this:

- The Cabinet is confined more to rubber-stamping decisions than to developing government strategy. Few decisions are made in Cabinet, the bulk being made in more specialized Cabinet committees, and being referred to the Cabinet only in the case of disagreement.
- Ministers are too concerned with the work of their departments – where their reputation will rise or fall – to be involved in other areas of policy.
- The Cabinet is less a place where strategy is developed than a place where departmental interests are protected.

The result has been to place the Prime Minister in an advantageous position over his or her ministers. At the same time, though, the support of the Cabinet and Parliament is still the critical element in the ability of Prime Ministers to govern, and – as the case of Margaret Thatcher shows – they forget this at their peril. Tony Blair dismissed 'all this president Blair rubbish', arguing that similar charges had been made about his more proactive predecessors. And the fact that Blair governed in tandem with Gordon Brown, his strong and opinionated Chancellor of the Exchequer, suggested that the idea of presidentialism may be overstated (see Heffernan, 2006).

Parliament

Parliament is the sentimental heart of the Westminster model, although the importance of its role in government is disputed. The conventional view, dating back many decades, holds that it is both marginal and in decline, with most real power lying in the executive and Parliament being squeezed in recent years by both its European and its regional counterparts. Because a Prime Minister with a good majority can normally count on the loyalty of party members, Parliament usually spends most of its time debating or confirming the government's programme. But Cowley (2006: 36ff.) argues that while Parliament may be marginal to the policy process, it has become more important in the last decade, and is set to become more important in the future; most of the shifts in power to the EU or the regions have been shifts in power not from Parliament but from the executive.

Parliament is the British legislature, where proposals for new laws are introduced, discussed and either rejected or accepted, where existing laws are amended or abolished, and where votes are taken on taxing and spending. Its main strategic advantage over the executive comes from being the link between citizens and the executive; it plays a key role in legitimizing government. It also has three other critical functions (see Leach *et al.*, 2006: 230–3, 239–40):

- It both recruits and maintains the government. Membership of Parliament is a prerequisite for membership of the government, and the support of Parliament is essential to the stability and success of the government.
- It scrutinizes the government, which must defend and explain itself in Parliament. This is particularly true of Question Time, when the

Prime Minister or key government ministers must account for their policies and actions.

- It acts as a forum for national debate. Although most parliamentary debates may be narrow and uninspiring, there are times when the government needs to involve Parliament in decision-making, particularly at times of crisis and war. Tony Blair, for example, made a point of several times seeking its support over his policies on Iraq.

Strictly speaking, Parliament consists of the monarch and the two houses of Parliament, but the monarch has only a symbolic role and the upper House of Lords has only limited powers over law and policy, so the real focus of political power lies with the lower House of Commons. As noted earlier, the principle of parliamentary sovereignty means that only Parliament has the authority to make laws, but this power has been reduced since 1973 by the new importance of European Union law: where British and European law conflict (in policy areas for which the EU has responsibility), British law must give way. The result has been that Parliament has lost power to the law-making bodies of the EU: the European Commission, the Council of Ministers, and the European Parliament. It has also lost power to the regional assemblies.

The British Parliament has two chambers:

House of Lords

The so-called Upper House, the Lords, is currently undergoing a messy process of reform that has brought changes to its structure without agreement on its final form. Once a powerful part of government, the chamber is a legacy of the days when Britain was ruled by aristocrats: for most of its history, its members were hereditary male peers, including dukes, barons and earls. Since the idea of hereditary privilege was at odds with modern democratic principles, the House steadily lost its powers in tandem with the diminishing role of the monarchy. In 1958, membership was expanded to include life peers: people who had been rewarded for public service with a title by the Queen (on the recommendation of the Prime Minister), the title dying with them. One result was the arrival of the first female members of the House.

Pressures grew in the 1960s and 1970s for more change, and the Labour Party promised during the 1980s to abolish the House when

Illustration 4.2   Houses of Parliament

The Houses of Parliament on the bank of the Thames in central London. Parliament is at the core of the British system of government, but it has lost powers as those of the Prime Minister have grown, and as European law has superseded British law in many areas.

it came to power. It later abandoned that pledge, but the Blair government launched a series of reforms to the chamber. The automatic right of all but 92 hereditary peers to sit in the House ended in 1999, and a government commission was appointed to offer suggestions for where to go next. It reported in 2000, recommending a mainly nominated chamber, limiting its members to 12–15 years of service, and retaining its existing powers. More proposals have since been touted, ranging from a fully elected to a fully appointed chamber, but none has yet been agreed and the debate over the final form of the new House of Lords continues. Meanwhile, the transitional House of Lords has about 730 members, made up as follows:

- A rump of 92 hereditary peers who were elected by their colleagues and allowed to remain pending the next stage in the process of reform.
- About 600 life peers. In the past these have typically included former Prime Ministers and Speakers of the House of Commons,

and people prominent in public life, such as actors, musicians, and entrepreneurs. Political appointments continue to be made, but since 2000 an Appointments Commission has been responsible for vetting 15 non-party political peers (or 'People's Peers'), chosen from applicants who must show that they can bring integrity and experience to the job.

• Religious leaders, or the Lords Spiritual, made up of the two arch-bishops and 24 bishops of the Church of England.

• The Law Lords: 12 nominated judges who function as the supreme court of appeal for civil and criminal cases (except criminal cases in Scotland). The House of Lords Constitution Select Committee also plays a role in legal issues, reviewing all public bills going through Parliament that have constitutional implications. The Law Lords will be replaced in 2008 by a new British Supreme Court (see below).

As well as being in a state of limbo, the Lords today has only limited power. About two to four of its members are usually appointed to the Cabinet, it has its own select and *ad hoc* committees (but no standing committees), and every parliamentary bill must go through the Lords, which spends most of its time revising bills sent from the House of Commons. The chamber can introduce and revise proposed legislation, but most of its decisions can be overruled by the Commons: money bills do not need the approval of the Lords, and while it can delay approval of other bills for up to a year, they can be reintroduced in the Commons which can pass them without the approval of the Lords. But it does have its uses: it has more time to debate issues than the Commons, it often debates controversial topics that the Commons would prefer to avoid, it can force concessions from the Commons, and it is a useful point of access for lobbyists. And given the weak-nesses of the Commons, the Lords – ironically – has been more of a block on the government in recent years (Cowley, 2006: 53).

House of Commons

Although it is the 'lower' house, the Commons is the more powerful chamber of Parliament, and the real focus of law-making. However, since the government so dominates the legislative process, it is ques-tionable whether Parliament any longer makes law, rather than simply discussing and voting upon government bills (Leach *et al.*, 2006: 233).

The House consists of 646 Members of Parliament (MPs) elected by direct universal vote from single-member districts. Debates are presided over by a Speaker, who is elected by the House from among its members, and usually comes from the majority party. The Speaker is not allowed to vote, and is expected to remain non-partisan. Party discipline in the House is tight, but discontent is not unusual; a breakdown of party cohesion – usually dubbed a 'backbench rebellion' if it is big enough – is normally interpreted as a sign of weakness, and can lead to the fall of a government, the resignation of a Prime Minister, or even a general election.

The chamber of the House is small, with benches rather than seats (see Figure 4.1). The governing party sits on the left when facing the Speaker's chair, with the Prime Minister and members of the Cabinet on the front bench, while MPs without government office, or with only junior office, sit behind the front bench and are known collectively as backbenchers. The next biggest party in Parliament sits across from the governing party. Its leader sits directly opposite the Prime Minister, beside a shadow Cabinet of opposition MPs responsible for keeping up with – and challenging – their counterparts in the Cabinet. The leader of the opposition and the shadow Cabinet are formally recognized and salaried positions. If the opposition wins a majority in an election and becomes the government, its leader typically becomes Prime Minister, and many members of the shadow Cabinet become the real Cabinet. In other words, the shadow Cabinet is a government in waiting.

The process by which a bill becomes a law begins in government departments, which – guided by the government – identify issues that merit changes in the law, and develop proposals that are circulated to all other interested departments, and are revised by experts and affected interests. This process may take a year or more. The Cabinet then looks over the proposals, and those that are accepted go to the Parliamentary Counsel, which drafts bills. The plan to introduce a bill is normally announced in the Queen's Speech at the State Opening of Parliament in October. The bill is then introduced to Parliament (either chamber), and after initial debate is sent almost immediately to the relevant standing committee, where most of the real work of Parliament is done: specialists go over the details, outside experts are invited to give testimony, and changes are made to the bill. Once a bill has passed through committee, it goes back to Parliament for more debate and amendments, and a final vote. Once accepted, it is sent to the Queen for her signature.

Figure 4.1 **Floor plan of the House of Commons**

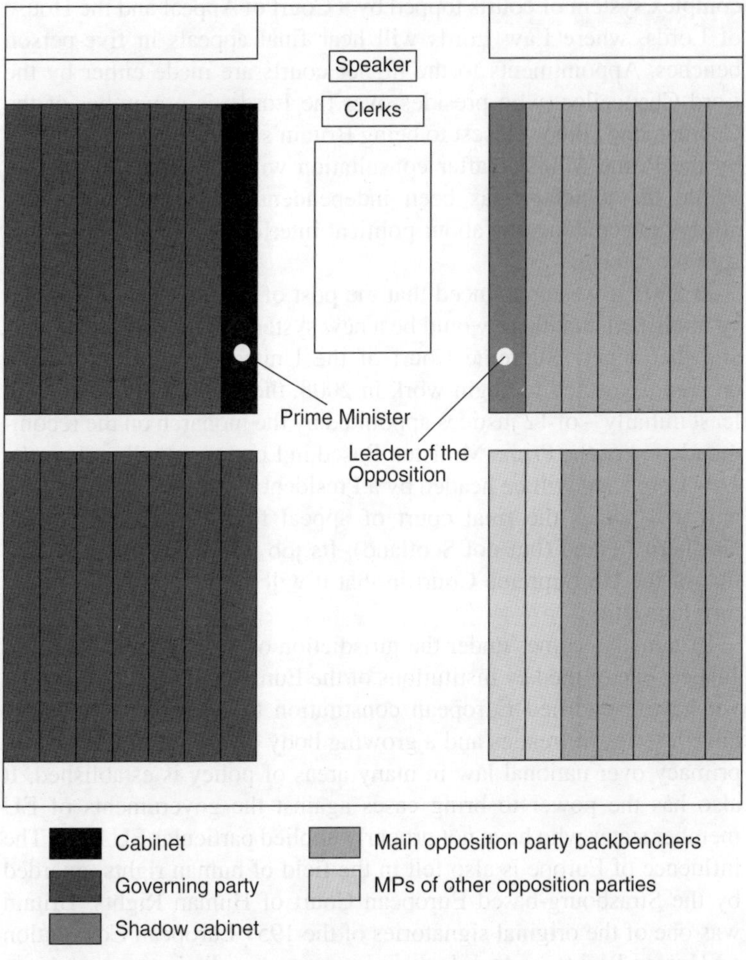
Speaker
Clerks
Prime Minister
Leader of the Opposition
Cabinet
Governing party
Shadow cabinet
Main opposition party backbenchers
MPs of other opposition parties

The Judiciary

Constitutional courts – such as those in the United States and Germany – typically exist to defend and interpret the constitution, and act as the final court of appeal on cases calling for judicial review: the process by which a judgement is made on the constitutionality of a law or the action of an elected official. Since Britain does not have a codified constitution, it does not have a distinct constitutional court. Instead, judicial review is carried out in a complex system of courts topped by a Court of Appeal and the House of Lords, where Law Lords will hear final appeals in five-person benches. Appointments to the higher courts are made either by the Lord Chancellor (who presides over the Lords, is a member of the Cabinet, and comes closest to being Britain's 'Minister of Justice') or by the Prime Minister after consultation with the Lord Chancellor. While the judiciary has been independent, this arrangement has always raised concerns about political interference, generating pressure for reform.

In 2003 it was announced that the post of Lord Chancellor would be abolished, that there would be a new system for appointing judges, and that a new Supreme Court of the United Kingdom would be created. Expected to begin work in 2008, the Court will consist – at least initially – of 12 justices appointed by the monarch on the recommendation of the Prime Minister. Based in London, it will replace the Law Lords and will be headed by a President and a Deputy President, and will act as the final court of appeal for England, Wales and Northern Ireland (but not Scotland). Its job will be distinctive from that of the US Supreme Court in that it will not be allowed to overturn legislation.

Britain also comes under the jurisdiction of the European Court of Justice, one of the key institutions of the European Union. It does not yet have a codified European constitution to interpret, but it does have a series of treaties and a growing body of European law, whose primacy over national law in many areas of policy is established. It also has the power to bring cases against the governments of EU member states who have not properly applied particular EU laws. The influence of Europe is also felt in the field of human rights, guarded by the Strasbourg-based European Court of Human Rights. Britain was one of the original signatories of the 1951 European Convention on Human Rights, and while this was not eventually incorporated into British law until 1998, many cases were successfully brought against the British government.

The Bureaucracy

Britain has about half a million bureaucrats (or civil servants), who carry out the typical responsibilities of bureaucrats everywhere: most are responsible for collecting government revenues (mainly in the form of taxes), for making payments in the form of benefits and pensions, and for running government services. Like most of its counterparts elsewhere, the British bureaucracy – sometimes known as Whitehall after the part of London where many government departments are headquartered – is hierarchical in structure and nature, and is expected to execute the laws of government and the wishes of government ministers.

The British civil service – like all other elements of government – has undergone profound change in recent years as attempts have been made to reform it by borrowing ideas from the private sector designed to make the service more efficient and responsive to consumers. The most important of these ideas have included the contracting-out of jobs previously done by bureaucrats, the tying of pay to performance, improvements in management methods, and techniques designed to provide a better service for less cost. In the view of Kavanagh (2000: 296–300), the effect has been a fundamental change to the characteristics of Whitehall:

- *Permanence*. Beginning in the early nineteenth century, bureaucrats were able to assume that their jobs were permanent. Careers in government and the civil service were treated as separate, and bureaucrats were regarded as servants of the monarch rather than of the political leadership of the day. In recent years, though, with the linking of performance to pay, and staff moving between the public and private sectors, the idea of jobs for life has weakened.
- *Neutrality*. As servants of the Crown, bureaucrats have been expected to be impartial and to recognize that their responsibilities are above party politics. For this reason, they are not allowed to stand for political office or to express political opinions in public, and – if they decide to enter politics – they must resign from the civil service, not just take a leave of absence as their counterparts in France and Germany are allowed to do. This impartiality was easier during the period of consensus government in the 1950s, 1960s and 1970s, but became less so with the growing ideological distance between the two major parties in the 1980s and 1990s. There are also allegations that recent governments have been more aggressive in involving themselves in decisions on the appointments of senior civil servants.
- *Anonymity*. The principle of responsible government means that ministers have traditionally received confidential advice from civil servants, but have been expected to take public responsibility for

the work of their departments, while bureaucrats have remained largely anonymous. This principle has been eroded by public enquiries that have been more willing to name names, by greater media inquiry into the workings of the bureaucracy, and by greater openness in the memoirs of former ministers and their aides.

The greatest changes to the bureaucracy were brought by Margaret Thatcher, who cut the number of civil servants by 28 per cent, launched a programme of departmental efficiency audits, questioned senior civil servants more aggressively about policies, took a close interest in high-level promotions, and more assertively imposed her views on the civil service (Jones and Kavanagh, 2003: 190). The most notable change in recent years has been a trend away from large government departments under the control of ministers to more than 150 small, independent agencies responsible for delivering services directly to the public. These include the Benefits Agency, the Environment Agency, the Health Development Agency, and the National Youth Agency. Instead of being subject to ministerial control, the agencies are led by chief executives who control budgets and staffing, and are held accountable by performance targets. Policy advice and the development of legislation are still the responsibility of government departments, but executive and administrative duties have been handed over to these agencies, where four out of five bureaucrats now work. The old notion of 'Whitehall' is increasingly at odds with reality.

Local Government

Britain has long been a unitary state, where political power has been focused at the national level, and local government has had few significant political powers. Local government until recently has been responsible mainly for providing a variety of basic services that most people take for granted, including refuse collection and road maintenance. Most Britons show little interest in local politics, turnout at local government elections is usually low, and local government officials are not as well known as national politicians. So weak is local government in Britain that it can be reformed, restructured or even abolished by the national government.

Changes made over the last 30 years (the most recent in 1998) have created a complex and confusing system of local government authorities. In England and Wales, most areas come under a two-tier system of counties and districts, each with locally elected councils responsible for such issues as education, transport, housing, highways, local services, refuse disposal, and the police. In selected areas, mainly larger cities, county and district functions have been combined into new unitary authorities. London has its own elected city government (see below), and six other metropolitan counties – such as Greater Manchester and Merseyside – have no county councils but are instead divided into district councils. Meanwhile, Scotland has unitary councils, Wales has unitary authorities, and Northern Ireland has unitary districts.

This untidy arrangement has been further complicated by the recent creation of elected regional assemblies for Scotland, Wales and Northern Ireland, but not for England. Thus, Britain – while still claiming to be a unitary state in which power is focused at the national level – has actually come to have a semi-federal system of government. The word 'federal' has negative connotations in Britain, mainly because of fears expressed by Eurosceptics about the possibility of a federal Europe in which many of the powers of British government are taken over by EU institutions. Interestingly, it is rarely mentioned in academic studies of the changes that have come to local government in Britain. It has instead been more fashionable to talk of 'multi-level governance', defined as 'negotiated exchanges between systems of governance at different institutional levels' (Pierre and Stoker, 2000: 30).

The Scottish and Welsh regional assemblies were created in 1998, following public referendums, and the first elections were held in May 1999. Both are elected for fixed four-year terms, and have powers over local issues such as education, health services, housing, transport and policing. The 129-member Scottish Parliament has control over most domestic policy matters, including health, education, justice, local transport and the environment, can make primary legislation in these areas, and has limited tax-raising powers. The 60-member National Assembly for Wales has control over a similar range of issues (except justice and policing), but has no taxing powers. Meanwhile, Northern Ireland – which had its own Parliament from 1921 to 1972 – has, since 1998, also had its own 108-member Assembly with powers over local issues, and also has two Ministerial Councils that address joint policy-making with Ireland and with the British Parliament. (The UK government retains control over economic, monetary, employment, foreign,

Parliament buildings at Stormont in Belfast, Northern Ireland. Once the seat of the Parliament of Northern Ireland (1932–72), it is now the seat of the new Northern Ireland Assembly, created as a result of the Good Friday peace agreement in 1998. Meetings of the Assembly have been suspended several times because of political disputes.

Illustration 4.3   Stormont

defence and security policy. But since the Northern Ireland Assembly has been suspended several times because of domestic political squabbles, the British government has – in practice – had greater powers.)

London – which, with its surrounding suburbs, is home to about one-third of the British population – was at one time governed by the Greater London Council, led by a left-wing Labour politician named Ken Livingstone. Illustrating the powers of national government over local bodies, Margaret Thatcher abolished the Council in 1986. The Blair administration felt that a city the size of London should have its own local government, so the ceremonial office of Lord Mayor of London (whose post is specific to the City of London) was joined by a new elected office for the whole of London. The first elections were held in May 2000, and – much to the chagrin of the Blair administration, which promoted its own 'official' Labour candidate – Ken Livingstone was restored to power. (He was elected to a second term in June 2004 as the Labour candidate.) The mayor governs with a 25-member London Assembly, elected using the additional member electoral system: 14 members are elected from individual districts, while 11 are elected on a London-wide party basis.

5

Politics and Civil Society

When most people think of politics, they think of government, and of leaders and institutions. But the lifeblood of politics in a democracy is provided by the people, and the way they use the opportunities provided to them to influence the way their government functions. They operate within a civil society, a community of individuals capable of acting separately from the state on the basis of pluralism, tolerance, civility and mutually accepted rules, and the patterns of association they endorse and accept. If the state consists of the rules and institutions by which a community is governed and controlled, then civil society is made up of all the voluntary and spontaneous forms of political association that evolve within that state, which are not formally part of the state system, but show that citizens can operate independently of the state (see Edwards, 2005).

Vibrant democracies such as Britain have many channels through which citizens can associate and work together, and can mobilize their numbers, values and goals to influence government, or to create organizations that either complement the work of government, or provide services where government has failed to do so. Citizens can also express themselves through elections, support for political parties or interest groups, the use of the mass media, and a host of other conventional and non-conventional forms of representation and participation, ranging from direct contact with elected officials to protests, boycotts, strikes and demonstrations. Like other democracies, Britain has a varied and active civil society through which its residents can engage with the political process. But – also as in those other democracies – many Britons choose not to participate, and this has caused growing concern.

This chapter begins with a survey of political culture in Britain, outlining the norms and attitudes of the British towards politics and civic responsibility: the views they hold regarding their role in the political system, their expectations of that system, and their opinions about their responsibilities to the political community in which they live. It then looks at elections and political parties, explaining the electoral process in Britain, comparing the structure and implications of the first-past-the-post system with those of the proportional representation systems used for elections to regional assemblies and the European Parliament, and examining the policies and the recent fortunes of the major political parties. It finishes with a discussion of the role of interest groups and the media in politics.

The chapter argues that the changes that have come to government – described in Chapter 4 – are reflected in civil society. Concerns about the fairness of the first-past-the-post electoral system have led to the introduction of proportional representation in local and European elections. The balance between the two major political parties has shifted as Labour has moved to the centre, and as the Conservatives have struggled to find a new identity in response. Meanwhile, the British have turned their backs in growing numbers on two of the most traditional forms of political participation – party membership and voting in elections – and have instead become more involved in the work of interest groups, and more willing to use unconventional channels to express their political views. The rise of the internet has changed the sources of political information and the channels for political participation and expression, and has obliged government to be more creative in the way it relates to citizens.

Political Culture

The term *political culture* describes the collective norms, values and expectations of a society as they relate to politics and government. Political culture helps explain what leaders and citizens regard as acceptable and unacceptable about the character of government, and about the relationship between government and people. Tying down the political values of a society is always a challenge, especially for a country like Britain, with its multinational identity and its long and convoluted history. A generation ago, most political scientists would have described the British as pragmatic, as having faith in their political system (if not necessarily politicians), as patriotic, and as politically moderate. But perceptions have changed in recent years, with new attention being paid to the decline of participation, trust, and faith in government, and to questions about the definition of national identity.

Pragmatism

The British tend to be pragmatic when it comes to their expectations of government and their aspirations for their own lives. They take an empirical approach to problem-solving, eschewing theory in favour of tried and tested approaches and assessments of the practical reality of policies. This is not to suggest that the British do not dream, or that they fear change, or that they are opposed to innovation. Quite the opposite is true, and the details of the political system have altered constantly over time, as they continue to do even today; most other European political systems seem quite staid by comparison to the changes that have recently come to the British model.

Particularly among older Britons, pragmatism has spilled over into pessimism. It often seems as though the national motto should be 'mustn't grumble', or 'things could be worse', given how often some Britons utter these phrases in response to the greeting 'How are you?'. The media have perpetuated the problem through their fascination with everything from lowered educational performance to rising crime and the mixed record of the English national cricket and football teams. Until recently at least, academics made the situation worse with their misplaced emphasis on the 'decline' of Britain. But the view that life was better and safer in 'the old days' is not supported by the facts; in terms of health care, education, economic wealth, individual freedoms, gender equality, consumer protection and the state of the environment, life for most Britons has improved greatly in the last 30 years. Fortunately, more people are beginning to realize this, and the gloom of the 1970s and 1980s is lifting.

Faith in the Political System

Despite this thread of pessimism, most Britons have high levels of faith in the political system. These feelings are tied closely to the long history of relative political stability and evolutionary change in Britain, which contrasts with the often revolutionary and violent change that has come to political systems in other European states. Faith in the political system was long bound up in the class structure and the strong feelings of political and social deference that this promoted. Cynics occasionally described Britain as a Nanny State, or one in which the government acted like the archetypal Victorian nanny, insisting that it knew what was in the best interests of the people, and preferring not to be questioned too much. Deference can be seen in traditional views about the monarchy and the class system, and in the willingness to obey authority figures representing the state, such as the police (see discussion in Moran, 2005: 83–4). However, deference has been on the decline (Hall, 1999: 453), for several reasons:

- Changes in the class system have weakened the authority of the Establishment.
- There is growing respect for succeeding through effort and hard work, and declining respect for privilege and old money.
- The British are becoming more self-reliant and less dependent on the state.
- The political system is seen as being less responsive than it should be.
- There has been less respect for elected officials.

These changes have been interpreted by some as a decline in faith in government, but they might equally represent a change in the *expectations* of government, tied in with a new belief in self-determination and support for alternative methods of engaging with government and expressing political opinions. On the one hand, membership of political parties has been falling, as has turnout by voters at elections (Box 5.1). At the same time, there has been a growth in the membership of interest groups, and recent studies have suggested that the British are more willing to use unconventional forms of political participation than the citizens of any other democracy: one survey in the mid-1990s found that 56 per cent were prepared to sign petitions, 35 per cent to attend lawful demonstrations, 25 per cent to join a boycott, 15 per cent to join a wildcat strike, 13 per cent to refuse to pay taxes, and 9 per cent to block traffic (Wallace and Jenkins, 1995).

It is important to make a distinction between levels of faith in political institutions and levels of faith in political leaders. With regard to institutions, the two for which there is the least public respect – the monarchy and the House of Lords – have undergone much change in recent years. At the same time, some of the criticisms of the political

Box 5.1 The disappearing British voter

The most fundamental property of democracy is the right to participate. Governments are the servants of the people, and are elected to represent the interests of the people. Elected officials may see themselves as delegates, who work to find out what their constituents want and need, and act accordingly, or as trustees, who act and vote according to what they feel is in the best interests of constituents, the party, and the country. Either way, government officials are there to *represent*. But to do so effectively demands that citizens participate in the democratic process, whether through voting, party activities, lobbying, joining interest groups, demonstrating, or any of the myriad ways in which they can make their decisions known. But recent evidence suggests that the British are not taking part in politics – or expressing their views on politics – as much as they once did.

A recent survey (Electoral Commission and Hansard Society, 2005) found that more than half of Britons felt that they knew either 'not very much' or 'nothing at all' about politics. About 13 per cent claimed to be 'very interested' in politics, 40 per cent were 'fairly interested', while 47 per cent were 'not very interested' or 'not at all interested'. These figures are not so different from those in several other democracies, and for many they have been reflected in falling voter turnout at recent British general elections. Electoral waters have been muddied by a blurring of the ideological distinctions among parties, by declining public identification with those parties, and by weakening links between class and voting (Bartle and Laycock, 2006: 77). But voter turnout has fallen from a high of 83–84 per cent in 1950–51, to 76–79 per cent in the 1970s, to 71 per cent in 1997, to a new low in 2001–05 of just 59–61 per cent. These figures are still respectable, placing Britain around the average for most European countries (with the notable exception of those where voting is compulsory such as Belgium and Italy). But they have sparked suggestions of a 'crisis' in British politics (Whiteley, 2001), and of declining faith in the political system (Bill Jones, 2003: 24). Were the 2001–05 results an indication of a new long-term trend in British politics, or were they an anomaly, to be explained by the particular circumstances of these two elections, in neither of which the opposition Conservatives were able to put up a real contest with Labour? It is not yet an issue that much concerns British political analysts, but this may change.

system have also been addressed: government has responded to concerns about the electoral process by introducing proportional representation in regional and European elections, and to complaints about too much power in Westminster and too much secrecy in government by passing legislation aimed at making government more open.

But faith and trust in political leaders has declined, much of it coming on the back of a string of scandals that have afflicted both the Conservative and the Labour parties. In 1994, two Conservative MPs received payments in return for asking questions in the House of Commons, in 1998 it was revealed that Britain's Trade Secretary Peter Mandelson (now European trade commissioner) had failed to declare a loan received from another member of the government for a house purchase, in 1998–99 there were charges that the Blair administration had given British citizenship to a wealthy Indian businessman who had made major donations to Labour Party funds, and in 2006 there was speculation about a 'cash for peerages' scandal after Tony Blair was accused of nominating for membership of the House of Lords four wealthy businessmen who had loaned the Labour Party several million pounds. Related accusations have been made against the Conservative Party. The cumulative effect of such incidents has been a tendency to see government leaders less as public servants and more as adversaries out for personal and political gain. But Britain is not unusual – similar trends can be found in other European countries and in the United States.

A Confused National Identity

Although they are not as patriotic as the Americans and the French, the British take pride in their history and traditions, which is part of the reason why so many have little enthusiasm for the European Union; it impinges too much on the sovereignty and separate identity of Britain for their comfort. Polls regularly find that the majority of Britons (80 per cent or more) are proud of being British. However, the notion of patriotism has been muddied by the rise of Scottish and Welsh nationalism (see Chapter 2), which has raised questions about the definition of 'Britain' and 'British'. Recent polls have found that about 65–75 per cent of Scots think of themselves primarily as Scottish and only 25 per cent as equally Scottish and British, and that 50 per cent of the Welsh think of themselves primarily as Welsh and only 30 per cent as equally Welsh and British. Identities are even more confused in Northern Ireland, where 65–75 per cent of Protestants regard themselves primarily as British, while 60 per cent of Catholics think of themselves mainly as Irish (figures quoted by Meehan, 1999; see also Curtice, 2004).

While the Scots, the Welsh and the Irish have long defined their identities in relation to their dominant neighbour, the English have

Illustration 5.1   Multiracial school

A multiracial class in a school at Deptford in Kent. The increased cultural
and racial diversity of Britain has led to a difficult debate about British
national identity, which has often served to confuse rather than to clarify,
and to emphasize the questions over the meaning of Britishness.

defined themselves more in the context of the meanings of 'Britain'
and 'British'. This has begun to change in recent years, though, with
more residents of England defining themselves as 'English' rather
than 'British' (Hazell, 2006), more overt displays of English patriotism in support of English national sports teams, calls for the recognition of St George's Day (23 April) as a national holiday, support for
greater recognition of what makes England different from Scotland
and Wales, and even – albeit among a minority – talk of the idea that
England might pre-empt the Scots by breaking away from the UK
first. For some, it was symbolic of the confusion that at the 2006 football World Cup, the *British* national anthem was played before
appearances of the *England* national team.

Discussions of the meaning of Britishness have been further
complicated in recent decades by the new racial and religious diversity of Britain. Where once there was a close association between the
history and cultural symbols of Britain and the British people, the
impact of recent waves of immigration has forced a reassessment of

national identity. Sadly, there is a perception that the British national flag – and even the English flag – may have been hijacked by racists and right-wing extremist groups bemoaning the growth of ethnic diversity. This has led some to associate both flags with intolerance, and even led one rather confused school head teacher to ban the display of English flags during the 2006 World Cup for fear that it would offend minority students. She backtracked following an outcry from her students.

A Closed Society

The British tend to be a private people, hence the old adage that an Englishman's home is his castle. Perhaps because Britain is such a crowded country where a premium is placed on personal space, the British can sometimes seem a little stand-offish to visitors. This sense of privacy was long reflected in the secrecy that often surrounded the functioning of government in Britain. Issues of national security are subject to secrecy in every democracy, but critics charge that state secrets have been too broadly defined in Britain, and that this has helped increase the power and reduce the accountability of the police, weakened the power of Parliament at the expense of the executive, promoted the use of surveillance, reduced the right to personal privacy, and allowed the government to interfere with media freedom.

Recent years have seen a movement for greater freedom of information, governments have given new emphasis to transparency, and information has become more freely available, particularly over the internet. The Freedom of Information Act, which came into force in 2005, provides a statutory right of access to recorded information relating to the work of Parliament, government departments, local authorities, the health service, and other publicly funded organizations. Critics charge that there are too many important exceptions – including information related to policy-making, and to matters where legal action may be likely or pending – and that the Information Commissioner responsible for enforcing the Act has powers only to recommend rather than compel the release of information. Nevertheless, the new law has helped make government more accessible, and has helped encourage citizens to be more interested in the activities of government and in gaining access to official information. But this new openness has come at a time when civil liberties are being curbed – and the powers of government expanded – in response to terrorism.

Social Liberalism

In line with many of their European neighbours, but in notable contrast to many Americans, the British as a whole tend to take liberal positions on social issues. The basic principles of the welfare state are unchallenged, capital punishment has been outlawed since 1964, homosexuality and abortion have both been legal since 1967, same-sex civil unions or partnerships have been allowed since 2005, there is little censorship on television, and unmarried couples living together and having children are not only tolerated but are steadily becoming the norm. Where political debates in the United States are often based around the question of the extent to which government should become involved in determining the personal choices of citizens – either through regulation on such relatively trivial matters as mandating the use of seatbelts by drivers, or through bigger issues such as access to legal abortion or prayer in schools – these are rarely discussed in Britain, if only because liberal social values are so ingrained in national life. Of course there is support also for conservative social positions, and attempts have been made to spark debates about the decline of 'family values' or to make access to abortion illegal, but such arguments attract little broad-ranging public support or sympathy.

Elections

Like all liberal democracies, Britain has many channels through which its citizens can take part in politics, express their opinions, and try to influence government policy. These include regular elections, political parties representing different ideological and regional positions, a large community of interest groups, and a diverse media establishment. The options have increased in recent years as the number of parties has grown, as new local and regional assemblies have been created, as the electoral system has diversified, and as the number of sources of political news has increased. Only about one in ten Britons has a sustained interest in politics, according to polls (see Electoral Commission and Hansard Society, 2005), but most take some periodic, intensive interest (usually in the lead-up to elections), and most are well-informed about national and international issues, if not necessarily interested in politics as such.

Elections serve the triple purpose of maintaining the legitimacy of the system of government, of offering cues for the direction of public policy, and of offering citizens a means of effecting peaceful political and constitutional change (Kavanagh *et al.*, 2006: 395).

British voters are faced with three sets of elections, as set out below.

The General Election

This is the contest by which members of the lower chamber of Parliament – the House of Commons – are chosen, and so by which the national government of Britain is determined. It is by far the most important event on the electoral calendar, and attracts the most political activity, and the greatest media and public interest. It is not held on a fixed schedule, but must be held at least once every five years, on a date chosen by the Prime Minister and confirmed by the monarch. The campaign is short, lasting just 18 days (excluding weekends and public holidays), and the election usually takes place on a Thursday.

The UK is divided into 646 constituencies (electoral districts), each represented in the House of Commons by a single Member of Parliament. All 646 seats must be contested in the general election, and voters make a straight choice among the candidates from the different parties standing in their district, the winner being the candidate with the most votes. Once the results are in, the monarch asks the leader of the party with the largest number of seats to form a government. If there is no clear winner, then the party leaders negotiate among themselves to form a coalition. Constituency boundaries are revised periodically to make sure that the number of voters in each is roughly the same. Until 2000, there were separate boundary commissions for England, Scotland, Wales and Northern Ireland, but they were then absorbed into an independent national Electoral Commission, which is also responsible for supervising the financial restrictions on parties and for overseeing referendums.

Britain is unusual within Europe in using the first-past-the-post (or winner-take-all) electoral system, under which a winning candidate does not need a majority, but prevails simply by winning more votes than any other candidate. Most other European countries use proportional representation (PR), under which parties win seats in proportion to the number of votes they win. First-past-the-post has the advantage of being quick and simple, and tends to produce stable and accountable one-party governments, but it also works in favour of parties that have large blocks of concentrated support, and against parties whose support is more thinly spread; the former tend to win seats, while the latter more often come second or third.

The kind of skewed results this can produce were most glaringly obvious in the 1983 general election, when the ruling Conservatives won 42 per cent of the vote but 62 per cent of seats in the House of Commons. Meanwhile, Labour won 28 per cent of votes and 32 per cent of seats (a more equitable result), while the third-placed Liberal–SDP Alliance won almost as many votes as Labour (25 per cent) but just 4 per cent of seats in the House. This meant, mathematically speaking, that the votes of Alliance supporters were worth only one-tenth as much as the votes of Conservative supporters. The imbalances appeared again in 2005, even if they were not quite so extreme: Labour won 35 per cent of votes but 55 per cent of seats, the Conservatives won 32 per cent of votes but 31 per cent of seats, and the Liberal Democrats won 22 per cent of votes but 10 per cent of seats.

The introduction of PR to Britain was first proposed as early as 1917, but until recently found few supporters within the Conservative and Labour parties, because they benefited the most from winner-take-all. However, pressure from within the European Union for a common EU-wide electoral system has combined with a change of heart within the Labour Party to bring about reform. British voters had their first taste of PR in 1998–99 with elections to the Scottish, Welsh and London assemblies and to the European Parliament (although Northern Ireland had already used PR for European and local elections). But there is little prospect of PR being used for the general election, because of a lack of public enthusiasm, opposition from the Conservatives, and antagonism even from members of the Labour Party (Fielding, 2000: 27).

European Elections

On a fixed five-year cycle, Britain elects 78 representatives to the 785-member European Parliament (EP) in Strasbourg, France. Candidates for EP elections are fielded by the same parties that contest general elections at home, and they run on a mixture of domestic and European issues. The first direct elections to the EP were held in 1979, since when British voters have shown a distressing lack of interest in turning out: after running at about 36 per cent (far below even the modest EU average of about 57 per cent), British turnout fell in 1999 to an all-time low of 23 per cent (less than half

Illustration 5.2   European Parliament

The European Parliament building in Strasbourg, France. British voters have had a less than stellar record in turnout for EP elections, as often as not using them as an opportunity to comment on the government in power in Britain rather than to vote on European issues, or to support the true party of their choice.

the EU average of 49 per cent), returning to a slightly more respectable 39 per cent in 2004. This lack of interest is explained by a combination of the Eurosceptic views of many British voters, and of the limited powers of the EP itself – it can neither introduce nor take the final decision on adopting new European laws.

European elections are striking for the extent to which opposition parties usually do better than the governing party. The main explanation for this lies in attitudes towards different kinds of elections. Elections that decide who runs the national government – or so-called 'first-order' elections – always draw the most media and public interest, and the highest turnout. By contrast, 'second-order' elections – such as European or local elections, where the stakes are lower – are usually seen as an opportunity to comment on the performance of the governing party. Thus, its supporters are less inclined to vote (adding to the low turnout figures), and many other voters will cast their ballots for parties they would not normally support (Hix, 2000: 64).

At the 1994 European elections, the governing Conservatives – plagued by divisions over Europe – won just 27 per cent of the vote and 18 of the British seats, while the opposition Labour Party won 43 per cent of the vote and 62 seats. By contrast, the 1999 elections were a major blow for Labour, by then in government, whose share of the vote fell to 28 per cent (which converted into 29 seats), while the Conservatives won 36 per cent of the vote and 36 seats. The balance was won by smaller parties including the Liberal Democrats (up from 2 to 10), the UK Independence Party (3), and the Greens (2). The turnaround was part of the typical inclination of voters to cast their ballots for the opposition, but it was also a reflection of a Europe-wide shift to right-wing parties calling for a slow-down in European integration, and was also affected by Britain's decision to adopt for the first time the same system of proportional representation used for EP elections in all the other EU member states. In 2004, with the total number of British seats down from 87 to 78 as a result of redistribution to take account of enlargement, Labour representation fell to 19 seats, the Conservatives were down to 27 seats, and the biggest gains were made by the Eurosceptic UK Independence Party, which won 12 seats, mainly at the expense of the Conservatives.

Local Government Elections

Because Britain is a unitary state (in theory, at least), and local authorities have limited power, local elections are seen as second-order contests, and have traditionally been ignored by most voters. Representatives are elected to district, county, city and town councils on a fixed four-year cycle, but the few voters who turn out usually make their choices on the basis of national issues and the performance of the national government, and turnout is rarely more than 40 per cent. Hopes that turnout might grow with the creation of new regional assemblies – which have their own powers over a variety of local policy issues – have been disappointed. Turnout at the first elections in 1998–99 was not inspiring (70 per cent in Northern Ireland, 58 per cent in Scotland, and 46 per cent in Wales) and was even worse in 2003 (63 per cent in Northern Ireland, 49 per cent in Scotland, and 38 per cent in Wales). Scottish and Welsh assembly elections are based on a combination of first-past-the-post and PR, while regional and European elections in Northern Ireland use PR.

Political Parties

Britain has a wide range of political parties, covering an assortment of ideological positions. However, while nearly 90 parties contested the 2005 general election, and 12 won seats in Parliament, Britain – thanks mainly to the arithmetic of the electoral system – has long been a two-party-dominant system. During the nineteenth century, it was the Conservatives and the Liberals that took turns at governing, their dominance occasionally threatened by Irish nationalist parties. Since the end of the First World War, Labour has replaced the Liberals, and they and the Conservatives have dominated, typically winning about 70–75 per cent of the vote between them and about 85–90 per cent of the seats in Parliament (see Table 5.1). The remaining share of votes and seats has been taken up by the old Liberal Party and its successors, and by regional parties; as well as Scottish and Welsh nationalists, Northern Ireland has its own parties which do not campaign on the mainland.

Labour

The Labour Party was founded in 1900 following debate about the need for a party to represent the interests of Britain's working-class population. In 1922 it replaced the Liberals as the opposition to the Conservatives, and headed its first coalition government in 1924 under Ramsay MacDonald. Labour won outright power for the first time in 1945 under Clement Atlee, and set about building a welfare state and a managed economy, nationalizing key industries, and creating a national health service, a social security system and a subsidized education system. It lost power in 1951, but returned in 1964–70 and again in 1974–76 under Harold Wilson, and in 1976–79 under James Callaghan. It went into opposition in 1979, losing four straight general elections and undergoing a crisis of confidence before finally regaining power in 1997 under Tony Blair.

Labour's failures in the 1980s were blamed on a combination of the political shrewdness of Conservative Prime Minister Margaret Thatcher, 'unelectable' party leaders such as the old-style socialist Michael Foot, and the growing unpopularity of many of its more traditional socialist policies, including state ownership of key industries, support of labour unions, and the redistribution of wealth through taxation. The extent of its internal problems was emphasized in 1981 when a group of moderate members of the party broke away

Table 5.1   Recent general election results

	1992		1997		2001		2005	
	% vote	seats	% vote	seats	% vote	seats	% vote	seats
Labour	35	271	43	418	41	412	35	355
Conservative	42	336	31	165	32	166	32	198
Liberal Democrat	17	20	17	46	18	52	22	62
Regional parties	4	24	5	29	5	27	6	27
Other	2	0	4	1	4	2	5	4
Total		651		659		659		646
Turnout (%)		76.3		71.4		59.4		61.4

Source: House of Commons web site, 2006.

to form the Social Democratic Party (SDP). This merged with the Liberal Party in 1988 after having helped encourage Labour to rethink its policies.

Tony Blair was elected party leader in May 1994, and moved quickly to 'modernize' Labour and to distance it from its more traditionally socialist ideas by adopting what he called a new left-of-centre agenda. In 1995 he encouraged the party to abandon the controversial Clause Four of its constitution, which pledged 'common ownership of the means of production, distribution and exchange'; Labour thereby gave up its promise to undo privatization, one of the most successful of Margaret Thatcher's policies. It went on to promote the 'third way' in politics, an approach to government, politics, economics and social issues that lies somewhere between the kind of right-wing conservatism/capitalism associated with the Thatcher government, and the left-wing liberalism/economic management associated with more mainstream European socialist parties.

The victory of 'New Labour' in May 1997 was remarkable in almost every sense. The party won a 177-seat majority, while the Conservatives lost half their seats in the Commons and all their seats in Scotland and Wales. The change of fortunes symbolized a widely felt need among Britons for new ideas in government, and a concern that Conservatives had paid too little attention to social problems. Labour had also moved itself towards the centre of the political spectrum (for example, promising not to raise income taxes), and the Conservatives had suffered from internal squabbles and the monetary crisis of 1992, when the pound was ejected from the European exchange-rate mechanism (Dunleavy, 2000: 131). There was also clearly much tactical voting in the election, with Labour and Liberal Democratic voters supporting each other's parties in districts where one of them was in a strong position to challenge the incumbent Conservative (Sanders, 1997). Finally, a new generation of young people who had known nothing but Conservative government was voting for the first time; some 52 per cent of under-25s voted Labour, up from 35 per cent in 1992. Many analysts also argued that the vote was ultimately less for Labour than against the divided Conservatives.

Labour under Blair went on to adopt many of the policies usually associated with the middle ground of politics, encroaching into traditionally Conservative territory: he embraced the market economy, opposed traditional socialist ideas of taxing and spending, developed a closer relationship with business, reduced the influence of trade unions in the party, committed his government to developing a balanced budget, instituted a more pro-European policy (Labour was for many years hostile to the idea of European integration), and moved Labour toward foreign policy positions that were pro-globalization, pro-NATO and pro-US. Blair also claimed that improved education, reform of the national health-care system, a tough position on crime, and constitutional reform were among his priorities.

Blair was able to prevent damaging in-fighting within the party between supporters of two currents of thought: left-wingers with a preference for public ownership and intervention in the economy, opposed to nuclear weapons, and cool on the transatlantic alliance, and right-wingers prepared to take a more pragmatic approach, favouring nuclear weapons, and supporting the transatlantic alliance. Labour maintained its commanding position at the 2001 election, when its majority was reduced by just 12 seats, and its percentage share of the vote fell from 43 to 41. However, voter turnout fell to 59 per cent, suggesting that enthusiasm for Labour was waning, and that it was being returned to office partly because the Conservatives had failed to offer a strong alternative.

All then changed during 2002–03 when Blair gave his support to the US-led invasion of Iraq. European publics were united in their hostility to the invasion – polls found 70–90 per cent opposition throughout the European Union (see Chapter 8) – but governments were divided, with Britain joining Spain and Italy in supporting the US plan, and France and Germany being vocal in their opposition. Mass demonstrations against the war were held in Britain, as elsewhere in Europe, and when it became clear that the pretext for invasion – that Iraq was developing weapons of mass destruction – was false, and as questions were raised about the real motives behind the war, and about the wisdom of British support for the US, Blair became increasingly unpopular.

As the 2005 general election approached, it was clear that the gloss had worn off his administration. In addition to Iraq, the Labour record on public services, crime and asylum was widely criticized, as was Blair's own governing style. But he had two important advantages: a strong economy, and the continued unpopularity of the Conservatives (see Bartle and Laycock, 2006: 84–8). The result was a third win for Labour, with a reduced but still impressive majority of 66. Unfortunately Blair had muddied the waters by declaring several months in advance that it would be his last election, sparking damaging debate in 2005–06 about how long he would stay in office, and generating calls from his critics for him to step down, which he eventually did in 2007.

The Conservatives

The origins of the Conservatives (also known as the Tories) date back to the late seventeenth century. Throughout the nineteenth century they alternated in office with first the Whigs, and then the Liberals, their most famous Prime Ministers including the Duke of Wellington, Sir Robert Peel, and Benjamin Disraeli. Since the end of the Second World War they have held power for a total of 36 years, under the leadership of Winston Churchill, Anthony Eden, Harold Macmillan and Alec Douglas-Home (1951–64), Edward Heath (1970–74), and Margaret Thatcher and John Major (1979–97). However, despite the number of their postwar election victories, and despite their status as one of the longest-serving political parties in any democracy, they have never won more than 45–50 per cent of the national vote; their share fell to a new low of 31–32 per cent in the 1997, 2001 and 2005 elections, and today they find themselves struggling to regain lost ground.

The Conservatives are a pro-business, anti-regulation party with so many shades of opinion that it is often charged that British conser-

Illustration 5.3   David Cameron

David Cameron speaking at the Conservative Party annual conference in 2006. Cameron had been elected party leader the year before on a wave of hopes that he could pull the party out of the rut into which it had fallen, and offer effective opposition to the Labour government. Critics initially charged that Cameron was too difficult to tie down, but supporters argued that more time was needed for him to establish his credentials.

vatism lacks consistency or coherence. Much like Labour, there have been two distinctive strands in Conservative thinking in recent years. Right-wingers in the party emphasize limited government, low taxes, self-reliance, social discipline, authority, continuity and morals, and are critical of the EU, while moderates emphasize the creation of wealth, efficient economic organization, a more active role for government in the economy, and a more progressive role for Britain in Europe. Between 1945 and 1975, Conservative policies changed little, irrespective of the leader. Then Margaret Thatcher took the helm and broke with tradition, and for more than a decade the party developed policies that reflected her values. She supported mone-tarist economic ideas (such as controls on government spending,

Box 5.2   David Cameron

Under the leadership of Iain Duncan Smith, the Conservatives had shifted too far to the right for the taste of many voters, and under the leadership of Michael Howard they had gone back to the old guard – he had been a government minister during the Thatcher and Major years. So it was with a sense both of renewal and of some trepidation that the party opted for the new and the moderate in 2005 when they elected David Cameron as their new leader. With just four years' experience as an MP, little was known about him, but his supporters clearly hoped that his youth and freshness would end the string of 'unelectable' party leaders, and he reportedly saw himself as 'the heir to Blair'.

Where the Conservatives had developed a modern tradition of electing leaders with middle-class origins, Cameron is something of a throwback to the days of the Tory Establishment. Born in London in 1966, he is the son of a stockbroker and is related to three nineteenth- and early-twentieth-century Conservative MPs. He was educated at Eton – one of Britain's premier public schools – and at Oxford, where he studied politics, philosophy and economics. He worked for the Conservative Party as an advisor and speech-writer before working for the television company Carlton in public relations for seven years, where he earned a reputation for being evasive.

Cameron won the leadership of the party in December 2005 at least in part by accident, following a lacklustre speech by David Davis, the front-runner. While he was almost immediately credited with reviving the fortunes of the Conservatives, Cameron's critics argued that it was difficult to know what he stood for (that he was all style and no substance), although his lack of specifics may have been deliberate: he was trying to win over Labour supporters – went the analysis – without providing too much detail on some of his party's more conservative positions, which might scare them off. The spectre of Europe continued to hang over his head, and to trouble him as it had troubled his predecessors: right-wingers in the party wanted him to take a tougher position on the EU, as well as on traditional Tory issues such as law and order.

There is evidence that he is moving to reposition the party, describing himself as a 'compassionate conservative', calling for a new style of politics, claiming that he will not oppose the government as a matter of course (but will offer support in areas of agreement), focusing on issues that have not been recent priorities of the Conservative Party (such as the environment and international development aid), and urging politicians to concentrate more on improving the general happiness and well-being of Britons.

reducing the role of government in the marketplace, low taxation and a free market), promoted private enterprise and private ownership, believed in a strong global role for Britain and close Anglo–American relations, and was hostile to many aspects of European integration.

Although the Conservatives under the leadership of Prime Minister John Major fought the 1997 election against the background of a strong economy, they faced an electorate that was tired of internal party squabbles. The party had become particularly divided over the issue of Europe, with some of its members arguing in favour of greater support for European integration, and some arguing that the process of integration had gone too far. The Conservatives had also been hurt by a number of financial scandals involving prominent backbenchers (the so-called 'sleaze' factor). Major was unable to pull the party together, it went into the election 20 percentage points behind Labour in opinion polls, and it sustained its worst election defeat since 1832.

Major resigned the party leadership, and was replaced in short order by three successors – William Hague (1997–2001), Iain Duncan Smith (2001–03), and Michael Howard (2003–05) – none of whom was able to make inroads into Labour's dominance. At least initially this was mainly because of Blair's popularity and strong political standing, but the Conservatives remained blighted by internal party divisions, by Labour's cooption of many of its more popular policy positions, and by the party's inability to broaden its appeal by reaching out to younger voters, women, the middle class, and ethnic minorities. It was hard not to compare the plight of the Conservatives with the plight of Labour in the 1980s, but – just as Tony Blair had rescued Labour in 1994 with fresh ideas and new thinking, so the Conservatives hoped that they could repeat history when – in December 2005 – they elected the 39-year-old David Cameron (b. 1966) as their new leader (see Box 5.2).

Liberal Democrats

A small, moderate centre party, the Liberal Democrats were created in 1988 when members of the Social Democratic Party (SDP) joined forces with the Liberal Party, one of the oldest parties in Britain and for many years until the 1920s the major opposition to the Conservatives. The last Liberal Prime Minister (David Lloyd George) left office in 1922, and Liberal support declined as the working class shifted its allegiance to Labour. Surprise by-election victories in the 1960s and 1970s had media pundits talking of a potential Liberal breakthrough, and for a while in the mid-1980s the SDP–Liberal Alliance seemed poised to take over from Labour as the major opposition party.

The Liberals and the SDP merged in 1988 to form the Liberal Democratic Party, which contested its first general election in April 1992. It won an impressive 17 per cent of the vote, but the quirks of first-past-the-post meant that this converted into just 20 seats (3 per cent of the total). In the 1997 election the party again won about 18 per cent of the vote, but more than doubled its representation in Parliament, winning 46 seats, the best result for a third party since the 1920s. New attention was paid to the Liberal Democrats by political analysts, especially given that their support and cooperation was being actively encouraged by the Blair government. They were led between 1999 and 2006 by Charles Kennedy, who was able to continue to build on party growth at the 2001 and 2005 elections. Kennedy claimed that the Liberal Democrats were on the verge of taking over from the Conservatives as the effective opposition to Labour, but critics asked how this could be when Liberal Democratic policies were so close to those of Labour in many areas. Kennedy stepped down in March 2006 after admitting a drinking problem, and was replaced by Sir Menzies Campbell (b. 1941).

Other Parties

There are many other smaller political parties in Britain, the most important representing regional interests, but among them they rarely win more than 3–5 per cent of the vote in general elections. The Scottish National Party (founded in 1934) campaigns for Scottish devolution and has undergone a revival since the 1950s, although it has never had more than 11 seats in the UK Parliament. It won 35 seats (27 per cent of the total) in the Scottish parliamentary elections in 1999, which allowed it to become the opposition to the Labour–Liberal Democratic coalition government. Its leader Alex Salmond went so far as to predict that Scotland would be completely independent by 2007, the 300th anniversary of the political union of England and Scotland. In spite of emerging as the largest party after the 2007 elections, it still fell short of a clear majority. Meanwhile, its Welsh counterpart Plaid Cymru (founded in 1925), which has in recent years had two to four seats in the UK Parliament, also won just over a quarter of the seats in the Welsh assembly in 1999, returning similar results in the 2003 and 2007 elections.

There are also nearly a dozen parties which are active only in Northern Ireland, and whose key differences revolve around their positions on the relationship with Britain. The biggest is the Democratic Unionist Party, which represents the Protestant cause of continued union for Northern Ireland with Britain, while Sinn Fein represents the Catholic/nationalist cause and has campaigned in the past for the reunification of Ireland (a goal officially rescinded by the 1998 Northern Ireland peace agreement). The Social Democratic and Labour Party meanwhile takes a more balanced line between the two positions.

While candidates for the larger parties must go through a rigorous selection procedure, British law allows almost anyone to stand for Parliament under almost any guise, unless they are long-term prisoners or peers or bishops in the House of Lords. They must be aged over 21, must be citizens of Britain, Ireland or a Commonwealth country, must have collected the signatures of ten local electors, and must have paid a deposit of £500 (about €750/$950), which is returned if the candidate wins more than 5 per cent of the vote. (A candidate who fails to cross the 5 per cent barrier is described as having 'lost their deposit'.) Everyone over the age of 18 and whose name is on the electoral register can vote except convicted prisoners, people with learning disabilities or mental illness who are incapable of making a reasoned judgement, and members of the House of Lords (but including citizens of Ireland or Commonwealth countries resident in the UK).

Interest Groups

As in most modern liberal democracies, interest groups play a key political role in Britain (Coxall, 2001). There are thousands of such groups, ranging from multimillion-member pressure groups to charities with more limited objectives. Several of Britain's mass movements and interest groups have spread to other countries. For example, the movement against cruelty to animals began in Britain, long famous as a nation of animal-lovers, and produced the Royal Society for the Prevention of Cruelty to Animals (RSPCA). (Ironically, it was founded in 1824, 65 years before the National Society for the Prevention of Cruelty to Children.) Similarly, Save the

Children, Oxfam (famine relief), the World Wildlife Fund, and Amnesty International were founded in Britain and have since become international.

As voters have become more disillusioned with elections and political parties, the number, variety, and membership of interest groups have grown: nearly one in three Britons are now members of at least one group, and many people belong to multiple groups (Pattie *et al.*, 2004). Interest groups have also become more professional and the methods they use have diversified. Where they once focused their efforts on ministers and bureaucrats, they have worked increasingly to mobilize media and public opinion, and have intensified their lobbying of Parliament, providing information to MPs, making presentations to parliamentary committees, and trying to influence the development of legislation. The European Union has provided new channels for influence, with groups trying to impact the development of new EU laws and policies, and reporting to the European Court of Justice failures by the government to implement EU law. This growth has led to more discussion about 'social capital', referring to the value of social networks, including their contribution to the effectiveness and stability of democratic government (Putnam, 2000)

Interest-group activity in Britain has occasionally added up to broader movements aimed at bringing political, economic or social reform, and there have been three particularly important movements in Britain in recent years.

The Labour Movement

Britain has about 300 trade unions, the biggest of which are affiliated to the Trades Union Congress (TUC), founded in 1868. Unions for a long time had a close relationship with the Labour Party, having a 40 per cent share in the electoral college that elected the party leader, and sponsoring about 40 per cent of Labour candidates in general elections. The TUC also had understandings with Labour governments whereby – in return for concessions – it agreed not to make big wage claims or to call strikes. By 1974, unions had so much political power that a general strike was called which ultimately obliged Edward Heath's Conservative government to call a general election, which it lost.

The failure of the Labour governments of Harold Wilson (1974–76) and James Callaghan (1976–79) to reach agreements with the unions on prices and wages led to another near-general strike in 1979. This made Labour so unpopular that it lost the 1979 election, ushering in a Thatcher government bent on reducing union power. Laws were passed requiring union leaders to ballot their members before taking strike action, and unemployment reduced union membership during the 1980s. In addition to a lengthy and divisive strike by coal-miners in the mid-1980s, print and journalists' unions also went on strike – all three groups failed to meet their goals. In recent years, unions have lost much of their support and many of their members, and their political influence has declined further as their influence on the Labour Party has weakened.

Business Groups

If the TUC represents workers, then employers are represented by the Confederation of British Industry (CBI), founded in 1965. Financial institutions are politically important in Britain, mainly because of the influence of the financial district of the City of London (see Chapter 6). While City interests are kept separate from those of industry, and while there are no formal links between business and the Conservative Party (such as those that once existed between unions and the Labour Party), many senior managers in the City and Britain's larger companies had significant influence within the Conservative Party during the Thatcher and Major years. They were not ignored by the Blair government, which made a point of cultivating contacts with business as part of its philosophy of increasing productivity and promoting British economic influence in the EU.

The Environmental Movement

Green political parties have not been as successful in Britain as they have in several other European countries, the pressure for environmental change instead expressing itself through support for a large community of environmental interest groups. Britain has what may well be the oldest and biggest (per capita) community of such groups in the world, with a combined membership of several million. Much of the growth in its size and levels of activity has come since the late 1980s, and the groups with the fastest growth include those that have been most activist, such as Greenpeace and Friends of the Earth. That growth has been accompanied by a new emphasis on the role of the individual in the creation of environmental problems, leading to a new level of activism among both groups and individuals (Rawcliffe, 1998, and Rootes, 2003). Three issues in particular are credited with

Illustration 5.4   Fox-hunting

Fox-hunting has been part of the English rural scene for centuries, opposed by its critics as barbaric, and justified by its supporters as a method of conservation and pest control, and as a staple of the rural economy. A 2004 law banned hunting with dogs, but also energized the fox-hunting lobby, which claimed a renewed interest in the pastime.

prompting much of the growth in the late 1990s: the anti-roads movement, direct-action protests in 1998–99 against the use of genetically modified foods, and concerns about rural issues and the state of the countryside (Margetts, 2000: 189–91). The latter issue prompted an estimated 100,000 people to turn out in a London protest in 1997, and 250,000 to turn out in 1998. A MORI poll found that 80 per cent of the participants in the 1998 protest were Conservative voters, a group not usually given to protest activity.

The Media

The British generally have a high level of political literacy and interest in national and international affairs, a situation which is sustained by one of the most diverse and well-respected mass media establishments in the world, catering to almost every taste and political persuasion. Like all European countries, Britain has mainly national or regional media, so people are interested less in local affairs than in national or international affairs. Important changes have come to the British media over the past decade: they are becoming more powerful political actors, they are becoming more polarized as competition increases, their independence from political parties is growing, and – thanks mainly to changes in technology – a greater variety of sources of information has become available (see Curran and Seaton, 2003).

Take the case of television. Until the late 1980s, British TV viewers had a choice of just four terrestrial channels: two state-owned but independent and commercial-free channels run by the British Broadcasting Corporation (BBC), and two independent commercial channels (ITV and Channel 4). (A new commercial channel – Channel 5 – was created in 1996.) All were editorially independent, were required to give equal air-time to the major political parties, and frequently became involved in political controversy. Despite being government-owned, the BBC has always had a reputation for being an impartial and dependable source of news both inside and outside Britain.

In the last quarter century, the television landscape has changed out of all recognition:

- Cable television was launched in 1984 and satellite in 1989, and the number of TV channels leapt from four to more than 60.
- Audience share for the terrestrial channels fell from more than 90 per cent to about 80 per cent, and was down to 70 per cent in 2005.
- Scotland increasingly opted out of carrying national programming, and instead aired more locally produced programmes.
- While there is more 24-hour news on offer, there is less prime-time political coverage on the mainstream commercial channels (Scammell, 2000: 171–8).

Under the circumstances, the public-service programming that was once provided by the BBC without much competition is now viewed by a smaller proportion of the audience, which is offered more entertainment options instead. The promotion of 'British' political issues has also declined as regional news plays a bigger role in the choices available to viewers. Finally, political parties have to work harder –

and use a greater variety of methods and outlets – to put their message across to viewers. Instead of enjoying the virtually undivided attention of viewers, they are now competing with the broadcasting fare of dozens of different channels.

The British broadcast market continues to undergo change, with the liberalization of the market, the deregulation of commercial radio, new rules allowing radio-owners to buy television stations and vice versa, the expansion of digital television (analog broadcasting is due to end in 2012), the merger of independent television (currently run by two separate companies), and permission for non-European companies to buy British companies. It is notable that the world's media have come to be dominated in recent years by seven major companies, four of which are American (including AOL Time-Warner and Disney), two continental European (Bertelsmann and Vivendi), one Japanese (Sony), and none British. Changes to British broadcasting law are designed in part to encourage the emergence of a world-leading British media company that could compete with the Big Seven. Critics charge, however, that too many other countries (notably the US) still bar foreigners from investing in their domestic industries, and that the existence of the BBC – a large state-owned corporation – could act as a barrier to the development of a large private competitor.

The print media are also experiencing change. For decades, British readers have been offered a choice of major regional daily newspapers (such as *The Scotsman* in Edinburgh or the London Evening Standard), and a range of London-based national morning papers:

- the five so-called 'quality' papers: *The Times*, *Telegraph*, *Independent*, *Guardian*, and *Financial Times* (all read predominantly by higher socio-economic groups)
- the five mass circulation tabloids: the *Daily Mail* and the *Daily Express* (read mainly by the middle class) and the *Sun*, the *Daily Mirror*, and the *Daily Star* (read mainly by the working class).

Where the 'qualities' provide a broader range of news and comment, several with a particular political or social bias, the tabloids tend to be more openly partisan and to offer an often simplified and exaggerated picture of politics. The popularity of the tabloids has also led to concerns that they give their owners too much political influence. Particular criticism has been directed at Rupert Murdoch, whose News International Corporation owns Sky

Television, *The Times* / *Sunday Times*, the *Sun*, and the *News of the World*. Murdoch's papers once took strongly anti-EU and pro-Conservative editorial positions, but since 1997 have in the main supported Blair, including at election time.

As in other industrialized countries, newspapers in Britain have lost readers and advertising revenues to online sources of news, leading to projections that several may close down in coming years. Some have responded – like their counterparts in television – by trying to attract new readers with a shift away from hard news on politics and economics, and towards soft stories on lifestyle and entertainment. Others have invested in new business in order to help sustain the costs of not-so-profitable print editions, or have invested in the development of free editions. Yet others have expanded the options available on their online versions, which have helped them pull in readers from more countries, and increase their advertising revenues.

Despite the changes, the British media still carry out the typical roles of helping form the national political agenda, providing people with information, helping determine political reputations, and providing the self-appointed role of watchdog. More recently, they have also been more openly manipulated by government for political ends. In this regard, Britain has lagged some way behind the United States, where media strategies have been a critical part of political campaigns since the 1950s. It has only been since the 1970s, for example, that Prime Ministerial press officers have become well-known public figures. Margaret Thatcher in particular was well-known for developing a media strategy, for employing an advertising agency to develop campaign advertising, and for changing her image (even to the point of taking voice-training lessons) in order to help convey her message. Tony Blair also had an active media programme, such that one of the most prominent members of his administration was the Prime Minister's one-time press secretary, Alastair Campbell (who stepped down in 2003).

The availability of political information – and the opportunity for political participation – have been greatly affected by the rise since 1999 of the internet, now the world's largest communications system. The British compete with Americans as the most internet-connected people in the world: the proportion of homes with internet access rose from less than 10 per cent in 1998 to nearly 60 per cent in 2006 (about the same proportion as in the United States), and many more people have access at work or in libraries, while virtually all schools in

Britain are connected. Recent surveys have found that nearly two-thirds of all British adults have used the internet. While only a small minority have used it for political purposes, it has become an important tool in political communication and in the promotion of civil society.

6

The Economy

Economic matters play a primary role in the public life of every society, but in few places has this been more true in the last 50 years than in Britain. From being the world's biggest economic and trading power, with its most powerful currency, Britain has seen itself outperformed by its competitors, and hurt by the policies of labour unions and management, many of the members of which were incapable of looking beyond their narrow horizons at the bigger economic interests of their country, and by the contradictory inclinations of different governments to play a greater or a lesser role in the marketplace. The result has been a series of unsettling shifts in British economic fortunes.

The postwar Labour government championed nationalization and welfare, policies that helped with the reconstruction of Britain but over the longer term contributed to a decline in productivity, efficiency and competition. By the late 1960s, Britain's economy was in trouble, and many bemoaned the spread of a 'British disease', usually blamed on an expensive welfare system, powerful trade unions, a large public sector, falling productivity, and a declining trade surplus. Conditions worsened during the 1970s, and for many the nadir came in 1978–79 with the 'winter of discontent', when it seemed that all the accumulating problems of the previous 20 years had brought the British economy to the brink of collapse. The media became fascinated by the booms and busts, feeding into popular misconceptions of the economic decline of Britain. When voters went to the polls, their decisions were driven as much as anything by concerns about that decline and by their opinions about which political party offered the best solutions to Britain's economic woes.

The Thatcher government took power in 1979 determined to reverse the trends, arguing that government was too involved in market decisions, and that the entrepreneurial spirit of Britons had been dulled by high taxes and too much reliance on the state. It cut taxes, sold off key industries to the private sector, and reduced the burden of regulation. Through a combination of these policies and broader changes in the global economy, the prospects for Britain by the 1990s were much improved. New wealth was created, new businesses were launched, productivity grew, and both inflation and unemployment fell. Today, in spite of the routine cyclical concerns that afflict all economies, Britain is wealthier and more buoyant, dynamic and productive than at any time since the 1950s. It is, however, also an expensive society in which to live, thanks mainly to a boom in property prices.

This chapter looks at the economic system of Britain and at the causes and effects of the recent changes. It begins with a survey of the structure of the economy, arguing that much of the hand-wringing about decline has been misplaced. It then examines economic trends since 1945, contrasting the boom years of the 1950s with the crises of the 1970s, assessing the content and impact of Thatcherism, and discussing the changes that have taken place over the last decade. Two in particular have had the greatest impact: large inflows of capital and investment that have strengthened the ties between Britain and the global economy, and the pressures, demands and opportunities of British membership of the European Union. It is debatable which has had the most influence.

The Structure of the Economy

Britain has all the classic features of a modern capitalist society. It is wealthy, it makes a diverse range of products, it offers its consumers a wide range of services, most of its economic wealth is generated by non-tangible services rather than industry, and it plays a key role in the international trading system. It is a free-market system in which prices are driven mainly by supply and demand, and in which private enterprise dominates the creation of wealth. Private enterprise was at the heart of the development of Britain's empire, but the postwar policies of an expanded public sector and greater government regulation broadened the frontiers of the state, which have contracted again since the 1980s as the government has withdrawn from the marketplace and placed greater emphasis on the private sector and individual enterprise.

The basic measure of national economic wealth is gross domestic product (GDP), or the total value of all goods and services produced by a country in the course of a year. Britain in 2004 had a GDP of just over $2.1 trillion, making it the fourth biggest economy in the world after the United States, Japan and Germany (see Figure 6.1). There was a time in the 1980s when Britain's GDP fell below that of France and even Italy – when Italy overtook Britain in 1986, the Italian press dubbed the event *il sorpasso*, a recognition of the extent to which the Italian economy had progressed and to which the British economy had regressed. However, the last few years have seen a remarkable recovery as economic growth has helped Britain overtake both Italy and France in GDP. Even when assessed by per capita GDP, Britain has done well, and today ranks ahead of Germany, France and Italy (but behind the United States or Japan).

In terms of how that GDP is generated, Britain's economic structure is typical of most other liberal democracies. Britain was once predominantly an agricultural society, but that changed with the industrial revolution, when the contribution of agriculture to economic wealth slipped as industry grew. Since the Second World War – in line with the USA, Japan and all other European countries – the contribution of services has grown as that of industry has declined. Many of Britain's factories have closed, and manufacturing jobs have been lost to cheap labour in Asia and Latin America. Where industry now accounts for just 32 per cent of Britain's GDP, and agriculture for 2 per cent of GDP, two-thirds of economic wealth is generated by services, such as retail activities, banking, insurance, financial services, tourism and entertainment.

Public spending in Britain in 2006–07 totalled £552 billion (€830/$995 billion). Income is derived primarily from income tax (28 per cent), national insurance (17 per cent) and value added tax (15 per cent), the balance coming from corporation, excise and local taxes (see Figure 6.2). There are two bands of income tax: a basic rate of 20 per cent, and a higher rate of 40 per cent for top-earners (a starting rate of 10 per cent was abolished in 2007). Income tax rates were significantly reduced during the Thatcher years, and the basic rate is now the lowest it has been in more than 70 years. Meanwhile, tax on the income and capital gains of companies runs at 30 per cent, the lowest rate of any of the major industrialized countries. Finally, like all European Union member states, Britain imposes value added tax on each stage in the production and distribution of goods, the standard rate being 17.5 per cent.

Figure 6.1   The British economy

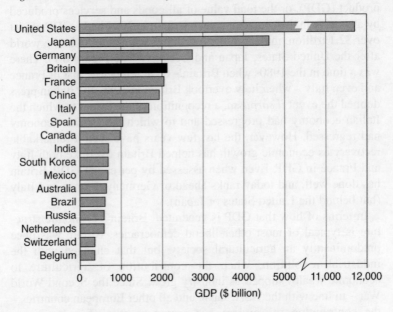

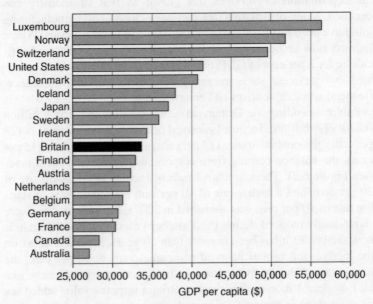

Source: World Bank web site 2006, http://web.worldbank.org. Figures are for 2004.

In terms of spending, the major items in Britain – as in most advanced industrial societies – are social security, health and education, which among them account for 57 per cent of government spending. Concerns about the cost and efficiency of public services have been at the top of the political agenda since the 1970s, encouraging the Blair administration to increase spending on health care, education, transport, law and order, and deprived neighbourhoods. It is debatable, however, whether the problem with public services is one of too little expenditure (the Labour analysis), or of too much government involvement in their management (the Conservative analysis) (Leach *et al.*, 2006: 380).

One of the most distinctive features of the British economy is the special role of finance (Gamble, 1999: 34). When Britain was the centre of the global economy in the nineteenth century, and sterling was the dominant currency, the position of London took on new strength, and even today the financial district of London – the City – has a role in the national and international economy which gives London a dominance unmatched by the capital city of any other country. Whenever key decisions need to be taken on economic policy, the question is often 'How will it play in the City?'. The key to the power of the City is that it has developed interests in a range of international commercial and banking services which do not depend for their profitability upon the state of the national economy (Ingham, 1984: 62–78). London and New York, according to one report, are the only two genuinely global financial centres in the world, and – in terms of factors such as availability of skilled personnel, access to international financial markets, and access to customers – have extended their competitive advantage over Frankfurt and Paris in recent years (Z/Yen, 2005). Among other things, London is the world's biggest market for gold, international insurance, international commodities, and foreign exchange, it has the world's third-largest stockmarket when measured by value, it has nearly half the global foreign equity market, and one-fifth of international bank lending is arranged in the City.

Perhaps the most notable change that has come to the British economy in recent decades has been in the structure of business. Nationalization and the expansion of the welfare state by the postwar Labour government greatly increased both taxation and the role of the state in the marketplace, an approach that initially brought benefits to a country exhausted by war, but that over the longer term created an atmosphere in which inefficient state-owned monopolies reduced

Figure 6.2   The national budget

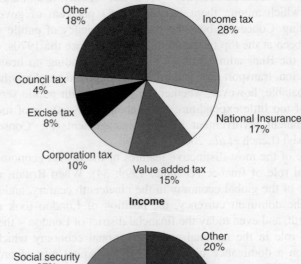

Income

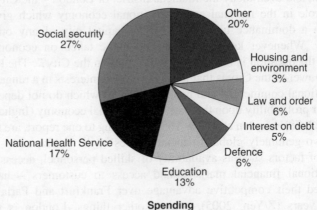

Spending

Source: HM Treasury web site 2006, http://budget2006.treasury.gov.uk. Figures are for 2006–07.

choice and stifled enterprise. The privatization undertaken by the Thatcher administration in the 1980s significantly cut back on the presence of the state in the marketplace, and helped revitalize the entrepreneurial potential of British business. There are now nearly 4 million businesses in the UK, and – as they once were – many of them are world-ranking. The *Fortune* magazine survey of the world's 500 biggest companies in 2006 found that nearly 40 were UK-based, and the *Financial Times* survey of Europe's 500 biggest companies found that nearly 150 were UK-based. They included BP, Aviva,

Illustration 6.1   City of London

The skyline of the City of London, with St. Paul's Cathedral on the left, the Thames in the foreground, and Tower 42 (once Britain's tallest building) on the right. 'The City' is the world's biggest market for gold, foreign exchange, and international insurance, and has been acclaimed – along with New York – as one of the only two genuinely global financial centres in the world.

HSBC, Vodafone, Tesco, Shell, Royal Bank of Scotland, Prudential, Barclays, GlaxoSmithKline, Lloyds TSB, Legal and General, AstraZeneca, BT, and Anglo-American.

The larger British companies have been behind an active programme of joint ventures, mergers and overseas acquisitions, reaching a peak in 2000 with more than $260 billion of spending, surpassing the previous record – in 1999 – by 63 per cent. Examples include the $200 billion takeover by Vodafone of the German company Mannesmann in 1999, the string of takeovers that have elevated the Royal Bank of Scotland to being the world's sixth largest bank, and the 2005 takeover by BAE Systems of United Defense in the United States, making BAE the biggest foreign company eligible for major US defence contracts. There have also been record levels of mergers and acquisitions in Britain involving foreign companies: when ranked by value, Britain is second only to the United States as a target. In both 1999 and 2000 there was nearly $100 billion-worth of activity, and similar high levels were being approached in 2005 and 2006 (figures from UNCTAD web site, www.unctad.org). Prime examples in recent years have included the 2006 takeover of airports operator BAA by the Spanish company Ferrovial, the 2007 takeover by India's Tata Steel of Corus Group plc (itself the result of a 1999 merger involving British Steel), and attempts by the US Nasdaq exchange to buy the London Stock Exchange after more than 300 years of British ownership.

Most of the key indicators suggest that Britain's economy is in good condition (see Figure 6.3):

- After running at a lower rate than that of its EU partners in the 1970s and 1980s, annual growth in GDP in the 1990s was the same as that for the EU and the G8 group of countries. Britain's economy in early 2007 was growing faster than those of France and Italy, and at about the same pace as that of Germany.
- The unemployment rate – after hovering in the range of 2–4 per cent between 1945 and 1975, then climbing to a peak of 11 per cent in 1985–86 – was back down in 2006–07 to just over 5 per cent, one of the lowest rates in the European Union.
- The inflation rate – which had peaked in 1980 at 21 per cent, fallen to 3–5 per cent in the mid-1980s, and risen again to 10 per cent in 1991 – has recently been in the range of 1–3 per cent, and Britain has enjoyed its longest period of sustained low inflation since the 1960s. There were concerns as this book went to press, however, that it was beginning to climb again, mainly on the back of increases in the price of fuel.
- The pound has been growing steadily in value for a decade. This has caused problems for exporters by making their products more expensive, and for tourists by making visits to the UK more expensive, but it has greatly increased the overseas purchasing power of British consumers and businesses.

Not all has been good news, however. Questions remain about Britain's productivity, there are concerns about the low rate of personal savings, and key public services are underperforming. Critics charge that too many barriers remain to the entrepreneurial spirit in Britain, and that while the relative decline of productivity may have ended, the British marketplace is still not as free as those of the United States and Germany. The cost of living has also grown, fuelled in particular by an increase in housing prices that

Figure 6.3   British economic performance

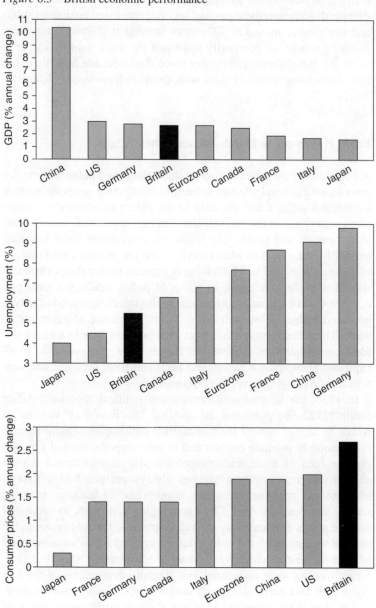

Source: *The Economist*, early 2007, various issues. Figures are for 2007.

many analysts regard as both unrealistic and unsustainable. But despite the characteristic pessimism of economists, business leaders and the media, most key indicators suggest that Britain has been enjoying a level of prosperity unknown for more than two generations. As one observer put it, 'For more than a decade now, there has been something seriously right with the British economy' (Kaletsky, 2002).

From Hands-off to Hands-on, and Back Again

All economies are mixed, meaning that private and public enterprises coexist, often interacting and sometimes competing with one another. Economies differ relatively only to the extent to which the government intervenes in the marketplace through regulation, taxes, subsidies, benefits and tariffs. The levels of intervention are determined mainly by the extent to which services and programmes are provided by government, and to which there is agreement that the government should help those in need. In terms of policy goals, the ideal is a combination of low inflation and unemployment, high productivity, a balanced budget, a low national debt, and a balance of payments on trade. There has been much debate over just how best to achieve this ideal combination of factors, and Britain – like governments in all capitalist economies – has moved back and forth between intervention and *laissez-faire* over the last century.

In 1776, the Scottish philosopher and political economist Adam Smith (1723–90) published his seminal *The Wealth of Nations*, in which he argued against the mercantilist philosophy of governments intervening to promote exports and to limit imports, instead supporting the idea of trade and competition. He argued that a market economy left to itself, while not always perfect, had a natural tendency to promote economic equilibrium (a balance between supply and demand), and – by encouraging capitalists to make and sell the goods demanded by the marketplace – it would promote the general welfare, with the individual worker 'led by an invisible hand to promote an end which was no part of his intention' (Smith, 1976). Smith's views were influential, but British governments of the late eighteenth and early nineteenth century were deeply conservative, and protected the domestic economy through tariffs on a variety of imports, notably grain. The Corn Law of 1816 – which prevented imports of foreign grain as long as the price of grain was below a particular level – was eventually repealed in 1846, helping bring an end to economic depression and sparking an era of growth and prosperity for Britain.

The prevailing view in industrialized countries for the next 80 years or so was to minimize government involvement in the marketplace, and to treat economic cycles as a natural and uncontrollable part of economic life. Then came the Great Depression in the early 1930s, which forced governments to rethink their approach. Influenced by the theories of the British economist John Maynard Keynes (1883–1946), who argued that governments could reduce unemployment through deficit spending, these countries' governments chose to address economic downturns by stimulating demand, to which end they cut taxes or increased spending on the public sector. The wisdom of Keynesianism seemed to be borne out by the economic boom of the 1950s, which in some countries extended into the 1960s and early 1970s.

The keyword in British economic policy after the Second World War was consensus: a tacit agreement between the Conservatives and Labour that – whichever was in power – they would work to maintain welfare, full employment and a mix of private and public ownership, and would agree on policies through compromise involving discussions between government and interest groups, particularly unions. There were in fact many disagreements over policy, so the existence of the consensus is debatable. But Britain nevertheless emerged from the brief era of austerity that followed the war, and in the 1950s enjoyed new prosperity, an era of mass consumption, and a growth in productivity and exports. Over the short term, at least, government intervention seemed both wise and productive.

By the 1960s, however, Britain was in trouble, and the words 'British disease' were often on the lips of economic and political analysts. Whether the disease was a real set of economic trends, or simply the construct of the press and popular opinion, is a debatable point, but there were clearly many critical problems afflicting the British economy:

- An overdependence on consultation as a method of governance. Most notably, the political Right felt that trade unions had become too powerful, leading to the repeated reliance of governments on consultation with – and appeasement of – the unions, the use of strikes as a first resort, and the loss of an increasing number of working days through industrial disputes.

- A welfare system that was proving expensive and was – to its critics – making too many people dependent upon the state, thereby reducing self-reliance and undermining incentives for self-improvement.
- A large public sector that had created inefficient state monopolies, and that was interfering with the ability or the motivation of entrepreneurs to start and build competitive private businesses. At the same time, there had been a failure to modernize the economy.
- A declining position in world trade. Britain's share of world exports had fallen from more than 26 per cent in 1950 to about 9 per cent in the mid-1970s.
- A relative decline in productivity. While British figures were up just over 3 per cent annually during the 1950s and 1960s, productivity grew at annual average rates of 5.6 per cent in West Germany, France and Italy. By 1973, the situation was even worse; growth was running at a paltry 0.2 per cent in Britain, compared to 3.8 per cent in France and 2.5 per cent in West Germany.
- A declining trade surplus. From a time in 1963 when Britain exported twice as much as it imported, its trade surplus had almost disappeared by the early 1970s.
- Little incentive for technological innovation, and a failure to apply such innovation to industry.
- For social conservatives, the problem extended to moral decline, reflected in the rise of a counterculture, a conspiracy to rebel, a weakening of 'family values', an increase in the incidence of crime, and the compromising of 'traditional' notions of law and order.

Booth (2001: 6, 88ff.; see also Box 6.1) takes issue with the notion of the 'British disease'. He argues that Britons were far better off at the end of the twentieth century than at the beginning, that judgements on the performance of British manufacturing trade were too harsh, that many historians are now prepared to argue that the economic weaknesses of the later twentieth century were exaggerated, and that many of the problems that caused so much concern in Britain were evident in other developed economies as well. But Margaret Thatcher was one of those who – at the time – supported the popular view of decline, and upon becoming leader of the Conservative Party in 1975 she argued that major changes were needed if Britain's problems were to be addressed. Her philosophy included several key economic goals:

Illustration 6.2 Urban dereliction

This abandoned terraced housing in Manchester is symbolic of the economic change that has come to Britain in recent decades, with older industrial areas declining (but recently undergoing a resurgence), and the wealth differential between north and south becoming more obvious.

- The promotion of an enterprise culture through a reduction in the size of the public sector, the encouragement of a free market-orientated economy, and the reduction of government subsidies so that businesses could find their natural economic level.
- The reduction or removal of government regulations on business, the privatization of many previously state-owned industries and services (such as British Telecom, Jaguar, British Petroleum, British Airways, and British Airports Authority), and the sale of government-owned housing – known as council houses – to its occupants. The effect of privatization was to triple the number of private shareholders between 1979 and 1989, and more people began to realize that making well-judged investments in the market could increase their net worth. Many of the privatized businesses also became more efficient and competitive, and more responsive to consumer demand.
- A freeing of the labour market through the curbing of trade-union power, and the introduction of trade-union reforms. In the mid-

1980s the Thatcher government fought and won battles with major unions, notably the National Union of Mineworkers, whose leadership charged the government with being intent on destroying the British coal industry, but which itself appeared bent on bringing down the government.

• The use of monetarist economic policies aimed at reducing the increase in money supply so as to reduce inflation, and cutting government expenditure so as to reduce public borrowing.

The reduction of taxes was designed to put more money in the pockets of British consumers, and thereby to promote savings, investment and entrepreneurial activity. At one time in the 1960s, the top rate of income tax (known as supertax) had stood at a remarkable 95 per cent, giving wealthy Britons little encouragement to start new businesses and new jobs, and creating a new class of tax exiles who left the country for parts of the world with lower tax rates. Under Thatcher, the top rate of income tax was reduced to 40 per cent, and the basic rate fixed at 35 per cent. Many new businesses were started, and while many failed, there was an average net increase of 500 new firms every week in Britain in the early 1980s, peaking at nearly 900 per week in 1987, and the number of self-employed grew from 7 per cent of the labour force to 11 per cent (Riddell, 1989: 53, 72, 75).

Thatcher's economic policies were typical of the trend among Western post-industrial countries since the early 1980s to reduce the level of government intervention in the marketplace. Support for Keynesianism declined, as support grew for the monetarist philosophy of free marketeers such as Milton Friedman and the Chicago school of economists, who argued that the role of government should be to promote the supply of labour and capital in order to promote economic growth. However, critics charged that such policies undermined key principles of the welfare state, and that they failed to take adequate note of the problems of the underclass.

Whether as a result of such policies, or for a more complex set of reasons, there is little doubt that there has been an aggregate improvement both in British economic health and in the attitudes of business towards customers. The relative decline of the 1960s and 1970s had been halted by the mid-1990s, when Britain had the fastest growing economy in the European Union. Building and road construction expanded, there were more private homeowners and shareholders, and the new levels of wealth were reflected in the growing number of luxury cars on British roads. Class distinctions declined as the middle

Box 6.1   The mythology of decline

Many of the studies of British politics and economics between the 1960s and the 1990s bemoaned the 'decline' of Britain. On the political front, the concern was that the political system was not as responsive or efficient as it might have been, and that British influence in the world was waning. On the economic front, commentators worried about falling productivity and Britain's failure to rise to the new business challenges posed by West Germany and Japan. Their arguments seemed to be supported by the data: in 1900, Britain managed the global financial and trading system, it had the highest per capita GDP in the world and by far the largest share of the world's manufactured exports (a remarkable 35 per cent), its share of world exports equalled that of the United States, and British worker productivity was second only to that of the US (and 150 per cent greater than the level in France) (Booth, 2001: 4). By 1973, however, Britain had dropped to fourth place on every list.

What most commentators failed to note in their analysis was that (a) Britain's global economic stature was bound to change given the end of empire, the costs of two world wars, and the accelerating growth of emerging economic powers such as the United States and Japan; (b) much of the decline could simply be attributed to other countries catching up with Britain, which had transferred resources out of agriculture much earlier than most of its competitors (Booth, 2001: 42); (c) the decline was almost entirely relative, and the absolute figures showed large improvements in Britain's productivity and its quality of life; and (d) the decline was not general, and Britain continued to dominate and prosper in many economic sectors.

Almost all the key indicators suggest that Britain's economy, despite its many problems in the 1960s and 1970s, has kept pace with its competitors, and 'has delivered unparalleled and sustained improvements in living standards and personal economic security for the majority of its people over the past half-century' (Middleton, 2000: 25). Postwar per capita GDP has grown in tandem with that of the USA, Germany, France and Japan, the distribution of wealth has broadened with the rise of the middle class, and the overall quality of life when measured by indicators such as infant mortality, life expectancy and access to education has improved dramatically, Britain has one of the freest economies in the world (when measured by such factors as personal choice, freedom to compete, and the protection of person and property), it is one of the least corrupt societies in the world, and it is both an aggressive source of – and attractive magnet for – foreign investment. Where, then, is the evidence of decline?

class grew, and competition helped improve the choices available to consumers and the quality of service provided by retailers.

At least part of the problem for many years was that business was not well-regarded as a profession. This was ironic for a country where the creativity of industrialists and inventors had first driven the industrial revolution of the eighteenth and nineteenth centuries, then underpinned the commercial revolution of the twentieth century. Attitudes in Britain stand in stark contrast to those in the United States, where some of the best-known names in public life have been entrepreneurs, ranging from the Rockefellers, DuPonts, Disneys and Waltons of the past to the more recent likes of Bill Gates, Steve Jobs, Charles Schwab, Donald Trump, and Warren Buffett. And yet the history of British business is peppered with names of comparable stature, including Cecil Rhodes (founder of the De Beers diamond corporation), William Lever (whose company became the foundation of Unilever), the Cadbury and Rowntree families of chocolate fame, Charles Rolls and Henry Royce, Jesse Boot (whose name lives on in Boots, the national chain of chemists), W. H. Smith (founder of the chain of news and stationery stores of the same name), Michael Marks and Tom Spencer (founders of the chain of clothing and food stores), William Morris (later Lord Nuffield) (one of the founders of the British automobile industry), and Anita Roddick (founder of The Body Shop).

Americans admire those prepared to work hard to build new enterprises and create opportunities, despite recent scandals in the United States that have tainted the reputation of corporate leaders and reduced admissions to postgraduate business schools. For their part, most Britons still do not particularly admire the business profession, and despite the economic freedom they enjoy the British are still less likely to start up a new business than their counterparts in most other industrialized countries. There are signs, however, that attitudes may be changing, and the owners and operators of large businesses are becoming increasingly prominent in public life, if not necessarily admired.

A prime example of the rise of the modern British business celebrity is offered by Sir Richard Branson, whose Virgin business empire has grown to include many different interests. Virgin began in the late 1960s as a cut-price record store in London. Branson then moved into the recording industry, becoming known more widely for the launch of the low-cost airline Virgin Atlantic, and expanding to areas as diverse as fashion, soft drinks, publishing, property, hotels, cinemas, and even railway services. Virgin Atlantic has been in a struggle against British Airways in its attempt to capture a greater

Illustration 6.3 Sir Richard Branson

Entrepreneur Sir Richard Branson at Euston Station in London, launching the first of the new tilting trains operated by his company Virgin Trains. Branson's celebrity is symbolic of a new attitude towards business and the creation of wealth, and of the relative value of 'new money' and 'old money'.

share of the transatlantic air travel market through an alliance with American Airlines. Branson's ventures have not always been success-ful, but a flair for publicity has made him a well-known public figure, contributing to a reassessment of public attitudes towards business, and of business as a career option.

Despite criticism that the Thatcher administration failed to take care of the needs of the underclass, and despite continued problems with poverty, a growing income gap between rich and poor, and homelessness (see Box 3.1 in Chapter 3), the free-market philosophy had become so popular and institutionalized by the time Thatcher left office that when Tony Blair became leader of the Labour Party in 1994, he set about 'modernizing' the party and committing it to the maintenance of some of the more popular aspects of Thatcherism, most notably privatization. Indeed, many of the elements of the Labour manifesto as it went into the 1997 general election sounded more conservative than socialist. They included a balanced budget, greater independence for the Bank of England, efforts to reduce welfare dependency, promotion of the work ethic, close ties to business, and a rejection of special deals for unions. At the same time, however, the Blair government emphasized the need to deal with the problems of the underclass.

The British are generally wealthier and better-off today than they were even 20 years ago, but debates continue about the areas in which they still lag behind their European counterparts. Of particular concern in recent years has been the declining quality of public services. The British once took great pride in the merits of their transport network (notably the railway system), the National Health Service, the education system and the police force, but recent decades have seen growing problems in almost all areas. The quality of the transport system has declined as railways have become more inefficient, with public faith undermined by frequent delays and cancellations of service, and by a worrying number of fatal accidents. Faith in the National Health Service has been shaken by patients having to wait a long time for non-essential surgery. Concerns have been raised about the education system as comparative studies have found British pupils lagging behind their counterparts in several other industrialized countries. Respect for the police has been undermined by charges of racism in several police forces, notably the London force (see Chapter 3).

The Blair administration increased spending on public services in response to the concerns, but critics continue to argue that the problem is not so much a lack of spending as too much government control and inefficient management. 'Compared with the way those services are run in mainland Europe', argued *The Economist* (14 July 2002: 51), 'health and education in Britain are run by centralized, egalitarian, socialist-style systems'. Critics argue that there is too much resistance in Britain to choice in both health care and education, and that the idea of running health care on a private or semi-private basis – or of filtering children into different educational streams according to their ability or desires – does not have enough political or public support in Britain to prompt the kinds of changes needed to make the provision of services more efficient. In this respect, Britain is on a different path from that of most of its European neighbours.

It is not just over the question of choice in public services that Britons differ, but also over the question of personal wealth and financial independence. Conspicuous consumption is an idea that has come quite late to the British, to some extent because of the residual effects of 'going without' during and after the Second World War, but also because of a preference since then for allowing the state to provide many basic services rather than opting for private alternatives. Most Britons prefer public health care to private health care, look to the state to provide social security rather than building their own retirement plans, and depend on state education for their children rather than private education. Among the effects of these attitudes is that Britons save little (typically less than 5 per cent of household disposable income), and also invest relatively little.

Britain in the International System

As an island state whose leaders and entrepreneurs have long understood the need for trade, and the opportunities it offers, Britain has always been an outward-looking society. It continues to be a major actor in world trade today: it has less than 1 per cent of the world's population but accounts for 5 per cent of world trade in goods and services. It is the world's eighth-largest exporter of goods (worth nearly $350 billion in 2004), and it is the second-largest exporter of services (worth more than $170 billion in 2004) (figures from World Trade Organization web site, www.wto.org). The value of its exports is equivalent to nearly 25 per cent of GDP, and it has the highest ratio of inward and outward investment of any major economy. It is also a leading member of all the main international trading and economic organizations, including the G8 group of countries, the European Union, the World Trade Organization, and the Organization for Economic Cooperation and Development (OECD).

British exports and imports have grown in tandem in recent years (although usually with an annual deficit), increasing from a combined value of about $560 billion in 1994 to about $1.12 trillion in 2004. Finished manufactured goods such as machinery, equipment, road vehicles and consumer goods make up nearly half of all exports, services account for about a quarter, intermediate goods such as chemicals, pharmaceuticals and metals account for about 20 per cent, and the balance is made up of food, drink, tobacco and raw materials, notably oil – Britain is a major exporter of oil, although its reserves are rapidly running out. The European Union is its biggest trading partner, accounting for about 57 per cent of exports and 50 per cent of imports. Asia, the Middle East and Australasia account for about 20 per cent of British trade, and the United States for about 12 per cent (see Table 6.1 and Figure 6.4).

Table 6.1   Britain's major imports and exports

Imports %		Exports %	
Road vehicles	11.2	Oil	9.4
Oil	7.6	Road vehicles	9.2
Telecoms equipment	6.8	Telecoms equipment	7.0
Office machines	6.6	Pharmaceuticals	5.8
Electrical machinery	6.1	Power generating equipment	5.7
Clothing	4.1	Electrical machinery	5.3
Pharmaceuticals	3.1	Office machines	4.6
Power generating equipment	3.0	Mineral manufactures	3.3
Mineral manufactures	2.7	Organic chemicals	3.2
Organic chemicals	2.6	Specialized machinery	2.9

Source: Office for National Statistics, *Monthly Review of External Trade Statistics*, May 2006. Ranked by value. Figures are for 2005.

One of the most notable features of the British economy is the volume of inward and outward foreign investment. In 1999, it was the world's largest outward investor, overtaking the United States for the first time since 1988. Meanwhile, in the period 1992–2001 it attracted nearly $450 billion in investment from overseas, ranking it second only to the United States as a target of inward investment. In 2004 it attracted nearly $80 billion in investment, or 36 per cent of all investment in the EU-25 (figures from UNCTAD web site). Its low levels of corporation tax are part of the explanation, but American and Japanese companies are also attracted to Britain because of the convenience of using English, which has become the international language of commerce. Concerns have been raised, though, about just how attractive Britain will remain as long as it opts to stay out of the euro zone (see below).

Britain traded with other parts of Europe centuries ago, and trade was at the heart of the development of the British Empire in the seventeenth century, when the first settlements were made in North America and the Caribbean, and the first trading stations opened in India. By 1700, Britain was already a dominating force in world manufactured trade, and in the commercial and financial services – and the nonfinancial services such as merchanting and brokering – that supported that trade. It imported primarily food and raw materials, and exported

Figure 6.4 Britain's major goods trading partners

Exports

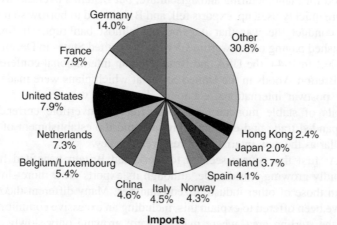

Imports

Source: Office for National Statistics, *Monthly Review of External Trade Statistics*, May 2006. Ranked by value. Figures are for 2005.

a select range of so-called export staples: machinery and transport equipment, cotton and wool textiles, iron and steel, and coal (Booth, 2001: 53). By 1900, Britain was the manager of the international financial and trading system, its corporations and manufactures dominated that system, and it had invested heavily in emerging overseas markets.

However, the early signs of Britain's eclipse had already begun to emerge. The heavy reliance on food imports meant that insufficient investment was made in the industrial sector, US industry expanded rapidly during the late nineteenth century, and German manufacturing power was on the rise. British industrial competitiveness fell dramatically during the First World War, and never fully recovered, while demand for export staples grew only slowly, undermined by growing competitiveness from Japan and the USA, and then hit by the market crash of 1929 and the depression that followed. Furthermore, Britain had entered the war as a creditor nation but emerged as a debtor (Booth, 2001: 59). From the early 1930s to the late 1950s, British trade was heavily orientated towards the Empire, and the use of sterling for international transactions within this group created an informal sterling area.

The economic recovery of the later 1930s, which allowed Britain once again to become a major creditor nation, was dealt another heavy blow by the Second World War. The wartime economy was good for manufacturing and agriculture, but Britain's overseas assets were quickly used up, exports fell, and Britain had to borrow so much to conduct the war that it came out almost bankrupt. (It finally finished paying off its wartime debt to the United States in December 2006.) In 1944, the USA and Britain led an international conference at Bretton Woods in the United States at which plans were made for the postwar international economy. Agreement was reached on the goals of stable monetary relations, freely convertible currencies, expanded trade and economic growth, and the establishment of the dollar as the new international reserve currency.

At first the system seemed to work and Britain benefited from rapidly growing world trade, although its exports grew more slowly than those of other industrialized countries. Many different theories have been offered to explain this, including an excessive commitment to the sterling area, where markets were growing only slowly, and disproportionately high spending on defence in order to prove British independence and its continuing status as a world power (Booth, 2001: 74–5). Whatever the reasons, the British share of global exports was cut by two-thirds between 1950 and 1973, and there was a similar fall in the British share of world trade in services.

Britain today is heavily invested in the fortunes of the global economy. It depends heavily for its economic well-being on inward investment, many of its biggest industries are foreign-owned, and it is heavily dependent on imports (Leach *et al.*, 2006: 376–7). As a result, one of the key pressures on the British economy is globalization: the growing interdependence of states, organizations, processes and people, with a resulting reduction in the freedom of national governments to make economic policy choices. At the same time, Britain has also been subject to the forces of Europeanization, and a debate has emerged about which of these two influences means more (see Hay, 2006: 261–7).

The Economic Implications of Europe

When six European countries launched an experiment in international integration in 1952 by merging their coal and steel industries, and then in 1958 by reaching agreement on the creation of a common market, Britain still saw its economic interests as lying primarily outside Europe; it attempted to rebuild its economy by concentrating on the sterling area, and trying to retain its status as a world power. By the end of the 1950s, however, the government had begun to realize that it would be in British interests to join the European Economic Community (EEC); the Community was enjoying fast growth and improved living standards, and its industrial strength was underpinned by growth in trade among its members. After two false starts, Britain finally joined the EEC in 1973, just 18 months after the United States took the dollar off the gold standard, signalling the end of the Bretton Woods system and tolling the death knell for the sterling area. Although the hope for a new boost for British trade did not at first materialize, membership of the Community (now the European Union) soon became the major influence on Britain's place in the global trading system, and brought much change to the domestic economy:

- Britain does more than half its trade with its EU partners, compared to about 12 per cent with the United States and 2–3 per cent with Japan.
- Many of the regulations that govern the behaviour of British industry come out of European law rather than domestic law.
- The EU has a Common Commercial Policy under which all the key decisions affecting trade are taken collectively by the member states, which act as a unit in negotiations with the Americans or the Japanese.

The EU may have 27 national members, but instead of a group of independent national economies (to the extent that any economy can really be independent), there is now a federal economy in Europe, or one where the national and the European economies have separate and independent powers, but neither level operates without the other. The most significant effect of European integration on economic activity has been the creation of a single European market in which there is all but uncontrolled movement of people, money, goods and services, and where national frontiers are almost invisible. The basis of the single market is the Single European Act, an agreement signed by the EU member states in 1986, and which came into effect in 1987, under which a five-year timetable was set for the removal of all the remaining non-tariff barriers to free trade among the member states. Those barriers took three main forms.

First, there were physical barriers such as customs and border checks, which allowed member states to control the movement of people, collect sales and excise taxes, enforce different health standards, control banned products, and prevent the spread of animal and plant diseases. Member states particularly wanted to control illegal immigration and the movement of terrorists and other undesirables. Under the Schengen Agreement, opened for signature in 1985, a computerized database of undesirables was developed, which helped address many political concerns. With effect from March 1995, virtually all border controls were finally eliminated by the signatories to Schengen, and the European Police Office (Europol) was created to help collect information and improve cooperation. Britain, citing its special concerns as an island state, has opted only into selected elements of Schengen, so its borders are not yet as open as those of other EU member states.

Second, there were fiscal barriers, the most important of which was different levels of indirect taxation (such as VAT, or value added tax), which caused distortion of competition and artificial price differences, posing a handicap to trade. There were also different levels of excise duties, driven mostly by varying levels of concern about human health. In the 1980s, for example, Spanish smokers paid half as much on cigarettes as those in France, a quarter of the rate in Ireland, and one-sixth of the rate in Denmark. Agreement was reached in the 1990s on a minimum rate of 15 per cent VAT, and on working towards a single rate of VAT, or at least variations within a very narrow band. Much more controversial has been the suggestion that the EU harmonize tax rates in other areas, notably corporation tax or the setting of withholding tax on savings. Tax harmonization is seen by many as the first step towards the development of EU authority over the setting of income tax, an idea that was opposed by the Blair administration.

Finally, there were technical barriers, including different regulations and standards based on personal safety, food safety, public health and environmental protection. Many of these regulations were in the interests of consumer safety, and so were welcomed, but others amounted to protectionism. The European Commission tried to develop EU standards and encouraged member states to conform, but this was a time-consuming and tedious task, and did little to discourage the common image of interfering Eurocrats. Several breakthroughs helped clear the political hurdles, notably a 1979 decision by the European Court of Justice establishing that a member state could not block imports from another member state on the basis of local health regulations. Member states have since had to accept products from other states that meet domestic technical standards. Progress has been made on removing technical barriers to the single market in a wide variety of areas, from safety and operating standards for road vehicles to the content of processed food.

By reducing or eliminating these barriers, the Single European Act remains one of the most radical of all the steps taken in the process of European integration since it made its first halting steps in the 1950s. Completion of the single market not only accelerated the process of economic integration, but it has also changed the lives of every European, making economic integration more real even to the most diehard British Eurosceptics. The changes it has brought include the following:

- With a few exceptions, residents of Britain can now live and work in any other EU member state, open a bank account, take out a mortgage, transfer unlimited amounts of capital, and even vote in local and European elections. At the same time, there has been a growth of immigration into Britain from other EU member states, notably those in Eastern Europe.
- The single market has helped remove many of the barriers that British corporations once faced, and has increased the number of consumers they can reach. Combined with privatization programmes in many countries and the general trend towards globalization, it has increased the number of opportunities for acquisitions, joint ventures and corporate mergers, both within the EU and between European and non-European corporations. The European mergers and acquisitions market is now bigger than that of the United States, and – as noted earlier – Britain has the biggest such market in the EU.

• Because integrated infrastructure – such as transport, energy and communications networks – is an important element in the successful operation of markets, the EU has promoted the development of so-called Trans-European Networks (TENs). Helped by the enormous growth in European tourism (which has been particularly important to Britain, one of Europe's top-four tourist destinations), and by the revitalization of rail transport as a cost-efficient and environmentally friendly alternative to road and air transport, the EU has been developing a high-speed train network connecting Europe's major cities. Key elements in this have been the opening of the Channel Tunnel, and investment in British railway tracks to bring them up to the quality of those in France and Germany; for example, €13 billion is being spent on a high-speed train link between Paris, Brussels, Cologne, Amsterdam and London.

A critical change spearheaded by Britain has been the loosening of regulations on air transport. Most European countries once had state-owned national carriers that had a national monopoly over most of the international routes they flew, so air transport was highly regulated, and expensive to consumers. When the Thatcher administration launched a liberalization programme in the mid-1980s that led to the privatization of British Airways in 1987, and negotiated bilateral agreements with other EU member states, the lid was taken off the air transport market. Big carriers have taken over smaller ones, national carriers have created international alliances, new cut-price operators such as Ryanair and easyJet have taken off, and consumers now have greater choice and can fly much more cheaply than before.

While the single market has brought generally positive change to the British economy, the critical question now – as noted earlier – is whether and/or when Britain will adopt the euro (Box 6.2). The relationship between the pound sterling and attempts to set up the single currency has not always been a happy one. Britain initially opted to remain out of the exchange rate mechanism (ERM) that was set up in 1979 as a prelude to the creation of the single currency, and required that member governments take the action necessary to keep their currencies stable relative to each other. It then joined in October 1990 against a backdrop of economic recession in Western Europe, and found that the high interest rates needed to keep the pound within the agreed range of exchange rates hurt exports and contributed to unemployment. On 16 September 1992 – otherwise

Box 6.2   The euro: to join or not to join?

In early 2002, after decades of anticipation and preparation, 12 of the 15 member states of the European Union undertook the single biggest currency conversion in history. Out went their national currencies – including francs, pesetas, lire, escudos, deutschemarks, and guilders – and in came the new single European currency, the euro. Talk of the need for a single currency had begun in the late 1960s when European leaders sought a response to the upheavals brought by the end of the Bretton Woods system, dominated by the US dollar. A feasibility plan was ordered in 1969 and a three-stage conversion was outlined, but plans were undermined by the oil crises of the 1970s. An attempt was made in the 1980s to achieve exchange-rate stability as a prelude to monetary union, but it was not until the 1990s that there was sufficient political support to proceed. When it finally came, the conversion went remarkably smoothly, and by the end of February 2002 some 302 million people had made the switch. The euro also became a popular currency alongside national currencies in several Eastern European countries, and in poorer non-European countries (such as Cuba) visited by significant numbers of vacationeers from the EU. (In January 2007, Slovenia became the 13th country to adopt the euro.)

British public opinion remains deeply hostile to the idea of giving up the pound, with just over half of respondents in recent opinion polls against the idea, and less than one-third in favour. The debate over the euro has created some strange political bedfellows (Kelly, 1997: 292). There is no straight party division for or against, but rather there are supporters and opponents on both sides, using different logic to back up their case. Those opposed include old-style members of the Labour Party, concerned about the development of a 'Banker's Europe' and about the loss of devaluation as a tool of economic policy, and the right wing of the Conservative Party, which argues the need to protect national sovereignty, and criticizes the concept of a 'fortress Europe'. Meanwhile, new-style members of Labour argue that joining the single currency could be a job creator, while more centrist Conservatives believe that joining would help control inflation, would promote the interests of the City of London and of the free market, and would undermine nationalism.

Since the 1950s, the US dollar has been the world's leading currency, underpinned by the size and stability of the US economy. But problems in the USA (including large budget and trade deficits) have combined with the rise of the European marketplace to bolster the international standing of the euro (see Levitt and Lord, 2000: Chapter 10). The economies of the eurozone are not as integrated into the global economy as that of Britain (Leach *et al.*, 2006: 377), but this is changing, and as the euro grows in stature so the pressures for Britain to join will also surely grow.

known as Black Wednesday – Britain was forced out of the ERM and the pound was devalued (for details, see Leach *et al.*, 2006: 367). The economy began an almost immediate recovery, a fact which played into the hands of opponents of British membership of the single currency.

The Blair administration argued upon winning office in 1997 that it would not take Britain into the single currency without a positive vote in a national referendum, which would be held after the next election, should Labour win. Labour did indeed win the 2001 election, but it quickly became clear that Blair was reluctant to move too quickly, instead launching a campaign to convince British voters of the virtues of joining the euro. The euro itself was introduced in January 2002, and – after a brief transitional phase – fully replaced the national currencies of 12 of the 15 EU member states in March 2002. Britain did not join, but Gordon Brown, then Chancellor of the Exchequer (Finance Minister), instead set five 'economic tests' for British membership of the euro:

- Are business cycles and economic structures compatible so that Britain and others could live permanently with euro interest rates?
- If problems emerge, is there sufficient flexibility to deal with them?
- Would adopting the euro create better conditions for businesses making long-term decisions to invest in Britain?
- What impact would adopting the euro have on the competitive position of the British financial services industry?
- Would adopting the euro promote higher growth, stability, and a lasting increase in jobs?

Those who thought that British public opinion might turn more in favour of the euro once it was adopted by other EU states, and once British travellers had become accustomed to using it, were disappointed by polls that showed a hardening of opposition. Their arguments were undermined as the pound gained strength, as it became clear that the British economy was performing well outside the euro zone, and as a number of countries that had adopted the euro continued to experience poor numbers on inflation, unemployment and growth. The credibility of the euro was also undermined by the 'growth and stability pact' agreed by European leaders prior to the launch of the euro, and designed to ensure investor confidence. Under the pact, member states agreed to control their budget deficits, limiting them to less than 3 per cent of GDP. However, several countries – including France, Germany and Portugal – experienced difficulties meeting these targets. The prospect of a referendum in Britain on adoption of the euro has been raised several times in recent years, but has so far come to nothing.

7

Culture and Lifestyle

Modern Western popular culture may have a strong American accent, but – as the birthplace of the English language, and a once aggressive colonizer – Britain has played a primary role in the evolution of the culture and lifestyle that we associate with 'the West'. Its impact has been greatest in the fields of literature, popular music, film and drama, no reference to which is possible without consideration of the impact of writers such as Chaucer, Shakespeare, Swift, Shelley, Austen, Wordsworth, Tennyson, the Brontë sisters, Dickens, Hardy, Kipling, Golding and Greene, or of musicians such as The Beatles, The Rolling Stones, The Who, David Bowie, Eric Clapton, Elton John, The Sex Pistols, Queen, Police, and Oasis. The impact of the former has been greater thanks to the spread of the English language, and of the latter thanks to the universal following for rock music. British cinema also plays an important supporting role to the popularity of American cinema, although just how the two are different any more is difficult to say.

Britain is less well-known for the visual arts and classical music, but has nonetheless had significant influence:

- It has produced great artists such as Thomas Gainsborough, Joshua Reynolds, John Constable, J. M. W. Turner, William Hogarth, Francis Bacon, Peter Blake and David Hockney, and has produced great sculptors such as Henry Moore and Barbara Hepworth, but its reputation is overwhelmed by the work of continental painters and sculptors.
- It has produced great architects such as Christopher Wren, Inigo Jones, Richard Rogers and Norman Foster, and great buildings are to be found in abundance in Britain, but the wealth of prewar archi-

176

tecture has been sullied by the frequent eyesores produced by bad postwar town planning. (Although recent developments have begun to right some of the wrongs, and London in particular has become an architectural trend-setter.)

• It has produced great classical composers and musicians, such as Henry Purcell, Edward Elgar, Frederick Delius, Gustav Holst, Ralph Vaughan Williams and Benjamin Britten, but few have achieved the same stature as their continental counterparts.

This chapter sets out to examine the features, personality and global impact of British culture, beginning with an overview of the definition of culture and of the dimensions and impact of the British version. It then offers an analysis of the meaning of 'Britishness', and of its impact on understanding national identity and its links with culture. It argues that the multifaceted nature of English, Scottish, Welsh and Irish culture has been further diversified by the postwar arrival of ethnic minorities, with the result that Britain today is more multicultural than it has ever been before, and diversity has become essential to an understanding of what makes Britain distinctive. The chapter then examines the state of the arts in Britain, with an emphasis on the theatre, film, television and popular music. This is followed by a discussion of the ways in which the British spend their spare time, including an examination of the undeservedly amorphous reputation of British cuisine. It ends with an examination of the role of sports and religion in national life.

Culture

For its size, Britain has had a remarkable influence on world culture, helped by the twin influences of imperialism and the role of English as the dominating global language (see Box 7.1). Even though the spread of English – particularly since the Second World War – has come largely out of the popularity of American culture and the power of American business, and even though English-language fiction is now a global phenomenon, it was generations of British writers who nurtured the language and made it so portable and attractive in the first place. It has since been easier for the reputations of British writers to be carried on the back of the spread of their language; there have been creative minds of equal or greater stature in many other European countries, but – unlike painters, sculptors, photographers and musicians – their impact has been limited by the fact that few communicate in English.

Despite the global significance of British culture – and of icons such as the royal family, James Bond, The Beatles, Monty Python and Harry Potter – it is, like all cultures, ultimately the product of home-grown values and experiences, not all of which can be understood by foreigners. Seen from the broad view, British culture is the result of a long and complex history in which politics, economics, religion, nationalism and the arts are all intertwined. The Second World War stands as a watershed, such that the idea of Britain can be broadly divided into two eras: the imperial 'glories' of the prewar years (even though these glories were often anything but, and their retelling has been polluted by myth and misconception), and the redefinition that has come with the postwar years, including the rise of the welfare state, the changing place of Britain in the world, the breakdown of the class system, and the increasingly multifaceted nature of British society.

During the opening decades of the twentieth century, Britain's national leaders were individuals of global stature, its corporations reached around the world, its products could be bought almost anywhere, and its music, literature and films were at the core of what was already being seen as an emerging Western culture. Then came the Second World War, and while Winston Churchill may have summed up the feelings of a generation when he proclaimed that the struggle against Nazism was Britain's 'finest hour', the war was to fundamentally alter Britain's place in the world, and the view that Britons held of themselves.

The debacle at Suez in 1956 combined with the early successes of European integration to compel the British to think less from a global perspective and more from a European perspective, and even ultimately to open a debate about the very identity of Britain itself: was it still a united kingdom, or was it a rusty amalgam of England, Scotland, Wales and Northern Ireland? A post-imperial melancholy set in, characterized by inward contemplation, nostalgia, conformism and arguments over everything from Britain's place in the world to relations between management and workers, economic 'decline', the class system, race, the monarchy, and relations with America and Europe. The tensions came to be reflected in literature, theatre and films, which moved from a celebration of British exceptionalism to a self-conscious examination of everything that seemed to be going wrong with the country.

Box 7.1   English: the global language

No-one knows for sure how many people in the world speak English, but it is generally recognized as the dominant global language (see Crystal, 2003), its stature based not so much on how *many* speak it as on *who* speaks it, and on how *widely* it is spoken. There are many more people in the world who speak Mandarin (probably 800–900 million), but most of them live in China and are relatively poor. Most estimates of the number of people who speak English range from 400 to 500 million, but they can be found in many different countries, notably the United States, Britain, Canada, the Philippines, India, Australia, New Zealand, South Africa and Nigeria. English has also become the language of political and business elites around the world, the language of international communications, technology, science, and education, the most commonly taught second language, and the language most commonly used by employees of all major international organizations, and of the European Union.

English is not only an official language in nearly 60 countries containing about one-third of the world's population, but English words and phrases have entered many other languages, so much so that in France there have been government-sponsored attempts for many years to develop French equivalents of English words and phrases that have entered daily conversation. In non-white former British colonies, the use of English has been criticized as a symbol of the colonial past, but despite attempts to restrict its use and champion local languages, it has prevailed. Furthermore, many English words have now become virtually universal, and are recognized all over the world; they include *airport*, *cigarette*, *hotel*, *OK*, *passport*, *stop*, *police*, *telephone* and *weekend*.

The status of English has been good for the British economy, notably in the sale of English-language training programmes: the British Council estimates that the teaching of English is one of Britain's largest sources of invisible earnings. It has also helped attract foreign students to British universities, seeking not just a British education but also the opportunity to learn or improve upon their English.

Why has English done so well? Part of the explanation lies in its long-standing role as the language of preference in international politics, diplomacy, and business. It is also a remarkably rich and diverse language; estimates of the number of words in English range from 500,000 to 1 million, compared to about 100,000 in French. Furthermore, simple English words and phrases convey often complex meanings, in a way that no other European language can match; this has prompted German corporations to encourage their executives to learn English, which is often better for communicating technical concepts than German. Interestingly, though, there are signs that the British are starting to make more of an effort to learn other European languages, probably inspired by a combination of the increased movement of Europeans around the EU, and of growing business and holiday travel by Britons to the continent.

The contrast is reflected in British films. In the late 1940s and early 1950s the Ealing comedies (named for the Ealing Studios) celebrated many of the hallmarks of being British, including simplicity, community, basic decency, and the ability not to take life too seriously. They were followed in the early 1960s by the bleak realism (or pessimism) of the British New Wave, and films such as *Saturday Night and Sunday Morning* and *The Loneliness of the Long-Distance Runner* emphasized isolation and social dysfunction, and are often depressing to watch today for what they tell us about the angst of that era. By the 1990s, British cinema had stopped being so self-conscious, and films were mining the rich seam of eighteenth- and nineteenth-century domestic literature, were celebrating the pleasures of being middle-class during a time of economic revival, were commenting on the new problems and inequalities brought by the free market, or had thrown social comment to the winds and were simply designed to entertain and to make money.

At the heart of the cultural changes taking place in the 1960s and 1970s was the changing class structure, and the greater willingness by Britons to question the assumptions made about their appropriate 'place' in the social hierarchy. Nowhere was this process more obvious than in the use of satire, which gave rise to a string of shows on radio, television and the stage in which poking fun at the class system was a central theme. A line can be drawn linking *The Goon Show* on BBC radio throughout the 1950s, to the stage show *Beyond the Fringe* in the early 1960s, to the cult television series *Monty Python's Flying Circus* (late 1960s and early 1970s). These were examples of an emerging countercultural trend which helped the British deconstruct and poke fun at many of the stereotypes that had until then coloured the class-driven values of much popular culture.

Further changes grew out of the new ethnic diversity of Britain. As the non-white population grew from the 1950s, black and Asian culture became an increasingly important part of the national culture. White Britons had to redefine themselves according to their response to the issue of race, which made its mark through the growth of minority neighbourhoods in the bigger cities, the spreading popularity of Asian cuisine, the entrance of minority themes into literature and the cinema, and the new religious diversity of Britain. Symbolically, fish and chips may still be seen (unfairly) as the quintessential representative of British cuisine around the world, but chicken tikka masala is probably more popular. It traces its origins to Indian tandoori chicken, but it was developed in Britain to meet

British tastes, and has become so much a part of national life that it was acclaimed in 2001 by then British Foreign Secretary Robin Cook as 'a true British national dish' and 'a perfect illustration of the way Britain absorbs and adapts external influences'.

Today, it is only older and/or more conservative Britons who recall the war, the empire, the class system at its height, pre-European Britain, and the political, economic and social troubles of the 1960s and 1970s. The last decade has seen the emergence of a newly confident and reformed Britain, whose culture reflects not so much the problems of the past as the opportunities and realities of the present. Younger Britons know and care little about the war or the empire, Britain has been a multicultural society and a member of the European Union as long as they have been alive, and most have enjoyed the benefits of an economy that has grown rapidly. The change in attitude is summed up neatly in two comments made by Americans. In 1962, former US Secretary of State Dean Acheson famously observed that Britain had lost an empire and not yet found a role. In 1999, a journalist for the *New York Times* commented that the British had 'finally stopped seeking a role and started getting a life' (quoted in *The Economist*, 6 November 1999).

The Identity of Britain

The task of understanding British culture is complicated by debates over the meaning of 'Britishness'. Culture is closely tied to national identity, but as noted in Chapter 2, one of the characteristics of life in Britain is the strength of regionalism and nationalism. National identity in Britain is diluted by the superimposition of separate English, Scottish, Welsh and Northern Irish identities, a phenomenon symbolized by the national flag (the 'Union Jack'), which combines the cross of St George (for England) with those of St Andrew (for Scotland) and St Patrick (for Ireland) (Figure 7.1). The concept of 'Britishness', which was always questionable, has come under increased scrutiny in recent years.

A 'nation' is usually defined as consisting of three components: a distinctive group of people with a common language and history; a specific territory occupied by those people; and a strong bond between the people and the territory (see discussion in Mohan, 1999: 28–33). There really is no British nation as such, because the people who make up the United Kingdom have separate (albeit overlapping)

Figure 7.1   The Union Jack

The British Union Flag, otherwise known as the Union Jack. It dates from 1606, shortly after the Scottish King James VI succeeded to the English throne as James I, when the flags bearing the crosses of St George and St Andrew were combined. The cross of St Patrick was added in 1801 following the Act of Union with Ireland. Wales is not represented in the flag because it had been united with England in 1282. No law has ever been passed to confirm the status of the flag; it has simply become the national flag through common usage.

histories and cultures, and they lack a common bond to a common piece of territory (see Weight, 2003 and Bryant, 2005). A number of developments in Britain since the Second World War have emphasized the contradictions in the concept of national identity and national culture, and have challenged the meanings of the symbols of Britishness:

- First among these is the empire. It no longer exists, but it was once one of the forces that brought Britain together, and encouraged the four nations of the United Kingdom to think of themselves as British.
- The second symbol is the monarchy. It may have lost much of its allure and some of its credibility, and is today regarded with less respect and reverence than perhaps at any time in its history, but it remains a representative of the unity of Britain. There is significance in the fact that the present royal family traces its ancestors to both Scotland and England, and that the male heir to the throne is invested as the Prince of Wales. However, there is still much about the royal family that is more English than British.
- The third symbol of Britain – its resistance to the forces of extremism, nationalism or fascism on the continent – has been diluted by the effects of European integration. British Eurosceptics have fought against integration by arguing that Britain is separate from

Europe, and that British distinctiveness – as symbolized, for example, by imperial weights and measures, and the pound sterling – should be preserved as a means of protecting the identity of Britain. But a generational shift is taking place, with younger Britons taking a more European view than older generations, and the distinctiveness of Britain is becoming less obvious.

- The fourth symbol is the shared history of the residents of the British Isles, but this has been complicated since the Second World War by the arrival of immigrants from the New Commonwealth, and more recently by the arrival of immigrants from continental Europe, and asylum-seekers from further afield. The resulting social diversity has added to the complexity of British identity. The political Right has often overtly or covertly identified 'Britishness' with 'whiteness', and the far-Right has aggressively adopted (and thereby demeaned) the symbol of the British flag in its protests against multiracialism.

Even if the British themselves may have some doubts about how to define their culture and identity, it is apparently not a problem for foreigners: the tourist trade is one of the biggest long-term economic growth sectors in Britain, attracting growing numbers of people from continental Europe, North America, and Asia, most of whom come in search of the history and culture that sometimes seems so hard for the natives to tie down. Travel and tourism were hurt by the fallout from the February 2001 outbreak of foot-and-mouth disease (which placed many rural areas out of bounds to visitors), by the September 2001 terrorist attacks in the United States, by the 2005 terrorist bombings in London, and by news of foiled terrorist plots before and since. However, Britain continues to hold its position among the top-six tourist destinations, bringing in about 25–28 million overseas tourists each year (see Figure 7.2), and about £15 billion (€22/$29 billion) in annual earnings.

The major countries of origin of overseas visitors to Britain (in order) are the United States, France, Germany, Ireland and the Netherlands. The majority come through London, where they often spend much or all of their time, attracted by its historical sights (such as the Tower of London, Westminster Abbey and Buckingham Palace), its museums and galleries (such as the British Museum, Madame Tussaud's, the National Gallery and the Natural History Museum), and its theatres and restaurants. Outside London, tourist attractions include cathedral towns (such as Canterbury, York and

Illustration 7.1   Broadway, Worcestershire

The charm and attraction of Britain's small towns and villages is captured
in this view of Broadway, which lies at the heart of the Cotswolds in
western England. Tourism – both internal and from abroad – is a major
source of income for Britain, although it is also a major source of traffic
and people congestion in the more popular attractions.

Chester), historic cities (such as Bath and Edinburgh) and royal
castles and palaces (such as Windsor Castle and Hampton Court).
Unfortunately, Britain is suffering the same effects from mass
tourism as other European countries: overcrowding, the rise of a
tourist culture at the expense of the native way of life, and rising
prices. Tourists everywhere tend to take their vacations at the same
time, and to congregate in the same places, so that cities like London,
Canterbury, Oxford, Cambridge and Bath have now become night-
mares of congestion during the summer season, particularly August.

The Arts

Britain's artistic heritage is both broad and deep. Britain is the birthplace of countless men and women who have become well-known far
beyond their national borders, and have contributed centrally to the

Figure 7.2   World's top 15 tourist destinations

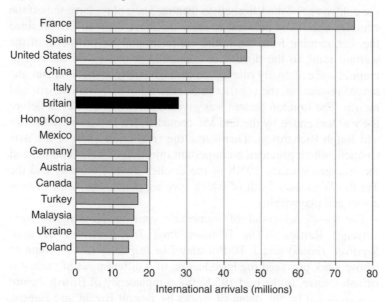

Source: World Tourism Organization, www.world-tourism.org. Figures are for 2004.

development of the Western cultural tradition. Their impact has been strongest in literature, film, popular music, theatre, poetry, painting and classical architecture, and perhaps weakest (but still considerable) in classical music and modern architecture.

Britain has a particularly rich history of theatre, dating back hundreds of years. The Elizabethan era saw the first great flowering of British theatre, with the work of playwrights such as Christopher Marlowe and Ben Jonson, but it was dominated by William Shakespeare (1564–1616), without question the most influential playwright in the history of the English language. He was so creative that he added to the language itself, and is credited with having coined more than 2,000 words, and many phrases that are still in daily use today (such as 'vanish into thin air', 'foul play', 'play fast and loose', and 'a tower of strength'). His plays are still routinely performed around the world in many languages, and continue to inspire modern interpretations in contemporary settings; for example the musical *West Side Story* was famously based on *Romeo and Juliet*.

The work of postwar British dramatists has often been compared to the golden age of the Elizabethan theatre. Their plays have fed off the complex social and political changes that have come to Britain since the war, ranging from the initial optimism and the prospects of the welfare state, to the dismay at continued austerity and the end of empire, and eventually running on through emerging nationalism, the sexual revolution, the conflict in Northern Ireland, Thatcherism and racism. The London theatre was given a reviving boost even before the war had ended by the Old Vic company, led by Laurence Olivier and Ralph Richardson. Then came the creation in 1946 of the Arts Council, which provided an important injection of state funding, and the emergence in the 1950s of the English Stage Company and the Theatre Workshop, both of which give support to the work of new actors and playwrights.

The most influential of immediate postwar playwrights were Terrence Rattigan (*The Winslow Boy*, *The Browning Version*, *Separate Tables*) and J. B. Priestley (*An Inspector Calls*), some of whose work presaged the introduction of a different set of values to British theatre. In the mid-1950s, the complacency of British theatre was shattered by the debut of works by Bertolt Brecht and Eugene Ionesco (whose play *The Lesson* was important in introducing absurdist theatre to London) and Samuel Beckett (whose *Waiting for Godot* raised controversial issues relating to censorship). In 1956, coincidentally the year of the Suez crisis, *Look Back in Anger* by John Osborne introduced a more radical tone into British theatre, representing a break with the past and a suggestion that the old world order was over (Shellard, 1999: 53). The middle-class virtues of theatre were replaced by a new strain of drama that was more issue-based, and rooted more in the realities of daily life for most Britons. This period saw the birth of the Angry Young Men, a group of writers who were deeply critical of the conformity they saw around them.

In the early 1960s, two theatrical companies were created that were to have a lasting impact: the Royal Shakespeare Company in 1960, and the National Theatre (now the Royal National Theatre) in 1963. These inspired the development of new companies and the opening of new theatres in most of the major regional cities of Britain, such as Chichester, Sheffield, Nottingham and Edinburgh. The decade also saw the staging of such groundbreaking plays as *The Birthday Party* and *The Homecoming* by Harold Pinter, *A Day in the Death of Joe Egg* by Peter Nichols, *In Celebration* by David Storey, and *Entertaining Mr Sloan* and *Loot* by Joe Orton. It also saw the development of the reputations of a string of new playwrights, including Peter Shaffer, Tom Stoppard, Alan Ayckbourn and David Hare, and a growing crossover between stage and television drama, notably by writers such as Trevor Griffiths and Dennis Potter.

An important change came in the late 1960s, when censorship came to an end. One of the frustrations faced by the theatre world until then had been the role of the Lord Chamberlain, one of whose tasks was to license new plays and so to act as a censor by deciding what was permissible and what was not. Strong language, nudity and themes such as homosexuality, abortion and satire involving the royal family were all limited by his decisions. Social changes brought growing support for revisions to the law, which eventually came with the Theatres Act of 1968, which revoked the Lord Chamberlain's authority over new plays. The rock musical *Hair* and the erotic review *Oh! Calcutta!* followed in short order, but the flood of permissiveness that supporters of censorship most feared never happened (Shellard, 1999: 147). Instead, a new spontaneity and sense of freedom was introduced to British theatre, which was followed by a new prominence for political and avant-garde themes, and more plays being written by women and ethnic minorities.

Meanwhile, Britain continued to be well-represented in stage musicals, building on the tradition begun in the Victorian era by W. S. Gilbert and Sir Arthur Sullivan, whose most popular creations – including *The Mikado*, *The Pirates of Penzance*, *HMS Pinafore*, and *The Gondoliers* – had lasting cultural impact. Many of the most commercially successful stage musicals of the last generation have been written or co-written by Andrew Lloyd Webber and/or Tim Rice; they include *Jesus Christ Superstar*, *Cats*, *Evita*, *Starlight Express*, and *Phantom of the Opera*. Some have achieved critical success, and have been credited with helping bring badly needed tourist income into London, but questions have been raised about the extent to which they detract from the more 'serious' goals of theatre.

Although it faced cuts in government subsidies during the Thatcher years, the theatre continued to prosper, and the West End of London continues to be one of the pre-eminent concentrations of drama in the world, with locals and tourists attending shows in increasing numbers, whether at the Adelphi, Aldwych, New Ambassadors, Royal Court, Young Vic or Theatre Royal. Nearly £250 million (€375/$480 million) was invested in the building of new theatres and the restoration of old theatres in the period 1995–2002, and the Blair government approved a substantial increase in the subsidy provided to theatre. Even regional theatres are mainly doing well, offering a variety of performances and attracting many of the leading actors of the day. There are more than 300 professional theatres in Britain, fed by a steady stream of world-class material ranging from Shakespeare through to the work of modern playwrights such as Michael Frayn, Steven Berkoff and Caryl Churchill. Britain's many actors and actresses are among the best-known names on either the stage or the screen, counting among their number Kenneth Branagh, Judi Dench, Ralph Fiennes, Hugh Grant, Ian Holm, Anthony Hopkins, Ben Kingsley, Ian McKellen, Alan Rickman, Maggie Smith and Emma Thompson.

There has been much crossover between theatre and film, and although the latter is another of the lynchpins of British culture, there is much less agreement about the health of British cinema. It has been argued by some that but for the intervention of the First World War, Britain – not the United States – might have become the dominating force in world cinema. Before the war, when cinema was in its infancy, British and other European directors were among the most innovative in the world, but after the war they lost their impetus, and the Americans not only better appreciated the commercial possibilities of cinema, but their technology was more advanced, and they quickly founded the conventions and genres that established Hollywood as the lynchpin of cinema (Alistair Davies, 2000). The United States also attracted many of the most talented British directors and actors, including Charlie Chaplin, Stan Laurel, Alfred Hitchcock and Cary Grant. This drain of talent handicapped the British film industry before it had the chance to flower. British cinema never fully recovered, and while Britons today have a presence in world cinema that is second only to that of Americans, they have achieved this not through a home-grown industry but rather by hitching a ride on – and contributing to – the dominance of American cinema. Street argues (1997: 197) that 'it is more or less impossible to think of British cinema without reference to its relationship to Hollywood'.

The British film industry was moderately successful between the 1930s and the 1950s, helped by healthy cinema attendance figures, government subsidies, and a reduction in the number of films coming out of the United States during the war. Production companies such as Gaumont-British, London Films (founded by Hungarian émigré Alexander Korda) and the Rank Organization had many commercial successes, and the work of British directors like Michael Powell,

David Lean and Emeric Pressburger, and of actors such as Alec Guinness, Noel Coward, Roger Livesey, James Mason, Leslie Howard and Peter Sellers, had a large domestic following. During the war there were successful films with appropriate themes, such as *In Which We Serve* (1942, an ode to the Royal Navy), *The Way to the Stars* (1943, an ode to the Royal Air Force), and *Brief Encounter* (1945, about how the war impacted the relationship between characters played by Trevor Howard and Celia Johnson). After the war there were comedies and films with social comment, many of them produced by Michael Balcon and coming out of Ealing Studios in London, including *Passport to Pimlico* (1949), *Kind Hearts and Coronets* (1949), *The Lavender Hill Mob* (1951), and *The Ladykillers* (1955).

The government tried to sustain the industry after the war, but British cinema was still too class-ridden, while American cinema provided the escapism that cinemagoers in an austere postwar Britain sought. Then the advent of television led to a sharp drop in cinema attendance, which fell in the period 1955–63 alone by a remarkable two-thirds (Richards, 1997: 149). British production companies became unwilling to invest in making films, and only the big American producers, such as Paramount, Twentieth Century-Fox (as it was then called) and Universal, could afford to take the risks and sustain the losses.

Perhaps the last truly home-grown genre in British cinema was the British New Wave of the early 1960s, a series of films which reflected the realities of postwar life in gritty detail, particularly for the working class; they included *Room At The Top* (1959), *Saturday Night and Sunday Morning* (1960), *A Kind of Loving* (1962) and *This Sporting Life* (1963) (Hutchings, 2001). They were all in black and white, and stood in stark contrast to the product then coming out of the United States, all of it in colour and some using new technology such as Cinemascope. The only commercially successful films being made in Britain were catering to the mass market, and included the horror films produced by Hammer Studios, and those in the *Carry On* series that were based on a particular brand of risqué British humour that had little prospect of being exported.

There was a brief change of direction in the early 1980s, headed by the work of the producer David Puttnam and the production company Goldcrest. They came together to make *Chariots of Fire*, which in 1981 unexpectedly won the Academy Awards for best picture and best screenplay, prompting its writer Colin Welland famously to declare that 'The British are coming'. Another Goldcrest film, *Gandhi*, won the best picture Academy Award in 1983, but in spite of its work, and that of Handmade Films, Channel 4, and Merchant Ivory Productions, and the revival of the English costume drama (see Higson, 2003), British films were unable to break into the American market in a sustained fashion. Nonetheless, the list of British films that have had either commercial and/or critical success on both sides of the Atlantic in recent decades has been impressive, and includes *Another Country*, *A Passage to India* and *The Killing Fields* (all 1984), *My Beautiful Laundrette* (1985), *A Fish Called Wanda* (1988), *Howards End* (1992), *The Remains of the Day* (1993), *Four Weddings and a Funeral* (1994), *Trainspotting* (1995), *Secrets and Lies* and *The English Patient* (both 1996), *The Full Monty* (1997), *Shakespeare in Love* and *Lock, Stock and Two Smoking Barrels* (both 1999), and *Bend it Like Beckham* (2002).

Ultimately, though, it is difficult to be sure any longer what distinguishes a *British* film from a film using a story based in Britain and featuring British actors but financed and produced by Americans. Walker (2005) notes the irony in the long list of impressive actors and directors produced by Britain, contrasting with its inability to sustain a native film industry. The British film industry has been almost entirely absorbed by Hollywood, as evidenced by the fact that the Academy Awards make no distinctions between American and British nominees and winners, but treat almost everyone else, except Canadians, Australians, and New Zealanders, as foreigners. There are still independent British films, it is true, but the definition of that independence is debatable. As in many other countries, the bulk of programming in Britain is American, and even the most well-known 'British' films of recent decades, such as the James Bond series, any of the costume dramas based on Victorian novels, the Harry Potter series, and the *Lord of the Rings* trilogy, have been produced and financed by American film companies.

A related medium is television, where British directors, writers and actors have developed a long and productive history, but have largely failed to break into the mass market outside Britain. The Scotsman John Logie Baird was one of the inventors of television, and the BBC in November 1936 launched the world's first television service, yet until the 1950s it was very much subordinated to radio, and until relatively recently British television viewers had few choices available to them. The BBC had a monopoly on programming until the launch of Independent Television (ITV) in 1955, but there were still only two channels available until the launch of BBC2 in 1964, and of the independent Channel 4 in 1982. British television has been a creative home for documentaries (such as *Civilization*, *The Ascent of Man*, and countless natural history programmes), for drama (notably historical series such as *Upstairs Downstairs*, *Brideshead Revisited* and *Jewel in the Crown*), for soap operas (such as *Coronation Street* and *East Enders*) and sitcoms (such as *Are You Being Served?*, *Fawlty Towers*, *Keeping Up Appearances*, *Only Fools and Horses* and *Absolutely Fabulous*), but few have broken into foreign markets. In the United States, British television either spawns copies – such as American versions of the sitcoms *Men Behaving Badly* and *The Office*, or of the quiz shows *Who Wants to be a Millionaire?*, *Whose Line is it Anyway?* and *Weakest Link* – or is restricted to non-commercial public television which has relatively few viewers.

The monopoly enjoyed by the BBC and ITV may have limited the viewing fare, but it arguably ensured a higher quality of output and more public affairs programming. As noted in Chapter 5, the television culture in Britain has been revolutionized in the last ten years with the advent of cable, satellite and digital television, which have expanded the choices available to viewers, but have also increased the competition for those viewers. The dangers of too much choice are clear in the United States, where the number of channels available on basic cable has increased in the last 15 years from no more than a dozen to typically more than 100. There is still much fine programming on American television, but in their fight to win viewers and finite advertising revenue, American producers have often sought out the lowest common denominator in the viewing public. The result has been a decline in public affairs programming or high quality dramas, and a growth in the number of chat shows, sitcoms, and reality programming. British television is following a similar path, and in fact has led the way in recent years with reality television and quiz shows.

While pre-eminent in theatre and film, Britain's most visible role in modern popular culture has been staked by rock music, one of the few art forms in which foreigners have really made any impact on American domestic culture. Until the late 1950s, Western popular music was dominated by Americans, whether through the big bands of the 1930s and 1940s or through the pioneers of rock and roll, such as Elvis Presley, Bill Haley and Buddy Holly. British singers of the 1950s – like Cliff Richard – either tried to ape their American counterparts, or developed their own home-grown form of music called

Lead singer Chris Martin performs with his group Coldplay at the Grammy Awards in Los Angeles in 2006. Popular music has been at the core of British culture and the British economy since the 1950s, making musicians among Britain's best-known public figures.

Illustration 7.2   Coldplay

skiffle. This all changed in 1962 when The Beatles developed a new and distinctive variation on rock which helped take Britain out of its postwar and post-imperial melancholy. Representing an emphatic response to what was widely seen as the decline of British popular culture in the face of overwhelming American competition, The Beatles first took their home city of Liverpool by storm, then the country, then – in 1963–64 – the United States (see Stark, 2006). The Beatles became the advance force of what was to become known in the United States as the British Invasion, opening the floodgates for a string of singers and bands from Britain to dominate popular music around the world, tracing a line through the punk rock years of the late 1970s and early 1980s to the Britpop years of the mid-1990s (see John Harris, 2004).

Rock music has not only been a mainstay of British culture, but has also been an important part of the British economy: in 2003, the

British music industry as a whole was worth more than £5 billion (€7.5/$10 billion), was worth nearly £2 billion (€3/$4 billion) in exports, and employed about 130,000 people. There are signs, though, that British popular music may not be having as powerful an effect on global culture as it once did, certainly if its popularity in the United States is any indicator. Between the rise of The Beatles and the end of the 1980s, not a year went by without British artists featuring prominently in the American charts. Over the last 12–15 years, however, British artists have failed to make the charts in the United States, where the home-grown variety has dominated. But this does not mean that British artists and bands – including Radiohead, Coldplay, Kaiser Chiefs and Arctic Monkeys – are not still at the heart of international popular music.

Sports and Leisure

The British are good at relaxing, although perhaps too good if recent studies are any indication. Where they would once leave the house regularly to attend sporting events, have a drink at the local pub, visit the theatre or an exhibition, or go for a walk in the country or a nearby park, they are becoming increasingly sedentary and staying at home. They have been discouraged by the increased expense of going out to restaurants, sporting events or the theatre, by worsening traffic problems, and by the declining quality of public transport, and encouraged by the greater ease of finding entertainment at home, whether on a growing number of television channels or the internet, and by a desire to invest in their homes by making improvements; little wonder that among the most popular recent programmes on television have been home improvement and gardening shows. Ironically, though, the amount of free time that the British have available has grown, and they are spending twice as much of their income on leisure as they did 50 years ago.

The increased focus on leisure is nowhere more evident than in the matter of where people go on holiday. The economic and social changes that followed the war allowed the British to become more mobile, by giving them more disposable income and more leisure time. Until the late 1960s, the typical holiday was spent at a seaside resort town such as Blackpool, Torquay or Brighton, the average family staying in a hotel and not doing much more than exploiting the simple pleasures associated with resorts: sitting on the beach, swimming, walking, and perhaps going to a show. The advent of cheap, mass tourism in the late 1960s and early 1970s changed all this, and the British started becoming more adventurous, often holidaying on the mainland of Spain, the Balearic Islands, the Canary Islands or the Greek islands. These still remain the destinations of choice for the majority of British package holidaymakers, but long-haul vacations to the United States (particularly Florida), the Caribbean, Australasia, Southeast Asia and southern and eastern Africa have become more popular, as has greater independence on the part of vacationers.

One of the country's most popular leisure activities is sport: about two-thirds of adults claim to take part in some kind of activity, the most popular being walking, cycling, swimming and football. The British are also keen followers of sport, choosing from a wide variety of options. The stature of sport is exemplified by Britain's contributions to global sports: it was the birthplace or nursery of football (the world's most popular sport), cricket, rugby, hockey, badminton, squash, golf, snooker, and the modern version of tennis. Other sports with a large following in Britain include boxing, equestrianism (particularly show jumping), horse racing, greyhound racing and sailing. Unique to Britain are the Highland Games pursued in Scotland (with events such as caber-tossing and hammer-throwing) and the Gaelic Games pursued in Northern Ireland.

If diversity is one of the hallmarks of sport in Britain, then the others are regionalism and the class basis of many sports (Holt and Mason, 2000: 168–72), two concepts which to some extent overlap. Cricket, for example, has always been primarily an English sport rather than a British one, and at least until the 1960s was closely associated with the upper class and the idea that playing the game was more important than winning, hence the famous put-down of ungentlemanly behaviour: 'It's just not cricket'. Equestrianism is associated with the landed gentry and the upper middle class, mainly because of its expense, which also explains why polo is often described as the sport of kings. The two different brands of rugby – rugby union and rugby league – are divided both by class and region. The more popular rugby union, which originated in the nineteenth century at Rugby School, an English private school, has its greatest support within the middle class, while rugby league, a breakaway version, is concentrated in northern England and has long been seen as a workingman's sport. Horse racing straddles class divisions, with some of the premier events – including the annual Derby at Epsom, and the Royal Ascot meeting every June – attracting aristocratic and

Table 7.1 Britain's main sporting events

Event	Sport	Venue
All England Lawn Tennis Championships	tennis	Wimbledon
Football Association Cup Final	football	Wembley
Open Championship	golf	various
The Derby	horse racing	Epsom
The Grand National	horse racing	Aintree
Henley Regatta	rowing	Henley
Cowes Week	sailing	Isle of Wight
Formula One Grand Prix	motor racing	Silverstone
Isle of Man TT Races	motorcycling	Isle of Man
Six Nations Championship	rugby	Twickenham Murrayfield Cardiff Arms Park
International test matches	cricket	Lord's The Oval Edgbaston
Badminton Horse Trials	equestrianism	Badminton

upper-middle-class interest, while routine weekly horse races will more often be supported by the lower middle and working class.

One of the great ironies about Britain is that despite the centrality of sport to British culture (see Table 7.1), the country has a less than stellar record in almost all the sports it invented or nurtured (international rugby being one of the exceptions). Consider the following:

- England has only won the football World Cup once (in 1966), and every four years the names of the heroes of the winning team – including Bobby Moore, Geoff Hurst and Bobby Charlton – are revived, as if to remind the British what none of their teams has been able to do since (see Ken Jones, 2003b). England's record at the 2006 World Cup – where it was knocked out in the quarter-finals after a performance that was lacklustre, conservative and tentative – was typical of its experiences. Meanwhile, none of the British national teams – England, Scotland, Wales or Northern Ireland – has won the quadrennial European Football Championship since its inception in 1960.
- Cricket was exported with success to many former colonies, including India, Pakistan, Sri Lanka, Australia, New Zealand, South Africa and Zimbabwe, but the English national team is

repeatedly defeated in international competition. One of the most famous rivalries in cricket is that between England and Australia. Following England's defeat by the upstart Australians in 1882, a joking obituary was written for the game of cricket, and a year later a cricket stump was burnt and its ashes placed in an urn. The two countries have since competed against each other for The Ashes. Despite the national pride that rides on an English victory, Australia won twice as many matches as England in the period 1980–2002. When England won the Ashes in an exciting five-match competition in 2005, the depth of national rejoicing was a reflection of how acute had become the desire for victory. But then in 2006–07, Australia beat England 5–0 for the first time in 85 years, leading to more soul-searching.

- Britain is home to some of the most hallowed golf courses in the world, such as St Andrews, Muirfield, Turnberry, and Royal St George's. But while British players have performed much better over the last 30 years, with players such as Tony Jacklin, Nick Faldo, Sandy Lyle, Ian Woosnam and Colin Montgomerie winning an impressive number of tournaments, it is difficult not to conclude that Britain has often played below its potential. The last British player to win a major was Paul Lawrie in 1999.

- Formula One racing is very much coloured by British influences: many of its teams are based in Britain, and many of its cars are built with British technology and by British designers and engineers. Yet while British champions have not been uncommon (Jim Clark, Graham Hill, Jackie Stewart and Nigel Mansell to name a few), British drivers in recent years have often been outwitted by their Brazilian, German and Scandinavian counterparts. Since 1976 there have only been two British world champions: Nigel Mansell in 1992 and Damon Hill in 1996.

- Wimbledon is one of the four events in the international Grand Slam of tennis, yet Britain has not had a men's champion there since Fred Perry in 1936 or a women's champion since Virginia Wade in 1977.

The United Kingdom Sports Council, a government body which coordinates support to sports in which Britain competes internationally, claims that Britain is one of the five most successful sporting countries in the world. To be sure, there are plenty of examples to add to the occasional triumphs in rugby, golf and Formula One, notably Britain's presence in track and field sports, where world records and titles are often held by Britons, and where Britain's dismal record at the 1996 Atlanta Olympics (15 medals, including just one gold) was eclipsed by its much better showing at Sydney in 2000 (28 medals, including 11 gold) and Athens in 2004 (30 medals, including 9 gold). But it is difficult not to conclude that Britain is again punching below its weight, particularly when compared with the three other major European countries (Germany, France and Italy), all of which

---

Box 7.2   The revival of British cuisine

In much the same way as Britain has been a creative inventor of new sports, but has not done well at them, so it has a rich and diverse cuisine for which it receives little credit. If the cuisines of France, Italy and Germany have deservedly strong reputations and identities, that of Britain is usually associated with stodge, a lack of variety or imaginative flair, and with the ubiquitous 'meat and two veg': an unimaginative dish of cooked meat and vegetables, with condiments added to provide flavour. So low has Britain's reputation fallen in the eyes of many that President Jacques Chirac of France infamously quipped in 2005 that only Finland produced worse food than Britain. Clearly he had never tried any of Britain's famous meat and game dishes, its many different meat pies, its wealth of cakes and desserts (from trifle to bread-and-butter pudding, spotted dick, and rhubarb crumble), or its many different cheeses, ranging from Double Gloucester to Stilton, Caerphilly, Red Leicester, Sage Derby, and Cheddar (the world's best-selling and most widely emulated cheese).

In fact Britain has a long and inventive culinary tradition (see Spencer, 2002), which suffered greatly from the effects of the Second World War, when rationing meant that preparing meals was driven more by practical necessity than by imagination and inventiveness. Fortunately this has all begun to change in recent decades as Britain has rediscovered its native cuisine, and has adopted influences from abroad. Britain has produced a long line of famous and influential cooks, from Eliza Acton in the nineteenth century to Fanny Cradock and Elizabeth David in the mid-twentieth century, to today's cookery authors and television celebrity chefs, including Delia Smith, Nigella Lawson, Gary Rhodes, Jamie Oliver and Gordon Ramsay, several of whom have picked up a following in other parts of Europe and in the United States. These writers have helped Britain rediscover its traditional dishes, and have also contributed to a new culture of creativity in restaurants and domestic kitchens. In 2005, a panel of 600 food critics writing for *Restaurant* magazine (albeit a British publication) placed 14 British restaurants among the world's 50 best, and gave the top spot to *The Fat Duck* in the town of Bray, Berkshire.

routinely outperform Britain at the summer Olympics. London's successful bid to host the 2012 Olympics may be an opportunity to boost Britain's record in track and field.

What are we to make of all this? There are probably two major factors at work. First, the government in Britain has been notorious over the years for its unwillingness to provide much funding for sports, or to support the kinds of training and scholarship programmes that are available in many continental European countries. Second, British sportsmen and sportswomen often seem to lack the 'killer instinct' that makes them go the extra mile in competition. For generations, the notion of good sportsmanship has meant that greater emphasis has been placed on taking part than on winning, and amateurism has been more admired than professionalism.

Perhaps the greatest change that has come to British sport in the last two decades has been commercialism. Where once it was considered almost indecent to have a link between sports and corporate interests, the outfits of team members in cricket, football and rugby are now emblazoned with the names of their sponsors, mainly electronics companies, banks, brewers, and – until they were barred from advertising – tobacco companies. The injections of cash from sponsors have been joined by increased government spending, by greater sums being paid to the governing bodies of key sports for television rights, and by income from the National Lottery. Started in 1994, the lottery was set up on the condition that 28 per cent of its income should go to 'good causes', including sports. Swimming, football, cricket and tennis have since benefited from the injection of millions of pounds from lottery income.

Religion

Religion plays only a marginal role in British national life, as it does in most of Europe. The majority of Britons – when asked – will claim one religious affiliation or another, but it is usually fairly weak, both absolutely and in relative terms (see Figure 7.3). For most people, religious activity typically involves no more than occasional attendance at church; most Britons are still baptised and married in a church, and most funerals are held in a church, but regular weekly attendance at church is low. Davie (1994) argues that the British have developed a habit of 'believing without belonging'; in other words, it is not belief in God that is challenged, but rather participation in orga-

Illustration 7.3   London's Olympic bid

Britain's Culture Secretary Tessa Jowell poses with former Olympic
athlete Sebastian Coe – now Lord Coe – who chaired London's successful
bid for the 2012 Olympics. As well as the economic boost expected from
the Olympics, it is also hoped that they will revitalize east London and
give a boost to British athletics.

nized religion. So while about 26 million Britons (nearly half the
population) identify themselves with the Church of England, less
than 2 million are active on a regular basis. Overall, fewer than one
in five Britons participate in religious activity in any kind of
sustained manner. The exception to the general rule can be found
among Britain's newer religions, such as Islam, Hinduism and
Sikhism; not only is support for these religions growing quickly, but
their followers generally have a stronger sense of identity with the
faith.

This restricted role for religion has not always been the case. Once
Roman Catholicism had been accepted as the state religion in 664, all
English kings maintained a close spiritual relationship with the Pope,
and the hierarchy of the church was an important part of government,
administration and law. However, the relationship changed forever in
1534 when King Henry VIII broke with the Roman Catholic Church.
The break was partly a result of a dispute over his attempt to divorce

Figure 7.3   Belief in God

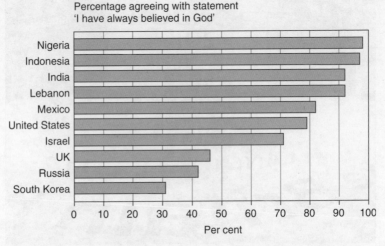

Source: ICM Research Limited survey undertaken for BBC programme 'What the World Thinks of God', 2004. BBC News Online, 26 February 2004.

his wife Catherine of Aragon, but it was also an attempt to restrict the power of the church. The ploy succeeded, and to this day the role of religion in public life is restricted to the monarchy: the British monarch remains the head of the Church of England (or Defender of the Faith, as he or she is formally known), which is regarded as the 'established' or national religion of England. (It is important to make a distinction between an established church and a state church; Anglicanism is regarded as the national religion, but the Church of England is not a state church, because it receives no financial aid from the government.) Meanwhile, the Church of Scotland is the national church there, but there are no established churches in Wales or Northern Ireland.

At first glance, the formal link between church and monarch would seem to compromise the idea of a separation of church and state, but it actually does the opposite, drawing attention away from any overlap between church and the elected government. The religious views of elected members of government, for example, are not usually a matter of public debate, and it is almost unheard of – in recent times at least – for the religion of a Prime Minister to be an issue of public debate; this was true even of Tony Blair, who – unusually – was quite open about his Christian beliefs. There are many reminders in the traditions of government about the links with religion, such as prayers in the House of Commons, but these are little more than symbolic gestures, or traditions that most members of government accept without much thought. In policy areas where religion might play a role – such as abortion, the teaching of religion in schools, or euthanasia (allowing a doctor to end a patient's life) – there is almost no overlap between religious values and government policy.

The Church of England is part of the international Communion of Anglican churches, which has 38 national members and claims to have a following of some 70 million people. It is divided into two provinces, one headed by the Archbishop of Canterbury and the other by the Archbishop of York. The former is regarded as the senior of the two, and has the title Primate of All England. The provinces are divided into dioceses overseen by 24 bishops, and these are subdivided into more than 13,000 parishes, each centred on a parish church overseen by a priest and (in larger parishes) assistants known as curates. The monarch appoints the leaders of the church on the advice of the Prime Minister, and those leaders have the right to sit in the House of Lords. Every ten years, the Lambeth Conference brings together Anglican bishops from the different countries where Anglicanism is practised, and decisions are made on doctrine and important policy questions.

The Church has about 13,000 ordained ministers, about 2,100 of whom are women. The ordination of women priests has only been allowed since 1994, and their advent has been symptomatic of a broader division within the Church of England (*The Economist*, 12 January 2002: 53). On the one hand there are Anglo-Catholic traditionalists (otherwise known as high-church Anglicans) who are opposed to the idea of female and gay priests, and many of whom left the church after 1994, leading to talk of a possible split. On the other hand, there are evangelicals who describe themselves as more progressive and more willing to accept change in the character and structure of the church. There has been an unspoken understanding over the years that the post of Archbishop of Canterbury should alternate between representatives of the two groups. However, when the evangelical George Carey retired in 2002 after 13 years in the post, he was replaced by another evangelical – Rowan Williams – who became the 104th Archbishop of Canterbury, and the first Welshman to hold the job in at least 1,000 years. Regarded as a liberal, Williams supports the idea that the Church of England should lose its established status and have a standing equal with the Catholic Church and other Christian churches in Britain. For many, his appointment represented the triumph of the progressive over the traditionalist element in the church.

While it has fewer overall members than the Church of England, the Catholic Church now has the largest active adult membership of any religion in Britain, with an average weekly attendance at mass of more than 1.2 million people. Where active participation among adults in the Church of England has fallen by nearly 45 per cent since 1970, participation in the Catholic Church has fallen more slowly, such that it is now the biggest church in the country. Organizationally, it is divided into eight provinces overseen by Bishops' Conferences for England and Wales, and for Scotland. It is subdivided into 30 dioceses, each with a bishop appointed by the Pope.

One of the most notable trends in British religion in recent years has been its growing diversity. For centuries, the British have been predominantly Christian, the only notable divisions being between the Churches of England and Scotland, and between Protestants and Catholics. But the arrival since the 1950s of immigrants from the Indian subcontinent has brought more Muslims, Sikhs and Hindus to Britain. While active adult participation in Christian religions has fallen by more than one-third since 1970, the number of Hindus has doubled, the number of Sikhs has quadrupled, and the number of Muslims has quintupled. There are now more than 1,000 Muslim mosques in Britain, more than 200 Sikh temples, and more than 140 Hindu temples. Unfortunately, the diversity has brought social tensions, in part because these new religions are identified with ethnic minorities (and thus are an element in the racism that has become a feature of society in Britain), and in part because of the broader conflict between Muslims and the West.

8

Britain and the World

In a speech to the Conservative Party in 1948, Winston Churchill argued that Britain was located at the intersection of three circles of influence: the British Empire/Commonwealth, the United States, and Europe. This notion was to have a lasting impact on British foreign policy, promoting the rather wishful idea that Britain could act as a bridge connecting the three circles. But the balance among them has changed since 1948, and so has Britain's international position; the empire is gone, the Atlantic Alliance is in trouble, and Europe has still not decided what it stands for. Britain today is faced with a Commonwealth that is weak, a United States whose foreign policies are discredited, and a Europe that is often divided. It may be able to continue to offer its services as a bridge, but the international system is not what it once was, and Britain is faced with a difficult choice.

Britain has long been an outward-looking society, interested and involved in events beyond its shores. As an island state, it might have followed the example of medieval Japan and cut itself off from the outside world. But migrations from the continent made it impossible to ignore events on the other side of the English Channel, the North Sea and the Irish Sea. The rule of monarchs with estates in France perpetuated the links, as did the need both to intervene in, and protect itself from, military and political events on the continent. Then came the industrial revolution, and the need for new sources of raw materials and new markets, along with the need to outwit its European competitors, encouraged Britain to expand its political and economic interests all over the world.

The growth of its empire gave Britain a vital historical role in global affairs, given substance by the spread of the parliamentary model of government, by the permeation of global culture by British literature, drama and music, and by the spread of English to become the most widely spoken language in the world and the standard for international commerce and communications. Britain's economy is today the fourth biggest in the world, it is a nuclear power, and its military – while relatively small – is efficient and well-respected. But Britain is no longer the dominating international power that it once was, and since the end of the Second World War has found itself trying to adjust to changed circumstances. Its equivocation over Europe has brought the biggest problems, but there has also been a rising chorus of criticism of its willingness to fall in step behind US foreign policy. The transatlantic 'special relationship' has some residual nostalgic attractions, but the critics charge that Britain receives little in return for its support of US policy, as was shown only too clearly by the experience of the Bush–Blair partnership in 2002–07.

This chapter looks at Britain's international position. It looks in turn at Churchill's three circles of influence, and at the competing pressures of the Commonwealth, the Atlantic Alliance, and the European Union. It assesses the significance of Britain's political and military role in the world, and analyses the effects of European versus Atlanticist pressures on British foreign policy. It concludes that Britain's place at the confluence of Churchill's three circles has changed profoundly over the past two generations, and will continue to change as the importance of the Atlantic Alliance declines and the pressures continue to grow for Britain to work more closely with its European partners.

The Changing British Role in the World

In spite of the distance that many Britons like to keep between themselves and their neighbours in continental Europe, Britain over the last millennium has been as much a part of the political and military history of Europe as any of those neighbours. Its territory was several times ruled by monarchs with interests in parts of France, it often had to fight off threatened invasions by its competitors (notably the French and the Spanish), and it was one of the dominating actors in the struggles that determined the continental balance of power; this drew it frequently into European conflicts, from the Hundred Years' War (1337–1415) to the War of the Spanish Succession (1701–14), the Seven Years' War (1756–63), the Napoleonic Wars (1799–1815), the Crimean War (1853–56), and the two world wars.

Britain first began to look beyond Europe to pursue its economic and political interests during the reign of Elizabeth I (1558–1603), and eventually built an empire that would stretch around the world. To maintain this empire demanded the construction and protection of trade routes, and the commitment of soldiers and bureaucrats, contributing in turn to the expansion of British political and military influence. By the nineteenth century, Britain was the dominating economic and military power in the world. Its factories were the engines of the global economic system, it traded with almost every part of the world, its troops were stationed on almost every continent, it took an active role in military operations in Europe, Asia and Africa, and it had a navy that dominated the world's oceans. The British Empire was the biggest the world had ever known, on which it was claimed that the sun never set. The world lived under the *Pax Britannica*, the expectation that Britain would take a leading role in maintaining global peace (see Roberts and Roberts, 2002: Chapter 25).

But all has changed in the last 50–60 years. Britain emerged from the Second World War with its economic resources stretched beyond their limit, with nationalist movements in many of its colonies agitating for independence, and without the ability or political agreement to support a large and widespread military. It took the shock of Suez to wake diehard supporters of British global power from their dreams of past greatness, but – when it came – the dismantling of the empire was carried out in a relatively peaceful and orderly fashion, the military was soon withdrawn from many of its former fields of activity, and Britain was reduced to a supporting actor in the Cold War. Dean Acheson's comment (see Chapter 7) that Britain had lost an empire but not yet found a role seemed to sum it all up, as did his argument that its attempt to play a role separate from Europe, as head of the Commonwealth, and based on a special relationship with the USA, was 'about to be played out'.

Britain has retained its strong internationalist credentials, as illustrated by its contribution to the work of six key international organizations:

- It was a founder member in 1945 of the United Nations, is one of the five permanent members of the Security Council with veto power (along with the United States, France, Russia and China), is the fifth largest contributor to the UN regular budget, and is a leading contributor to UN peacekeeping operations (Britain's biggest troop contributions in recent years have been in Cyprus and Kosovo).

- It is the second-largest economy in the European Union after Germany, and while it was not a founder member of the EU, and has a not always entirely deserved reputation as a reluctant European (see later in this chapter), it nevertheless has considerable influence on the policy-making processes of the EU, and is essential to the development of common European policies on trade, industry, defence and foreign affairs.

- It was a founder member in 1949 of the North Atlantic Treaty Organization (NATO), and is second only to the United States in the extent of its influence over NATO policy and its contribution of military resources to the organization. Most Royal Navy ships are committed to NATO operations, and 55,000 British troops are committed to NATO's Allied Rapid Reaction Corps.

- It is a member of the most exclusive international economic club in the world, the Group of Eight industrialized countries (G8), whose leaders meet at well-publicized and increasingly well-guarded annual summits, and where it plays a central role in the development of G8 policies.

- It is a member of the Organization for Security and Cooperation in Europe (OSCE), a regional security organization founded in 1994 that brings together 55 states to promote security, prevent conflicts developing, observe elections and provide post-conflict rehabilitation.

- It is the leading actor in the Commonwealth, a 53-nation association of mainly former British colonies and dominions that includes nearly one-third of the world's population.

But despite its interest and role in international affairs, Britain is not the power it once was, and most of its contemporary influence is exerted not unilaterally, but in concert with other groups of states. Just which of those groups of states – or circles of influence – is most crucial to Britain's future interests remains a matter of debate.

The Commonwealth

Although it is the least significant of the three circles, and is perhaps more important for nostalgic cultural reasons than for hard political reasons, the Commonwealth nonetheless helps mould the way Britain

Table 8.1 Members of the Commonwealth

Antigua and Barbuda	Kenya	Seychelles
Australia	Kiribati	Sierra Leone
Bahamas	Lesotho	Singapore
Bangladesh	Malawi	Solomon Islands
Barbados	Malaysia	South Africa
Belize	Maldives	Sri Lanka
Botswana	Malta	Swaziland
Brunei	Mauritius	Tanzania
Cameroon	Mozambique	Tonga
Canada	Namibia	Trinidad and Tobago
Cyprus	Nauru	Tuvalu
Dominica	New Zealand	Uganda
Fiji	Nigeria	United Kingdom
Gambia	Pakistan	Vanuatu
Ghana	Papua New Guinea	Zambia
Grenada	St Kitts and Nevis	
Guyana	St Lucia	
India	St Vincent and the Grenadines	
Jamaica	Samoa	

defines its position in the world. A legacy of the British Empire, the Commonwealth is a loosely structured and voluntary organization that consists of 53 countries, most of which were once British colonies or dominions (see Table 8.1). Members include Australia, Canada, New Zealand, many Caribbean states, India, former British African colonies, and two countries that were never colonized by Britain: Namibia and Mozambique. Based originally around the old white dominions, the Commonwealth grew and became increasingly multiracial in the 1950s and 1960s as Britain's African, Caribbean and Asian colonies won their independence. It now has a collective population of 1.8 billion people (about 30 per cent of the world total).

The Commonwealth Secretariat is based in London, its staff coordinating policy and operating the many educational, economic assistance and cultural-exchange programmes run by the Commonwealth. It promotes sustainable economic development, and manages regional investment funds designed to encourage trade within the Commonwealth. Its economic interests are heavily influenced by the perspective of the relatively poor African and Asian states that make up the bulk of its membership; thus, its priorities tend to be driven by issues such as poverty, economic development, trade, and aid to underdeveloped countries.

The Queen is head of the Commonwealth, and *de jure* head of state in 15 member states, including Australia, Canada and several Caribbean states such as Grenada and Jamaica, where she is represented by a governor-general. There are biennial summits of the Commonwealth heads of government of the member states, and every four years the Commonwealth Games brings together athletes from the member states in a mini-Olympics (the most recent games were held in Melbourne, Australia, in 2006, the next will be held in Delhi, India, in 2010). The Commonwealth also has an important cultural role in world affairs, thanks in part to its use of English as the sole official language, and in part to the contribution it makes to the promotion of diplomatic ties among its member states.

However, the Commonwealth is by no means a convincing power bloc in the world, and still less a vehicle for significant British influence (Jones *et al.*, 2004: 39). To make matters worse, it has sometimes been defined more by what divides it than what unites it, with the competing interests of its richer white members and its poorer non-white members occasionally causing strains. For example, while it may have expelled South Africa in 1961 because of its policies of apartheid (it rejoined in 1994), suspended Nigeria in 1994 because of the authoritarian policies of its military government, and suspended Pakistan and Fiji from its councils in 1999–2000 following military coups in those countries, the Thatcher government was unwilling to agree in the 1980s with Commonwealth arguments in favour of imposing sanctions on South Africa.

More recently, its claims to being a champion of democracy, human rights, and the rule of law have rung hollow in light of its prevarication on the issue of Zimbabwe. During 2001–02, Britain spearheaded attempts to punish the authoritarian regime of President Robert Mugabe for its seizures of white-owned farmland, its intimidation of the judiciary and opposition political parties and journalists, and its manipulation of the 2002 presidential election. Although agreement was eventually reached in March 2002 to suspend Zimbabwe from the Commonwealth for one year – a move which was more symbolic than practical, and had little impact on the policies of the Mugabe regime – it came only after months of disagreement that saw white members falling out with black African members. While some felt that the decision over Zimbabwe would restore some credibility to the Commonwealth, others argued that the damage had already been done. Zimbabwe took matters into its own hands in December 2003 by withdrawing from the Commonwealth.

The Commonwealth has also had less significance for Britain since the latter became part of the European Union. Prior to joining what was then the European Economic Community (EEC) in 1973, Britain had preferential trading agreements with several Commonwealth states that were either abandoned or significantly rewritten when Britain joined the Community (Clarke, 1996: 279, 343). Furthermore, as Canadian interests switch towards the economic integration of North America, Australian interests switch to Southeast Asia and the Pacific Rim, and British interests switch to the European Union, the old cultural ties that defined the relationship between Britain and key members of the Commonwealth continue to weaken, raising questions about the future direction of the organization.

As for Britain's colonial interests, few remain. From a time when the British Empire included a quarter of the world's population, it has shrunk to a pale shadow of its former self (see Fogle, 2004). Following the return of Hong Kong and its 7 million residents to Chinese control in 1997, there were just 15 Overseas Territories left, containing a total of 180,000 people: Anguilla, the British Virgin Islands, the Cayman Islands, Montserrat, and the Turks and Caicos Islands (all in the Caribbean), Bermuda, the Falkland Islands, St Helena, Ascension Island, Tristan da Cunha, South Georgia and the South Sandwich Islands (all in the Atlantic), Gibraltar on the south coast of Spain, British Antarctic Territory, British Indian Ocean Territory, and four small islands in the Pacific, including Pitcairn.

Most have a high degree of self-government, with locally elected legislatures responsible for domestic affairs, and governors or commissioners who are appointed by the Queen and are responsible for foreign affairs and security. None of the Territories has asked for independence, although the future of Gibraltar (a British possession since 1713) has been the subject of debate for many years. Under the 1969 constitution, Britain is committed to the principle that it will never pass the sovereignty of Gibraltar to another state (that is, Spain) without the support of Gibraltar's people. But the Spanish have long made clear their desire to see Gibraltar returned to their control, and there have recently been controversial discussions about a new relationship between the three parties. Meanwhile, the thorny issue of the Falklands (Malvinas) refuses to go away. Sovereignty has been disputed between Argentina and Britain ever since the latter asserted its claim to the islands in 1833. The two countries fought a war over them in 1982, since when they have maintained their competing claims to possession while trying to cooperate – not always with success – on practical issues such as fishing rights and commercial flights between Argentina and the Falklands. The problem has been complicated by studies suggesting the presence of rich oil reserves in surrounding waters.

The Atlantic Alliance

Throughout the Cold War (roughly 1945 to 1990), Britain was a partner with its Western European allies, the United States and Canada in the ideological, military and political engagement with communism. But despite the common belief of its members in the value of democracy and capitalism, the Atlantic Alliance was always a marriage of convenience: the United States needed Western Europe as a market and as the first line of defence against the Soviets and their allies, while the Western Europeans needed American economic investment and security guarantees. The two sides often disagreed – for example, over Suez, Vietnam, the Middle East, and nuclear weapons – but the Alliance survived and the disputes were rarely made public (see Lundestad, 2003).

Much has changed since the end of the Cold War (for discussion, see McCormick, 2007: Chapter 2). Europeans have become more politically assertive, more economically competitive, and less dependent upon American investment and security. They have also become increasingly aware of the many ways in which they differ with the United States on political priorities, policy positions, and even cultural norms. The result has been to raise many questions about the current health and future direction of the Alliance, posing fundamental challenges to Britain's future foreign policy options, and casting doubt (once again) on the future of its 'special relationship' with the United States (see Box 8.1).

For much of its life, security issues were at the heart of the Alliance. Along with Canada, the United States and most other Western European countries, Britain has been committed to the common defence policies of NATO, created in 1949 against a background of threatening behaviour by the Soviet Union, notably its refusal to work with the Western powers on the administration of postwar Germany, and its institution of the Berlin blockade of 1948–49. Under the terms of the treaty, an armed attack on one member state was to be considered an attack on them all, and each member promised to take 'such action as it deems necessary ... to restore and maintain the security of the North Atlantic area'. The treaty was signed by the United States, Canada, and ten Western European countries (excluding West Germany, which did not join until 1955) (see Sloan, 2005).

Britain joined in supporting the US-led coalition against Iraq following its invasion of Kuwait on 2 August 1990, and for a few months at least the Atlantic Alliance seemed to be stronger than the European alliance. Margaret Thatcher adopted the most hawkish stance among EU leaders, and in her last few weeks in office played a key role in convincing President Bush of the merits of a rapid counterattack. Britain placed its troops under US operational command, its commitment of 35,000 troops, 60 warplanes and 15 naval vessels being second only to that of the United States, and bigger than that of France (the next biggest EU member state, which committed 12,500 troops, 40 warplanes and 14 naval vessels). British policy stood in stark contrast to that of several EU member states, including Belgium (which refused to sell ammunition to Britain) and Spain and Portugal (which allowed its naval vessels to be involved only in minesweeping or enforcing the blockade against Iraq).

Britain was also alone in participating in – and supporting – US efforts to enforce the no-fly zones over southern and northern Iraq after the 1991 Gulf War, took part in the UN regime imposed in 1991–99 to inspect sites within Iraq where weapons of mass destruction were thought to have been under development, and played the leading role in providing political and military support for US efforts to pressure Iraq into removing obstacles to UN arms inspectors during 1998. Elsewhere, Britain was a full-fledged member of Operation Allied Force, the NATO attack on Serbia in March–April 1999 that came in response to the ethnic cleansing visited on the predominantly Albanian province of Kosovo by the regime of Slobodan Milošević. European leaders were quick to condemn what was happening, and there was general support in the EU for the bombing war that took place in March–May, although levels of support varied. In the absence of American resolve, Tony Blair won a reputation as the leader most in favour of the attack, committed British air, sea and ground forces to the operation, and went so far as to suggest the use of ground troops before the bombing had ended. With the end of hostilities, the British military played a central role in reconstruction, making up one-third of the peacekeeping force sent in to Kosovo.

With the end of the Cold War, and the collapse in December 1991 of the Soviet Union, the underlying rationale of NATO – to neutralize

Box 8.1   The special relationship: Can it survive?

In the famous 1946 speech in which he warned of an iron curtain descending on Europe, Winston Churchill also spoke of the importance of the 'special relationship' between Britain and the United States. The term has since been used regularly (see Dumbrell, 2006), but rarely without being contained in quotation marks, indicating doubt about just how 'special' the relationship really is. While the two countries might have a common history and cultural heritage, and have been allies in many wars, there have also been times when they have been at odds.

Shortly before finally stepping down as Prime Minister in 1955, Churchill warned his Cabinet colleagues: 'Never allow yourselves to be separated from the Americans'. Since Suez, British leaders have taken those words to heart, regularly supporting US foreign policy even in the face of public opposition at home, and at the expense of good relations with Britain's EU partners. The French in particular have often charged that Britain is being used by the United States as a conduit for its ties with the rest of Western Europe, and their wariness of US influence in European foreign and security policy has stood in contrast to Britain's Atlanticism.

At no time was the relationship more controversial than during the Bush-Blair years. How could George W. Bush, a neoconservative unilateralist and the most reviled US president in Europe in modern times, find common ground with Tony Blair, a reformed socialist and champion of multilateralism? One of Blair's key diplomatic aims was to remain close to the US (Wallace and Oliver, 2005), and he made much of the 'pivotal' role that Britain could play in world affairs, with its twin loyalty to the USA and to the EU. But his support for the 2003 invasion of Iraq was unpopular at home and hurt British relations with France and Germany (which both opposed the war). Blair might have reasoned that having the ear of the Bush administration was better than being given the cold-shoulder, but this would have been true only if Britain had been able to influence US policy, or had earned some advantage in return, and there was little evidence of this; Bush clearly planned to pursue his own definition of policy priorities with or without British backing. Support for the war in Iraq, charged Blair's critics, had done little more than associate Britain with a bankrupt policy, and had drawn the ire of Islamic militants.

West German Chancellor Helmut Schmidt once quipped that the Anglo-American relationship was so special that only one side knew it existed (quoted in Garton Ash, 2004: 183). At the time of Iraq, Chancellor Gerhard Schroeder suggested that the transatlantic bridge only seemed to run in one direction (quoted in Cox and Oliver, 2006: 178). Today, more than ever before, there is reason to question the viability of the special relationship, and for the British to ask if it is worth pursuing at the cost of closer relations with its EU partners.

Illustration 8.1   Blair and Bush

Tony Blair's decision to support American president George W. Bush and the 2003 invasion of Iraq was controversial in Britain, and had important implications for the 'special relationship'. Here, protestors taking part in an anti-war demonstration wear Blair and Bush masks, emphasizing the extent to which the two men will probably always be associated together in discussions about the war in Britain.

the threat posed by the USSR and its allies – disappeared. At the same time, many new possibilities emerged in the realm of foreign and security policy. In rallying support for the response to the Iraqi invasion of Kuwait in August 1990, President George H. W. Bush made a speech in which he argued that 'Out of these troubled times a new world order can emerge ... freer from the threat of terror, stronger in the pursuit of justice and more secure in the quest for peace.' He never explained what he meant by 'new world order', and the world has been far from orderly since 1990, but the phrase seemed to draw a line in the sand between the old insecurities of the Cold War and the new insecurities of a world facing multiple new threats.

With the Cold War is over and several former adversaries – including Bulgaria, Hungary, Poland and Romania – now members of NATO, questions have been raised about NATO's purpose. Questions have also been raised about the health of the Atlantic Alliance, which has been strained by disagreements on two critical fronts:

- There is the new economic might of the EU: its combined GDP is greater than that of the USA, its population is 40 per cent bigger than that of the USA, and its share of world trade is about three times that of the USA. The new European confidence can be seen most clearly on the trade front, where the Europeans have faced off with the Americans with growing frequency since the creation of the World Trade Organization in 1995 over issues such as the US embargo on Cuba, the US imposition of tariffs on steel imports in 2001, and the question of subsidies to farmers.
- There have been many disagreements on policy between the USA and the EU. In addition to the dispute over Iraq starting in 2003, which saw France and Germany being openly critical of US policy, and strong majority public opinion throughout Europe opposing the American venture, the Europeans have also been at odds with the Americans on a wide range of more limited issues, including the problems of Israel and Palestine, the most effective response to international terrorism, dealing with rogue regimes such as Libya, Iran, and North Korea, and international agreements on issues as varied as climate change, land mines, and the work of the International Criminal Court.

In light of such disagreements, it seems logical to many that the Europeans should follow up their more independent and assertive role in international economic matters with greater independence on security and defence issues. European integrationists in particular want to see the EU developing a common foreign and security policy as a means of providing a counterbalance to US influence in the world. The challenge, however, has been to encourage EU member states to build agreement on foreign policy as effectively as they have on international trade policy. Doubters point to the many instances where EU states have been unable to rise to important challenges (such as in the Balkans in the 1990s) or have disagreed over policy (as with the issue of Iraq). But optimists note that there has been much progress since the 1990s in moving the EU towards common positions. As a close ally of the United States, and a member of the European Union, Britain now finds itself torn between two competing sets of pressures, where compromises are increasingly difficult to find.

Britain and the European Union

If the importance of the Commonwealth has waned, and the future of the Atlantic Alliance is under new scrutiny, there is no question any longer that the most important circle of influence for Britain today is the European Union. Europe may still be regarded as 'foreign' by many Britons and their leaders, and the EU may not yet have a common foreign and security policy, but EU membership has had vital implications for domestic politics and policy in Britain, which has been pulled irresistibly – if not always willingly – into the heart of European matters. This process of Europeanization has changed the structure and character of the British political system, has meant the introduction of a new tier of law that has demanded changes at the national level, and has introduced a new level of government (or perhaps governance) with powers over domestic matters. The British still equivocate over the extent to which they are British and the extent to which they are European, but there is no question that Britain – like all EU member states – is today defined less in national terms and more in the context of its membership of the world's biggest capitalist marketplace, its most important emerging political actor, and its newest superpower.

When Europeans began building ties of economic cooperation among themselves in the 1950s and 1960s, they concentrated on reducing the barriers to trade and on building a single European market, with common external tariffs on goods coming into that market, and free movement of money, people, goods, and services within its borders. European integration has since broadened and deepened significantly. There are few remaining barriers to internal trade, EU citizens can live and work in any of the member states (and can even vote and run in local and European elections), intra-European investment and corporate takeovers and mergers have grown, internal transport networks are expanding, and the member states have brought domestic laws into line with European law in many different policy areas, including agriculture, transport, trade, competition, immigration and consumer policy.

The EU now has 27 member states, the membership applications of three more (Croatia, Macedonia, and Turkey) have been accepted (making them 'candidate countries'), and the remaining four Balkan countries (Albania, Bosnia, Montenegro and Serbia) have strong longer-term prospects for membership. The member states among them negotiate common laws and policies through six major European institutions:

- A *European Commission*, responsible for proposing new European laws, and for implementing them once they have been adopted. The Commission is a small (20,000-person) bureaucracy headquartered in Brussels, headed by a team of 27 commissioners, one from each of the member states. The work and powers of the Commission are widely misunderstood and misrepresented in Britain, where it is often wrongly described by Eurosceptics as a powerful and expensive decision-making body. In fact it cannot make final decisions on new laws and policies, and can only do what the treaties of the EU allow it to do. And its budget is quite modest given the size of its task.

- The *Council of Ministers*, which is also headquartered in Brussels, shares decision-making powers on new laws with the European Parliament. The Council has a rotating membership, so that depending upon the issue under discussion, the appropriate group of ministers from each of the member states is convened: agriculture ministers will discuss agricultural proposals, environmental ministers will discuss environmental proposals, and so on. Typically, ministers use either a simple majority to make decisions, or a qualified majority where each is given a different number of votes in rough proportion to the population size of each state. Thus, Britain and Germany have 29 votes, Spain and Poland have 27, Austria and Bulgaria have 10, and so on.

- A 785-member *European Parliament*, which is directly elected by the voters of the EU for five-year terms, and divides its time between Strasbourg (France) and Brussels. Unlike conventional legislatures, it cannot develop new legislation, but instead shares responsibility with the Council of Ministers for voting on the adoption of legislative proposals developed by the Commission. Seats in the EP are distributed among the member states very loosely on the basis of population – Britain has 78 members, Poland and Spain have 54 each, Portugal and Hungary have 24 each, Denmark and Finland have 14 each, and so on.

- Judicial matters are addressed by the *European Court of Justice*, based in Luxembourg. When a member state has a question about the application of EU law, or if there is a dispute over the meaning or application of that law (involving EU institutions, member states, individuals or corporations), a case may be heard before the Court, whose job is to provide clarity and consistency to the governing treaties of the EU. There are 27 judges on the Court, one from each member state. It works in association with a *Court of*

Map 8.1 Political map of the European Union

First Instance, set up in 1989 in response to the growing workload
of the Court of Justice, and designed to be the first point of decision on less complicated cases.

- The *European Council* is a forum that brings the heads of government of the member states together for summit meetings at least
twice each year, in Brussels. The job of the Council is to make
broad decisions regarding the future direction and priorities of the
EU.

- Decisions relating to the euro are taken by the *European Central Bank*, which is based in Frankfurt and is responsible for overseeing monetary policy in the eurozone, conducting foreign exchange operations, and managing the foreign reserves of eurozone states. The national central banks of all the EU member states are members of the European System of Central Banks, but non-euro states such as Britain do not take part in decision-making.

Britain has long had a reputation for being a reluctant European (Box 8.2), and has developed an unfortunate habit of often being late to join its European partners in new ventures, and of being less than enthusiastic in engaging itself with Europe. Eurosceptics see Britain's reticence as admirable caution, some even arguing that Britain should never have joined the Community in the first place, and that its key interests continue to lie outside Europe. (One of the more bizarre suggestions that have been proffered is for Britain to leave the EU and to join instead the North American Free Trade Area.) For their part, Europhiles argue that Britain's dilatory attitude to European integration has prevented it from taking part in the critical planning stages of EU initiatives, so denying it the opportunity to mould the process more to its liking and advantage.

The extent to which British public opinion is out of step with that in much (but not all) of the rest of the EU is reflected in the regular polls carried out by Eurobarometer, the EU polling service (see Figure 8.1). These reveal a low level of psychological attachment to the EU by most Britons, who are also less enthusiastic about the benefits of EU membership than the citizens of almost any other member state. There are several possible explanations:

- Britain's physical separation from the continent has helped make the British feel that they are somehow different from other Europeans, and that they are not really European at all. Even today, many Britons still talk about Europe as something quite distinct from Britain.
- At the time that continental European leaders were planning the first steps in the process of integration, Britain still had many interests outside Europe: it had an empire, it had strong cultural links with its dominions and colonies (many of which still saw Britain as the mother country), and it had a strong relationship with the United States (in contrast to the distrust with which the French viewed – and continue to view – the US).

Box 8.2   Britain: really such a bad European?

It has become almost trite to describe Britain as the 'reluctant European' or the 'awkward partner' (George, 1998), and to quote the many examples of its failure to agree with its EU partners, or its insistence on changing the rules of the game. It was late joining the Community (although this was not entirely its fault), it was late joining the exchange rate mechanism that predated the single European currency, it remains outside the eurozone today, British voters have desultory turnout at European Parliament elections and low levels of enthusiasm for membership of the EU, and Britain's tabloid press persists in misleading and jingoistic attacks on the EU. Even Tony Blair – otherwise progressive on European matters – protected the 'red lines' (on issues such as taxation and immigration) beyond which Britain has not been prepared to venture.

Yet there may be reason for questioning the conventional wisdom:

- Because Britain has been so widely branded as a Eurosceptic, it tends to attract more attention than other member states with similar leanings. It is often forgotten, for example, that there was little enthusiasm for the euro in Germany, Denmark and Sweden. Similarly, Britain has never voted against a European treaty, as did Denmark in 1992, Ireland in 2001, or France and the Netherlands in 2005. Indeed, Denmark has developed a strong record of Euroscepticism, but is less visible in its actions.
- France has done more to seriously disrupt the work of the EU. It was France (or at least Charles de Gaulle) that twice vetoed the membership applications of Britain, Ireland and Denmark, and that set off the Community's most serious crisis in 1965 when it refused to take part in joint decision-making for six months. France is also the architect and dogged defender of the controversial and expensive Common Agricultural Policy, has been out of step with most of its EU partners over policy on NATO, engaged in an unseemly nationalistic squabble in 1997–98 over who should be appointed first president of the European Central Bank, and refuses to allow the chamber of the European Parliament to be moved to Brussels (with the farcical and expensive result that Parliament must move for one week per month to Strasbourg).
- Britain is criticized for negotiating hard on the development of new EU laws and policies, but it is driven less by stubbornness than by a philosophy that it should not make agreements that it cannot honour. Other member states, by contrast, may say 'yes' and then find themselves unable to deliver on their promises (Italy being the prime example). It is often forgotten that Britain has one of the best records in the Union on changing national law to fit with EU law.
- Britain since the early 1990s has often been an active leader of developments on the EU foreign and security policy front, pushing for greater emphasis on defence issues, contributing to EU military ventures, and taking the lead on a number of diplomatic initiatives, particularly the Israeli–Palestinian question (Smith, 2006).

Figure 8.1   British public opinion on the European Union

Percentage for whom the EU conjures up a positive image

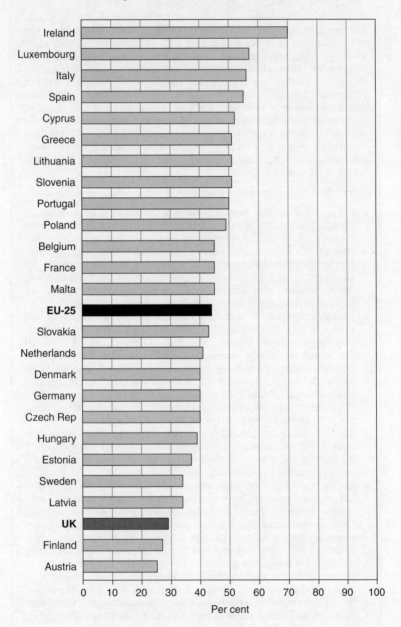

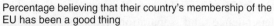

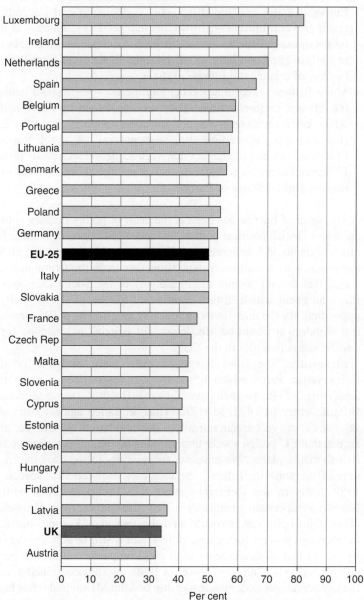

Percentage believing that their country's membership of the EU has been a good thing

Per cent

Source: Eurobarometer 64, December 2005.

- Where nationalism and the nation-state had been discredited on the continent by two world wars, they were vindicated in Britain by its independence and separation (Kavanagh, 2000: 70). Where European states concluded that only cooperation and integration could prevent future wars, it was its independence which – in the minds of many Britons – helped Britain avoid becoming caught up in the kinds of conflicts which brought so many changes to the borders of continental European states.

- Many Britons – like many other Europeans – understand neither the EU nor its implications. They are not helped by mass media which often promote myths and misunderstandings about the EU (for example, misrepresenting the powers of the European Commission), and by the fact that even academic specialists on the EU cannot agree on whether it is an international organization or a nascent United States of Europe.

The issue of Europe has been at the heart of policy debates within the major British political parties, and indeed has become a cause for much division and disagreement. In the early 1980s, it was Labour Party policy to withdraw Britain altogether from the Community, a stance that helped prompt the breakaway of the Social Democratic Party, an event which in turn contributed to Labour's long spell in opposition. By the mid-1990s Labour had reversed its policy, arguing that withdrawal would be 'disastrous' for Britain, and pushing for a more constructive role in the EU.

Meanwhile, the issue has been even more divisive for the Conservative Party, which ironically was responsible – under the leadership of Prime Minister Edward Heath – for negotiating Britain's entry in 1973. Margaret Thatcher railed against what she saw as excessive bureaucratization and regulation by Europe, and argued that EU policies were undermining her attempts to free up the British marketplace. 'We have not successfully rolled back the frontiers of the state in Britain', she famously declared in a speech in 1988, 'only to see them reimposed at a European level, with a European superstate exercising a new dominance from Brussels'. (This philosophy rather overlooked the fact that 'Europe' has few independent powers for making policy, and is still largely the sum of its parts.) Her disagreements with pro-Europeans within her party contributed to her fall from power in 1990, the split continued to dog the Conservatives under the leadership of John Major, and it has been a key factor in all recent party leadership contests. Some Britons

Illustration 8.2   Javier Solana

Javier Solana, foreign policy chief for the EU (or, more formally, High Representative for the Common Foreign and Security Policy). To the extent that the EU has been able to develop a foreign policy – or even common positions on specific foreign policy problems – Solana's office represents the international face of the EU. But just how substantial that face has been, or is likely to be, is debatable.

remain hostile to the 'federalist tendencies' of the EU, but many misunderstand the notion of federalism and fail to realize that it actually involves the retention of often substantial independent powers for the member states. At the same time, though, increasing numbers (particularly professionals and those in their twenties and thirties) are now convinced of the benefits of membership.

As noted earlier, one area in which the EU has made only mixed progress has been the development of a common foreign and security policy (see White, 2001; Marsh and Mackenstein, 2005). Backed by the vast size of the European market – which now accounts for about one-third of global economic production – the 27 member states have learned to work as one on global trade issues. They have also adopted common positions on a variety of headline international issues – such as the Israeli–Palestinian question and tensions between India and

Pakistan over Kashmir – and have increasingly voted as a block in the United Nations General Assembly. However, they have so far lacked the political unity always to work together on the most critical foreign and defence issues. Several member states (such as Finland and Ireland) are neutral, and the two major military powers – Britain and France – disagree on whether to defer to the NATO alliance and US leadership (Britain), or to take a more independent European line on security issues (France).

These different sets of allegiances and priorities illustrate one of the persistent characteristics of European integration: the competing interests of member states often pull the EU in contradictory directions, and as often undermine attempts to reach common policy positions. But cooperation on foreign and security issues has been habit-forming, and the political disagreement in the EU over the US-led invasion of Iraq should not distract us from the widespread public opposition to the invasion (70–90 per cent of the public in every EU member state) or from the strong public support for a common European security policy: according to Eurobarometer, 77 per cent of Europeans favour such a policy, with support highest in France, Germany, and several Eastern European member states (all 80 per cent or more), and majorities in favour even in Britain and Ireland (58–59 per cent).

Britain's role in the debate has been critical. Where Britain long opposed attempts to promote greater European military integration, Blair was sympathetic to the suggestion made in 1996 that the EU develop a defence and security 'identity' within NATO. The idea was that the Europeans would be able to mount peacekeeping or monitoring operations without necessarily looking for the support of the United States or other NATO member states; interested countries would contribute military forces that would come together under a joint command system. When Blair met with French President Jacques Chirac at St Malo in France in December 1998, the two leaders agreed that the EU should have the capacity for autonomous military action, and suggested the creation of a European Rapid Reaction Force (RRF). In 1999 the European Security and Defence Policy (ESDP) was announced, under which the EU would promote the 'Petersberg tasks' (agreed in 1992, and including humanitarian, rescue, peacekeeping, and other crisis management operations), and build a 60,000-member RRF that could be deployed at 60 days' notice, be sustained for at least a year, and carry out those tasks. When this proved overly ambitious, the focus shifted to more rapidly deployable 1,500-member battle groups.

Blair argued that it was not a straight choice between an EU defence capability on the one hand and continued cooperation with the Americans on the other – he argued instead that both were possible. The political costs of this were dragged into the harsh light of day by the hawkish position taken during 2002–03 by Blair on the question of plans by the United States to attack Iraq and remove Saddam Hussein from power. While there had been an outpouring of support and sympathy for the United States following the September 2001 terrorist attacks, the tide began to turn as the Bush administration shifted the spotlight of the 'war on terrorism' away from Afghanistan and towards Iraq. Bush claimed that Saddam was building weapons of mass destruction, and was supporting the al-Qaeda terrorist network. Questions were raised about the lack of hard evidence, about the wisdom of setting a precedent of pre-emptive strikes, about how such an attack would fit with international law, about the extent to which such an attack would further destabilize an already unstable region, and about the real motives of the Bush administration.

As events unfolded in mid-2002, European leaders began withdrawing support from the Bush administration. The French equivocated, the Germans were positively hostile to American 'adventurism' (a position that was undoubtedly influenced by the closeness of the September 2002 German general election), while the conservative Berlusconi government in Italy gave its blessing. Meanwhile, the world was treated to the peculiar sight of Britain's Labour Prime Minister leading the chorus in support of a divisive policy pursued by a neoconservative American president. Forcefully arguing his case that Britain played a 'pivotal' role in world affairs, Blair gave vocal support to the Bush administration, analysts suggesting that at least part of his thinking was that it was better to be involved – and to have influence – than not to be involved and to have little or no say in a policy that might end up damaging Britain's interests (*The Economist*, 9 March 2002: 60).

It is too early to know what the long-term effects of the fallout over Iraq will be, but inevitably the dispute will – as noted earlier – help encourage Britons to wonder anew about the Anglo–American special relationship, and to ponder in more depth the implications of closer foreign policy cooperation between Britain and the EU. Just as there has long been clear support for EU states working together on trade policy, so the widespread unpopularity within Europe of many

US foreign policy positions will likely shift governments and publics more towards the idea of common European policy positions. While the United States tends towards a uniquely American view of problems and their solutions, and has had an unfortunate inclination to use its enormous military power to achieve change, without thinking through the longer-term political implications, Europeans take a more multilateral, universal and inclusive view of the world, and reject military options in favour of negotiation, encouragement and incentives. The more the United States pursues its unique and often unpopular policies, the more Britain will gravitate towards the European circle of influence (for more discussion see McCormick, 2007).

The Changing Role of the British Military

Britain was once the pre-eminent military power in the world, and its history is peppered with great military leaders and celebrated victories that are at the heart of the mythology of British history. From Edward III's decisive victory over the French at the Battle of Crécy in 1346 to Henry V's victory at Agincourt in 1415, to Sir Francis Drake and his defeat of the Spanish Armada in 1588, to the Duke of Marlborough (who never lost a battle and defeated the French at Blenheim in 1704), to Lord Nelson and the Duke of Wellington, who between them contributed so much to ending Napoleon's aspirations for European hegemony, to General Bernard Montgomery, who inflicted the first major defeat on the Nazis at El Alamein in 1942, the list is impressive, and the British are always quick to use anniversaries to roll out the ghosts of their military heroes as a means to celebrate past achievements. Of course there are also plenty of examples of military blunders and failures, but these are routinely overlooked, or occasionally turned to advantage: how many other countries could turn the Charge of the Light Brigade, when nearly 700 cavalrymen were mistakenly ordered to charge Russian artillery in the Crimea in 1854, into an example of glorious failure?

The Second World War may have been Britain's finest hour, but it also struck a blow to Britain's status as a great power, and it soon began to withdraw from its military commitments around the world, the Suez crisis of 1956 finally confirming its reduction to a second-rank power. It had played a leading role in the development of nuclear weapons during the closing years of the war, but was quickly overtaken by the United States, and while it still has an independent nuclear deterrent it is a relatively small one. From a time when British troops were committed all over the world to protect British interests and promote British policy, the British military by the 1970s was a shadow of its former self.

Emphasizing its reduced condition, it came perilously close in 1982 to failing in a minor war against an inferior enemy. On 20 April of that year, Argentina invaded the Falkland Islands (Malvinas), a British possession in the south Atlantic since 1833, inhabited by less than 2,000 people. The Thatcher government responded by despatching a task force of 100 ships and 25,000 soldiers and sailors, supported by a small number of aircraft-carrier-based fighters. The troops fought bravely, but resources were spread so thinly that the task force had to commandeer commercial ferries and luxury cruisers to transport soldiers, the Royal Navy lived in danger of sustaining crippling losses from a handful of French-made Exocet missiles fired by the Argentinean air force, and enough ships and helicopters were lost that the task force came close to losing the logistical support it

Table 8.2   The British military

Personnel:	210,900 regular (114,000 Army, 53,000 Royal Air Force, 42,900 Royal Navy and Royal Marines) and 282,000 reserves. Total: 492,900
Nuclear warheads:	Less than 300, all sea-based, carried on four nuclear-powered submarines, no more than one of which is on patrol at any time with no more than 48 warheads
Aircraft:	183 Tornado fighter-bombers, 42 Harrier fighters, 26 Jaguar fighters, and about 300 helicopters (including Merlins, Pumas, Lynx, Chinooks and Sea Kings)
Ships:	3 aircraft carriers, 25 destroyers and frigates, 16 mine countermeasure ships, 4 nuclear-powered Vanguard-class ballistic submarines armed with Trident missiles, 11 fleet submarines armed with Tomahawk cruise missiles, 3 amphibious assault ships. Two new carriers on order, to enter service in 2012
Defence spending:	2.5 per cent of GDP

Source: Mainly Ministry of Defence, 2006, www.mod.uk. Figures are for 2006.

needed to fight the war. But Britain prevailed, and the war ended with the surrender of Argentinean forces on 14 June.

Just before the Falklands, there had been 320,000 personnel in the four branches of the regular forces: the Army, the Royal Air Force, the Royal Navy and the Royal Marines. The number went up slightly after the Falklands, but by 2001 had fallen to just under 211,000, a reduction of nearly one-third. Some of the slack was taken up by regular reserves, whose number increased over the same period by about one-third, to 282,000. At the same time, defence spending as a percentage of GDP was halved between 1985 and 2001, falling from 5.1 per cent to 2.5 per cent.

Soon after coming to power, the Blair administration developed the Strategic Defence Review (SDR), aimed at outlining Britain's options in the period until 2015. Published in 1998, it was the first such study in 17 years and the first to consider the needs and possibilities of the post-Cold War world (see Spear, 2000: 282–3). It concluded that there were no direct military threats to Britain, but that the end of the Cold War had introduced instability and uncertainty, and that there was a variety of new non-military threats faced by Britain, including the potential proliferation of nuclear, chemical and biological weapons, organized crime, and issues related to drugs, natural-resource issues and ethnic conflict. It argued that British forces would have to be ready to respond to a major crisis of a similar scale to the 1991 Gulf War, while being prepared for more extended commitments on a lesser scale, such as peacekeeping and relief operations. It also concluded that Britain should have the capacity to commit small and highly trained groups of personnel into different situations at short notice. In support of the latter, the Blair administration gave its blessing to the development of the EU Rapid Reaction Force.

Alongside its role in the conflicts in the Gulf in 1990–91, and in Serbia in 1999, the British military has been a key element in NATO rapid reaction forces, to which it has committed three aircraft carriers, 54 naval vessels, 12 nuclear-powered submarines, 55,000 troops and 140 aircraft. Meanwhile, it has been involved in UN peacekeeping operations in the Congo, Cyprus, East Timor and Georgia, international relief or evacuation operations in Angola, Eritrea, Mozambique, Rwanda and Somalia, as well as the following:

• After the breakdown of security in Sierra Leone in May 2000, and the taking hostage of UN peacekeepers by rebels, Britain deployed

Members of the Royal Marines being redeployed by Chinook helicopter from Laskar Gah in Afghanistan. The British military plays a key role both in international peacekeeping operations and in dispute resolution in former British colonies.

Illustration 8.3   Royal Marines

4,500 troops to the war-torn country, and subsequently helped restore order and train a new army and police force.

- Britain contributed about 1,700 troops to the Stabilization Force (SFOR) set up to help implement the 1995 peace accords in Bosnia and Herzegovina, as well as police officers taking part in the UN International Police Task Force. It participates today in EUFOR, the EU stabilization force which replaced SFOR in December 2004. It has also made the biggest contributions (about 19,000 troops) to KFOR, deployed in Kosovo in 1999 to help restore peace following the NATO attack on Serbia.

- Following its small supporting military role in the attack on the Taliban regime in Afghanistan, launched by the United States in the wake of the September 2001 terrorist attacks in New York and Washington DC, Britain played the lead role in peacekeeping operations before handing over responsibility to Turkish forces in June 2002.

- Britain had the second-largest commitment of troops to the invasion of Iraq, with 46,000 troops active at the height of operations in March/April 2003, reduced to just over 7,000 by mid-2006. The bulk has been based in and around the city of Basra in southeast Iraq. As of January 2007, 128 British military personnel had been killed in action in Iraq.

Ironically, the SDR was criticized for not dealing effectively with so-called 'asymmetric threats', such as terrorism and the threats posed by weapons of mass destruction, and also avoided the question of the development of a European defence identity. Yet these are the very issues which have now come to dominate discussions about the future of British defence policy. The new role of terrorism in international affairs was most graphically illustrated by the September 2001 attacks. Among the nearly 2,750 victims of the destruction of the World Trade Center in New York were 67 British citizens, making the event the biggest single loss of British lives in an attack of its kind. The Blair administration provided diplomatic and moral support to the new 'war on terror' declared by US President George W. Bush, and – as noted earlier – Tony Blair himself became the most visible and active of national leaders in support of US policies. On 7 July 2005, the new brand of terrorism struck home when four separate bomb explosions in central London killed 52 people and injured more than 770. Two weeks later, four more attacks failed to materialize when only the detonators exploded. Then in August 2006 news broke of a plot to use liquid explosives to blow up nearly a dozen airliners flying from Britain to the United States.

For some, Britain has become a target of such attacks mainly because of its support for US policies, which – if true – raises fundamental questions about the future of British defence policy. White (2001: 119) argues that the one area in which British governments have welcomed Europeanization has been on defence policy, but that this predates membership of the EEC, and has been driven more by a desire to strengthen the European commitment to NATO in order to keep the USA committed to European security. But the examples of Iraq, of the 'war on terror', and of Lebanon in July 2006 – when the Blair administration was unable to convince the Bush administration of the merits of calling for a ceasefire following the outbreak of hostilities with Israel – raise questions about whether the United States will ever really listen to Britain. Cox and Oliver (2006: 187) conclude that British ambivalence about the role of the EU in the world is matched only by unease about whether the USA will listen to British concerns. In defence policy, as in foreign policy, the exact location of Britain within Churchill's three circles of influence remains a troubling issue for debate.

Conclusions

With its long history and many traditions, it is easy to think of Britain as stable and unchanging, and as forming the bedrock of the elements we associate with parliamentary government, capitalism, and Western society. And yet nothing could be further from the truth. Few countries have gone through the kind of near-revolutionary changes that Britain has witnessed in the last two generations, evidence of which can be found everywhere. It can be found in the remodelling of the political system, the upheavals that have altered the structure of the British economy, changes in the make-up of British society, the redefinition of the place of family, national identity, race and religion, changing views on the place of Britain in the world, and a review of approaches to almost every area of public policy, from welfare to education, health care, transportation, economic issues and foreign affairs.

If there is anything that briefly sums up Britain and the British experience today, it is change. The people of Britain have had to become used to adjustment, innovation, diversity, reconstruction, novelty, revision, transition, and transformation, in almost every aspect of their lives:

- On the political front, the heritage of the parliamentary system can be traced back more than 800 years, giving Britain a political continuity that is virtually unmatched in the world. Yet the role and the powers of the monarchy, of the office of Prime Minister, of Parliament, and of the bureaucracy have undergone fundamental change, as has the relationship among local, regional, national and European levels of government.
- On the economic front, Britain has had to make an adjustment that has taken it from being the pre-eminent economic and trading power in the world, the birthplace of the industrial revolution, and the nursery of capitalism, through experimentation with competing approaches to managing the marketplace, to meeting the challenge

of adjusting to both steady growth and rapid integration into the European marketplace. The scale and the variety of change have outpaced almost anything seen in the rest of Europe or North America.

- On the social front, the predictable patterns of the class system have become blurred, the meaning of 'British' has been redefined on the back of waves of immigration and questions about the future of the United Kingdom, and social relations have changed in the wake of the decline of the nuclear family, the growth of the middle class, a transformation of occupational structure, and the aging of the British population.

The most important influence on postwar Britain has been the redefinition of the meaning of Britain's national identity. Externally, the British have had to adjust themselves to the idea that they are no longer a great power. From Suez to the collapse of the Berlin Wall, Britain was one of a group of middle-range powers that stood on the periphery of Cold War disputes between the superpowers. Today, it is torn as never before between trying to maintain an increasingly difficult relationship with the United States, and throwing in its lot with its partners in the European Union. Fortunately, the angst of post-imperial decline has been replaced by greater congruence between reality and aspiration. Instead of frustrating itself by trying to punch above its weight, Britain has reached the point where it is comfortable with its reduced role in the international system. Despite the resistance of many Britons, the future will almost certainly see their country acting more closely in concert with its European neighbours in its relationship with the rest of the world, and it will be defined less as a distinct political or economic entity, and more for its location within Europe.

Internally, the dominance of England over Scotland and Wales has declined. The last two generations have seen a newly assertive nationalism in all three countries that has raised questions about the future health of the union. Although peace now reigns in Northern Ireland, it is a troubled peace, compromised by ill-feelings that will continue to impact the way its different communities see each other indefinitely. Meanwhile, the jury is still out on the level of support for independence in Scotland, and on the significance of the rise of English nationalism. Along the way, the definition of 'Britishness' continues to change as Britain becomes increasingly multicultural, and as Asian, Caribbean and African minorities are joined by waves of new arrivals from the continent, coming either as asylum-seekers or in the wake of eastward expansion of the EU. There is still much ground to be covered in the debate over the definition of 'Britain' and the 'United Kingdom'.

The second important influence on postwar Britain has been the European Union. Whether they like it or not, and many do not, the British are daily being further integrated into the networks that have pulled the states of Europe closer together since the early 1950s. European law permeates British law, European policy plays a central role in areas as diverse as agriculture, consumer protection, the environment, fisheries, trade, transport and working conditions, and Britain makes its internal and external political and economic choices less in isolation and increasingly in concert with its European partners. While membership of the EU is voluntary, and Britain could theoretically leave if anti-European sentiment reached a sufficient pitch, even outside the EU it would be impossible for Britain to resist the gravitational pull of the continental European economic colossus. Eventual membership of the euro is all but inevitable, as are the creation of a European military force and the development of common European foreign and security policies. If for no other reason than to provide a counterbalance to the unilateralist and militarist tendencies of the United States in the world, it is essential that Europe (with Britain) exerts its political, diplomatic and economic influence on the global stage.

The third important influence on postwar Britain has been the economic and social impact of Thatcherism. The Prime Minister herself left office in 1990, but her influence continues to be felt. While not all of her ideas may have been original, she – unlike some of her Conservative predecessors – was able to see those ideas implemented, and the combination of the changes made by her administration, some of them calculated, some of them opportunistic, dramatically altered both the style of government and the economic and social character of Britain. Most notably, the government has stepped back from the marketplace. State monopolies have been replaced by competing private corporations, individuals have a greater direct role in the economy through ownership of shares and property, consumerism has grown, and British businesses now actually care about what consumers want. Furthermore, instead of citizens expecting the state to provide, the state now asks citizens what they have done to merit that provision, and encourages greater self-reliance.

The changes that have come out of these three broad forces have been overwhelmingly positive. The British are healthier, wealthier and more self-sufficient than they were in 1945, they have rediscovered their competitive and entrepreneurial spirit, greater emphasis is given than perhaps ever before to merit and social equality, and there is much greater general awareness of the difficulties that society faces and how they might be addressed. Many problems remain, it is true, including poverty and social exclusion, racism, economic inequalities, public services of mixed quality, and crime. However, there is always a danger in focusing on short-term trends rather than taking the longer view, and there will always be a mixture of the good and the bad in those trends. Overall, Britain today is a dynamic and forward-looking society with a global influence that is remarkable for a country of its size. It has undergone considerable change, and there is more to come as it both redefines itself, and redefines its place in the context both of Europe and the wider world.

Recommended Reading

The literature on Britain is extensive and constantly changing, with many new books and articles being published every year on the different topics covered by this book. The selection that follows is no more than representative: it emphasizes the most recent general introductions to each topic, and is designed to point readers in the right direction for further and more detailed study.

1 The Historical Context

By far the best general history of Britain is Fraser (2004). She offers an excellent and well-written survey of Britain since Roman times, which can be read and digested at any pace. The multiple volumes in the *Short Oxford History of the British Isles* (various authors) offer valuable studies dealing with different eras in British history, Schama (2003) has a three-volume survey published to accompany a BBC-TV series, and single-volume surveys are offered by Norman Davies (2000) and Morgan (2001a). A political and social history of Victorian Britain can be found in Rubinstein (1998), which can be followed up by histories of the twentieth century written by Clarke (1996), Marwick (2000) and Robbins (2002). There are numerous studies of developments in postwar British political history, including Coxall and Robins (1998) (which includes chapters on political parties and key policy issues), Marsh *et al.* (1999), and Morgan (2001b). The literature on Thatcher and Thatcherism is extensive, but a good general survey is provided by Young (1990).

2 Land and People

Good introductory surveys of the geography of Britain include Johnston and Gardiner (1997) and Hardill *et al.* (2001). For books on the geology and natural resources of Britain, see Toghill (2004), and Hunter and Easterbrook (2004). Hawkes (1991) is a reprint of a book published in 1952 that is still regarded as an important study of the formation of the British landmass. Thomas (1996) offers a history of the changing relationship between people and nature in Britain, Hoskins (2005) provides a study of how the character-

236

istic English landscape has evolved, and Soffe (2005) is an edited collection on the rural economy in Britain. Surprisingly little has been published on environmental policy in Britain (see Garner (2000) for an exception), mainly because the focus has shifted to the Europeanization of British policy; see Lowe and Ward (1998) and Jordan (2002). Winder (2004) offers a useful history of immigration to Britain. For a study of English national identity, see Kumar (2003) and for the equivalent on Scotland, see Pittock (2001). Adolino (1998) provides an assessment of the political context in which ethnic minorities find themselves.

3   The Social System

Two classic historical studies of class in England – which are still worth reading for context – are Engels (various years) and Thompson (1966). A broader historical survey, assessing changes in the class system up to the Blair administration, is provided by Cannadine (2000), while Marshall *et al.* (1989) look at class structure and different conceptions of class. Books making the case that class divisions are alive and well include Mount (2004). Singer (1999) has written a book that goes with the fascinating TV documentary *42 Up*, which looks at a group of Britons every seven years and watches how they change, providing insights into British society (the film *49 Up* was released in 2006). Davies (1998) offers an indictment of the underside of life in Britain, and the results of a study of poverty and social exclusion in Britain can be found in Pantazis *et al.* (2006). McKay and Rowlingson (1999) offer a study of social security in Britain, while studies of health care and the National Health Service are offered by Klein (2001), Webster (2002), Baggott (2004), and Ham (2004). For a survey of education policy in Britain, see Chitty (2004); otherwise, much of the literature on education is critical or focused on making the case for reform, one example being Woodhead (2002). Croall (1998) looks at the links between crime and society, Davies *et al.* (1998) offer a guide to the criminal justice system in England and Wales, and Reiner (2000) has written a well-known text on the history and organization of the British police.

4   Government and the Political System

There are numerous (and often lengthy) introductory surveys of British politics, including Jones and Kavanagh (2003), Jones *et al.* (2004), Moran (2005), Kavanagh *et al.* (2006), and Leach *et al.* (2006), all of which cover the key government institutions and political processes. Good edited collections offering recent analyses of key institutions and issues include Holliday *et al.* (1999), Budge *et al.* (2003) and Dunleavy *et al.* (2006). An edited collection of essays on public policy during the Blair administration can be found in Savage and

Atkinson (2001). Smith (1999) writes a thought-provoking analysis of the 'core executive' in Britain, and Hennessy (2001) is the primary source on postwar Prime Ministers and their different governing styles.

5   Politics and Civil Society

Surveys of parties, elections, interest groups and the media can again be found in the introductory sources listed for Chapter 4. Leonard and Mortimore (2001) provide an introduction to the electoral system, while Baston and Henig (2002) have written a lengthy reference book with plenty of statistical data on the political characteristics of Britain. Butler and Kavanagh (2001) and Worcester and Mortimore (2001) offer analyses of the 2001 general election, while Geddes and Tonge (2005) review the 2005 general election. There are numerous studies of individual parties and their histories, but an overview is provided by Ingle (1999). Studies of the types and methods of pressure groups in Britain can be found in Grant (2000) and Coxall (2001). For a guide to the British media, see Curran and Seaton (2003), while the relationship between politics, the media and public relations is examined by Bartle and Griffiths (2001) and Davis (2002).

6   The Economy

Middleton (2000) provides an assessment of British economic performance since 1945. A general survey of British economic policy is offered by Grant (2002), while responses to the idea of economic decline in Britain are offered by Booth (2001) (who also gives the broad view of the British economy during the twentieth century) and by Bernstein (2004). There are numerous studies of the economic impact of Thatcherism, including Evans (1997) and Heffernan (2001) (the latter looks at the impact of her philosophy on Blair's Labour Party). Temperton (2001) looks at the pros and cons of Britain adopting the euro.

7   Culture and Lifestyle

For a study of national identity in Britain, see Bryant (2005). Overall surveys of the state of British cultural studies – with an emphasis on the relationship between England, Scotland and Wales – are offered by Morley and Robins (2001), Bassnett (2003), and Turner (2003). The way in which landscape has inspired art is the subject of *A Picture of Britain*, a first-rate television series hosted by David Dimbleby, whose accompanying book (Dimbleby, 2005) is both evocative and instructive. A general assessment of theatre in Britain since

1945 is offered by Shellard (1999), a history of English literature can be found in Sanders (2000), and studies of British cinema are provided by Street (1997), Aldgate and Richards (1999), and Murphy (2001). British pop culture is the subject of a book by Calcutt (2000), the cultural and social impact of The Beatles is assessed by Inglis (2000), and a review of Britpop is provided by John Harris (2004). Two assessments of sport in Britain since 1945 are offered by Polley (1998) and by Holt and Mason (2000), while the history of British cuisine is reviewed by Spencer (2002), and an inventory of its traditional foods can be found in Mason and Brown (2004).

8 Britain and the World

There are few recent studies of the Commonwealth, but Kitchen (1996) provides a history, and Larby and Hannam (1993) provide a (now) dated study of the organization. The few analyses of Britain's place in NATO are now also dated, but the literature on NATO itself is extensive; examples include Asmus (2002) and Sloan (2005), while the Anglo–American special relationship is examined by Dimbleby and Reynolds (1989), Bull and Louis (1997), Riddell (2003), and Dumbrell (2006). The literature on the European Union is large and growing, with general surveys provided by McCormick (2005), Dinan (2005), Wallace *et al.* (2005), and Nugent (2006), and studies of Britain's relationship with the EU are provided by Gowland and Turner (1999), Young (1999), Geddes (2003), and Watts and Pilkington (2005). Turner and Gowland (2000) offer a collection of key documents relating to Britain's relationship with the EU, and Gamble (2003) offers an analysis of Britain's relationship to Europe and the United States. For a study of the impact of EU policy on national defence policy, see Howorth and Menon (1997).

Britain Online

In terms of the number of web sites available, and the proportion of people connected to the internet, Britain is second only to the United States. This means that there is a wealth of information that can be found electronically, and the list that follows barely scratches the surface. Links to all these sites (and new ones as I find them) can be found on my web page at mypage.iu.edu/~jmccormi.

General

Directgov: www.open.gov.uk
Office for National Statistics: www.statistics.gov.uk

Society

National Health Service: www.nhs.uk
Department of Health: www.dh.gov.uk
Department of Education and Skills: www.dfes.gov.uk
Church of England: www.cofe.anglican.org
Church of Scotland: www.churchofscotland.org.uk
Commission for Racial Equality: www.cre.gov.uk
Law Society: www.lawsociety.org.uk
Home Office: www.homeoffice.gov.uk

Government

British monarchy: www.royal.gov.uk
Office of the Prime Minister: pm.gov.uk
Houses of Parliament: www.parliament.uk
Scottish Parliament: www.scottish.parliament.uk
National Assembly for Wales: www.wales.gov.uk
Northern Ireland Assembly: www.niassembly.gov.uk
Local Government Association: www.lga.gov.uk

Civil society

Electoral Commission: www.electoralcommission.gov.uk
European Parliament: www.europarl.europa.eu
Labour Party: www.labour.org.uk
Conservative Party: www.conservatives.com
Liberal Democrats: www.libdems.org.uk
Trades Union Congress: www.tuc.org.uk
Confederation of British Industry: www.cbi.org.uk
BBC: www.bbc.co.uk
ITV: www.itv.com
The Times: www.timesonline.co.uk/global
Telegraph: www.telegraph.co.uk
Guardian Unlimited: www.guardian.co.uk
The Economist: www.economist.com

The Arts

Royal National Theatre: www.nt-online.org
Royal Shakespeare Company: www.rsc.org.uk
British Film Institute: www.bfi.org.uk
Britmovie: www.britmovie.co.uk

Lifestyle

UK Sport: www.uksport.gov.uk
British Olympic Association: www.olympics.org.uk
Football Association: www.thefa.com
England and Wales Cricket Board: www.ecb.co.uk
International Rugby Board: www.irb.com
UK Tourist Information: www.uktouristinfo.com
British Tourist Authority: www.visitbritain.com

International

Foreign and Commonwealth Office: www.fco.gov.uk
Ministry of Defence: www.mod.uk
Department of Trade and Industry: www.dti.gov.uk
The Commonwealth: www.thecommonwealth.org
European Union: www.europa.eu
North Atlantic Treaty Organization: www.nato.int

Bibliography

Note: Unless otherwise indicated, most statistics used in this book come from the web site of the Office for National Statistics at www.statistics.gov.uk.

Adolino, Jessica (1998) *Ethnic Minorities, Electoral Politics and Political Integration in Britain* (London: Pinter).

Adonis, Andrew and Stephen Pollard (1997) *A Class Act: The Myth of Britain's Classless Society* (London: Hamish Hamilton).

Alcock, Pete (2000) 'Welfare Policy', in Patrick Dunleavy, Andrew Gamble, Ian Holliday and Gillian Peele (eds) *Developments in British Politics 6* (Basingstoke: Palgrave (now Palgrave Macmillan)).

Aldgate, Anthony and Jeffrey Richards (1999) *Best of British: Cinema and Society from 1930 to the Present* (London: I.B. Tauris).

Anderson, Fred (2000) *Crucible of War: The Seven Years' War and the Fate of Empire in British North America 1754–1766* (New York: Alfred A. Knopf).

Asmus, Ronald (2002) *Opening NATO's Door* (New York: Columbia University Press).

Aughey, Arthur (2001) 'British Policy in Northern Ireland', in Stephen Savage and Rob Atkinson (eds) *Public Policy Under Blair* (Basingstoke: Palgrave (now Palgrave Macmillan)).

Bagehot, Walter (2001) *The English Constitution* (Oxford: Oxford University Press).

Baggott, Rob (2004) *Health and Health Care in Britain*, 3rd edition (Basingstoke: Palgrave Macmillan).

Banister, David (1998) *Transport Policy and the Environment* (London: Spon).

Bartle, John and Dylan Griffiths (2001) *Political Communications Transformed: From Morrison to Mandelson* (Basingstoke: Palgrave (now Palgrave Macmillan)).

Bartle, John and Samantha Laycock (2006) 'Elections and Voting', in Patrick Dunleavy, Richard Heffernan, Philip Cowley and Colin Hay (eds) *Developments in British Politics 8* (Basingstoke: Palgrave Macmillan).

Bassnett, Susan (ed.) (2003) *Studying British Cultures: An Introduction*, 2nd edition (London: Routledge).

Baston, Lewis and Simon Henig (eds) (2002) *Political Map of Britain* (London: Politico's).

Benn, Tony (1980) 'The Case for a Constitutional Premiership', *Parliamentary Affairs* 33(1), Winter: 7–22.

Bernstein, George L. (2004) *The Myth of Decline: The Rise of Britain Since 1945* (London: Pimlico).

Bogdanor, Vernon (2001) *Devolution in the United Kingdom* (Oxford: Oxford Paperbacks).

Booth, Alan (2001) *The British Economy in the Twentieth Century* (Basingstoke: Palgrave (now Palgrave Macmillan)).

Brimblecombe, Peter (1989) *The Big Smoke: A History of Air Pollution* (London: Taylor & Francis).

Bryant, Christopher (2005) *The Nations of Britain* (London: Open University Press).

Budge, Ian, Ivor Crewe, David McKay and Ken Newton (2003) *The New British Politics*, 3rd edition (Harlow: Longman).

Bull, Hedley and William R. Louis (eds) (1997) *The Special Relationship: Anglo–American Relations Since 1945* (Oxford: Clarendon Press).

Buller, Jim (1999) 'Britain's Relations with the European Union in Historical Perspective', in David Marsh *et al.* (eds) *Postwar British Politics in Perspective* (Cambridge: Polity Press).

Butler, David (1999) *The British General Election of 1951* (Basingstoke: Macmillan (now Palgrave Macmillan)).

Butler, David and Dennis Kavanagh (2001) *The British General Election of 2001* (Basingstoke: Palgrave (now Palgrave Macmillan)).

Calcutt, Andrew (2000) *Brit Cult: An A–Z of British Pop Culture* (London: Pion).

Cannadine, David (2000) *The Rise and Fall of Class in Britain* (New York: Columbia University Press).

Chitty, Clyde (2004) *Education Policy in Britain* (Basingstoke: Palgrave Macmillan).

Clarke, John, Mary Langan and Fiona Williams (2001) 'The Construction of the British Welfare State, 1945–1975', in Allan Cochrane, John Clarke and Sharon Gewirtz (eds) *Comparing Welfare States*, 2nd edition (London: Sage).

Clarke, Peter (1996) *Hope and Glory: Britain 1900–1990* (London: Penguin).

Corera, Gordon (2006) 'The Evolving Threat of al-Qaeda', *BBC Online*, 19 October.

Cowley, Philip (2006) 'Making Parliament Matter?', in Patrick Dunleavy, Richard Heffernan, Philip Cowley and Colin Hay (eds) *Developments in British Politics 8* (Basingstoke: Palgrave Macmillan).

Cox, Michael and Tim Oliver (2006) 'Security Policy in an Insecure World', in Patrick Dunleavy, Richard Heffernan, Philip Cowley and Colin Hay (eds) *Developments in British Politics 8* (Basingstoke: Palgrave Macmillan).

Coxall, Bill (2001) *Pressure Groups in British Politics* (Harlow: Pearson Longman).

Coxall, Bill and Lynton Robins (1998) *British Politics Since the War* (Basingstoke: Macmillan (now Palgrave Macmillan)).

Croall, Hazel (1998) *Crime and Society in Britain: An Introduction* (Harlow: Longman).

Crossman, Richard (1963) 'Introduction' to Walter Bagehot, *The English Constitution* (London: Fontana).

Crystal, David (2003) *English as a Global Language* (Cambridge: Cambridge University Press).

Curran, James and Jean Seaton (2003) *Power Without Responsibility: The Press, Broadcasting and the New Media in Britain*, 6th edition (London: Routledge).

Curtice, John (2004) 'Restoring Confidence and Legitimacy? Devolution and Public Opinion', in Alan Trench (ed.) *The State of the Nations 2004* (Exeter: Imprint Academic).

Davie, Grace (1994) *Religion in Britain since 1945: Believing Without Belonging* (Oxford: Blackwell).

Davies, Alistair (2000) 'A Cinema In Between: Postwar British Cinema', in Alistair Davies and Alan Sinfield (eds) *British Culture of the Postwar* (London: Routledge).

Davies, Malcolm, Jane Tyver and Hazel Croall (1998) *Criminal Justice: An Introduction to the Criminal Justice System in England and Wales* (Harlow: Longman).

Davies, Nick (1998) *Dark Heart: The Shocking Truth About Hidden Britain* (London: Vintage).

Davies, Norman (2000) *The Isles: A History* (London: Macmillan (now Palgrave Macmillan)).

Davies, Wendy (ed.) (2003) *From the Vikings to the Normans* (*Short Oxford History of the British Isles*) (Oxford: Oxford University Press).

Davis, Aeron (2002) *Public Relations Democracy: Politics, Public Relations and the Mass Media in Britain* (Manchester: Manchester University Press).

Dimbleby, David (2005) *A Picture of Britain* (London: Tate).

Dimbleby, David and David Reynolds (1989) *An Ocean Apart: The Relationship Between Britain and America in the Twentieth Century* (New York: Vintage Books).

Dinan, Desmond (2005) *Ever Closer Union: An Introduction to European Integration*, 3rd edition (Basingstoke: Palgrave Macmillan).

Douglas, Roy (2002) *Liquidation of Empire: The Decline of the British Empire* (Basingstoke: Palgrave Macmillan).

Dumbrell, John (2006) *A Special Relationship: Anglo-American Relations from the Cold War to Iraq*, 2nd edition (Basingstoke: Palgrave Macmillan).

Dunleavy, Patrick (2000), 'Elections and Party Politics', in Patrick Dunleavy, Andrew Gamble, Ian Holliday and Gillian Peele (eds), *Developments in British Politics 6* (Basingstoke: Palgrave (now Palgrave Macmillan)).

Dunleavy, Patrick, Richard Heffernan, Philip Cowley and Colin Hay (eds) (2006) *Developments in British Politics 8* (Basingstoke: Palgrave Macmillan).

Edwards, Michael (2005) *Civil Society* (Cambridge: Polity Press).

Electoral Commission and Hansard Society (2005) *An Audit of Political Engagement 2* (London: Electoral Commission and Hansard Society).

Engels, Friedrich (various years) *The Condition of the Working Class in England* (various publishers).

English, Richard and Michael Kenny (eds) (1999) *Rethinking British Decline* (Basingstoke: Macmillan (now Palgrave Macmillan)).

Evans, Eric J. (1997) *Thatcher and Thatcherism*, 2nd edition (London: Routledge).

Ferguson, Niall (2002) *Empire: The Rise and Demise of the British World Order and the Lessons for Global Power* (London: Allen Lane).

Fielding, Steven (2000) 'A New Politics?', in Patrick Dunleavy, Andrew Gamble, Ian Holliday and Gillian Peele (eds) *Developments in British Politics 6* (Basingstoke: Palgrave (now Palgrave Macmillan)).

Finer, Catherine Jones (1997) 'Social Policy', in Patrick Dunleavy, Andrew Gamble, Ian Holliday and Gillian Peele (eds) *Developments in British Politics 5* (Basingstoke: Macmillan (now Palgrave Macmillan)).

Fogle, Ben (2004) *The Teatime Islands: Adventures in Britain's Faraway Outposts* (London: Penguin).

Foley, Michael (2001) *The British Presidency*, 2nd edition (Manchester: Manchester University Press).

Fort, Tom (2006) *Under the Weather: The Story of our National Obsession* (London: Century).

Fox, Kate (2004) *Watching the English: The Hidden Rules of English Behaviour* (London: Hodder and Stoughton).

Fraser, Rebecca (2004) *A People's History of Britain* (London: Pimlico).

Gamble, Andrew (1999) 'State, Economy and Society', in Ian Holliday, Andrew Gamble and Geraint Parry (eds) *Fundamentals in British Politics* (Basingstoke: Macmillan (now Palgrave Macmillan)).

Gamble, Andrew (2003) *Between Europe and America: The Future of British Politics* (Basingstoke: Palgrave Macmillan).

Garner, Robert (2000) *Environmental Politics: Britain, Europe and the Global Environment*, 2nd edition (Basingstoke: Palgrave Macmillan).

Garton Ash, Timothy (2004) *Free World: America, Europe and the Surprising Future of the West* (New York: Random House).

Gaunt, Peter (ed.) (2000) *The English Civil War* (Oxford: Blackwell).

Geddes, Andrew (2003) *The European Union and British Politics* (Basingstoke: Palgrave Macmillan).

Geddes, Andrew and Jonathan Tonge (eds) (2005) *Britain Decides: The UK General Election 2005* (Basingstoke: Palgrave Macmillan).

George, Stephen (1992) *Britain and the European Community* (Oxford: Clarendon Press).

George, Stephen (1998) *An Awkward Partner: Britain in the European Community* (Oxford: Oxford University Press).

Gillingham, John (2001) *The Angevin Empire*, 2nd edition (London: Edward Arnold).

Gowland, David and Arthur Turner (1999) *Reluctant Europeans: Britain and European Integration, 1945–1998* (Harlow: Longman).

Grant, Wyn (1989) *Pressure Groups, Politics and Democracy in Britain* (London: Philip Allan).

Grant, Wyn (2000) *Pressure Groups and British Politics* (Basingstoke: Palgrave (now Palgrave Macmillan)).

Grant, Wyn (2002) *Economic Policy in Britain* (Basingstoke: Palgrave Macmillan).

Hague, William (2004) *William Pitt the Younger: A Biography* (London: HarperCollins).

Hall, P. A. (1999) 'Social Capital in Britain', *British Journal of Political Science* 29(3): 417–61.

Ham, Christopher (2004) *Health Policy in Britain*, 5th edition (Basingstoke: Palgrave Macmillan).

Hardill, Irene, David Graham and Eleonore Kofman (eds) (2001) *Human Geography of the UK: An Introduction* (London: Routledge).

Harris, Bernard (2004) *The Origins of the British Welfare State: Social Welfare in England and Wales, 1800–1945* (Basingstoke: Palgrave Macmillan).

Harris, John (2004) *The Last Party: Britpop, Blair and the Demise of English Rock* (London: HarperPerennial).

Hawkes, Jacquetta Hopkins (1991) *The Land* (Boston: Beacon).

Hay, Colin (2006) 'Managing Economic Interdependence: The Political Economy of New Labour', in Patrick Dunleavy, Richard Heffernan, Philip Cowley and Colin Hay (eds) *Developments in British Politics 8* (Basingstoke: Palgrave Macmillan).

Hazell, Robert (2006) *The English Question* (Manchester: Manchester University Press).

Heffernan, Richard (2001) *New Labour and Thatcherism: Political Change in Britain* (Basingstoke: Palgrave (now Palgrave Macmillan)).

Heffernan, Richard (2006) 'The Blair Style of Central Government', in Patrick Dunleavy, Richard Heffernan, Philip Cowley and Colin Hay (eds) *Developments in British Politics 8* (Basingstoke: Palgrave Macmillan).

Hennessy, Peter (2001) *The Prime Minister: The Office and its Holders since 1945* (New York: Palgrave (now Palgrave Macmillan)).

Higson, Andrew (2003) *English Heritage, English Cinema: Costume Drama Since 1980* (Oxford: Oxford University Press).

Hix, Simon (2000) 'Britain, the EU and the Euro', in Patrick Dunleavy, Andrew Gamble, Ian Holliday and Gillian Peele (eds) *Developments in British Politics 6* (Basingstoke: Palgrave (now Palgrave Macmillan)).

Holliday, Ian, Andrew Gamble and Geraint Parry (eds) (1999) *Fundamentals in British Politics* (Basingstoke: Macmillan (now Palgrave Macmillan)).

Holt, Richard and Tony Mason (2000) *Sport in Britain 1945–2000* (Oxford: Blackwell).

Horrox, Rosemary and W. Mark Ormrod (2006) *A Social History of England 1200–1500* (Cambridge: Cambridge University Press).

Hoskins, W. G. (2005) *The Making of the English Landscape* (London: Hodder and Stoughton).

Howorth, Jolyon and Anand Menon (1997) *The European Union and National Defence Policy* (London: Routledge).

Hunter, Arlène and Glynda Easterbrook (2004) *The Geological History of the British Isles* (London: Open University Press).

Hutchings, Peter (2001) 'Beyond the New Wave: Realism in British Cinema,

1959–63', in Robert Murphy (ed.) *The British Cinema Book*, 2nd edition (London: British Film Institute).

Ingham, Geoffrey (1984) *Capitalism Divided? The City and Industry in British Social Development* (Basingstoke: Macmillan (now Palgrave Macmillan)).

Ingle, Stephen (1999) *The British Party System* (London: Continuum International–Pinter).

Inglis, Ian (2000) *The Beatles, Popular Music and Society: A Thousand Voices* (Basingstoke: Macmillan (now Palgrave Macmillan)).

Johnson, Nevil (1999) 'The Constitution', in Ian Holliday, Andrew Gamble and Geraint Parry (eds) *Fundamentals in British Politics* (Basingstoke: Macmillan (now Palgrave Macmillan)).

Johnston, Ron and Vince Gardiner (1997) *The Changing Geography of the United Kingdom* (London: Routledge).

Jones, Bill (2003) 'Apathy: Why Don't People Want to Vote?', *Politics Review* 12(4): 23–7.

Jones, Bill and Dennis Kavanagh (2003) *British Politics Today*, 7th edition (Manchester: Manchester University Press).

Jones, Bill, Dennis Kavanagh and Michael Moran (2004) *Politics UK*, 5th edition (Harlow: Pearson Longman).

Jones, Ken (2003a) *Education in Britain: 1944 to the Present* (Cambridge: Polity Press).

Jones, Ken (2003b) *Jules Rimet Still Gleaming? England at the World Cup* (London: Virgin Books).

Jordan, Andrew (2002) *The Europeanization of British Environmental Policy: A Departmental Perspective* (Basingstoke: Palgrave Macmillan).

Kaletsky, Anatole (2002) 'Sour Noises, but What a Sweet Taste', in *The World in 2003* (London: The Economist).

Kavanagh, Dennis (1987), *Thatcherism and British Politics: The End of Consensus?* (Oxford: Oxford University Press).

Kavanagh, Dennis (2000) *British Politics: Continuities and Change*, 4th edition (Oxford: Oxford University Press).

Kavanagh, Dennis, David Richards, Martin Smith and Andrew Geddes (2006) *British Politics*, 5th edition (Oxford: Oxford University Press).

Kelly, Gavin (1997) 'Economic Policy', in Patrick Dunleavy, Andrew Gamble, Ian Holliday and Gillian Peele (eds) *Developments in British Politics 5* (Basingstoke: Macmillan (now Palgrave Macmillan)).

Kendall, Ian and David Holloway (2001) 'Education Policy', in Stephen Savage and Rob Atkinson (eds) *Public Policy Under Blair* (Basingstoke: Palgrave (now Palgrave Macmillan)).

Kerr, Peter (1999) 'The Postwar Consensus: A Woozle that Wasn't?', in David Marsh *et al.* (eds) *Postwar British Politics in Perspective* (Cambridge: Polity Press).

King, Steven and Geoffrey Timmins (2001), *Making Sense of the Industrial Revolution* (Manchester: Manchester University Press).

Kitchen, Martin (1996) *The British Empire and Commonwealth: A Short History* (Basingstoke: Macmillan (now Palgrave Macmillan)).

Klein, Rudolf (2001) *The New Politics of the NHS*, 4th edition (Harlow: Prentice-Hall Thorne).

Kumar, Krishan (2003) *The Making of English National Identity* (Cambridge: Cambridge University Press).

Larby, Patricia and Harry Hannam (1993) *The Commonwealth* (Piscataway, NJ: Transaction Publishers).

Leach, Robert, Bill Coxall and Lynton Robins (2006) *British Politics* (Basingstoke: Palgrave Macmillan).

Leonard, Dick and Roger Mortimore (2001) *Elections in Britain: A Voter's Guide* (Basingstoke: Palgrave (now Palgrave Macmillan)).

Levitt, Malcolm and Christopher Lord (2000) *The Political Economy of Monetary Union* (Basingstoke: Palgrave (now Palgrave Macmillan)).

Levy, Shawn (2002) *Ready, Steady, Go! The Smashing Rise and Giddy Fall of Swinging London* (New York: Doubleday).

Lewis, Philip (2002) *Islamic Britain: Religion, Politics and Identity Among British Muslims* (London: I.B. Tauris).

Louis, William Roger and Roger Owens (eds) (1989) *Suez 1956: The Crisis and its Consequences* (Oxford: Clarendon Press).

Lowe, Philip and Stephen Ward (eds) (1998) *British Environmental Policy and Europe: Politics and Policy in Transition* (London: Routledge).

Lundestad, Geir (2003) *The United States and Western Europe since 1945* (Oxford: Oxford University Press).

Margetts, Helen (2000) 'Political Participation and Protest', in Patrick Dunleavy, Andrew Gamble, Ian Holliday and Gillian Peele (eds) *Developments in British Politics 6* (Basingstoke: Palgrave (now Palgrave Macmillan)).

Marquand, David (1988) 'The Paradoxes of Thatcherism', in Robert Skidelsky (ed.) *Thatcherism* (London: Chatto & Windus).

Marsh, David, Jim Buller, Colin Hay, Jim Johnston, Peter Kerr, Stuart McAnulla and Matthew Watson (1999) *Postwar British Politics in Perspective* (Cambridge: Polity Press).

Marsh, Steve and Hans Mackenstein (2005) *The International Relations of the European Union* (Harlow: Longman).

Marshall, Gordon, David Rose, Howard Newby and Carolyn Vogler (1989) *Social Class in Modern Britain* (London: Routledge).

Marwick, Arthur (2000) *A History of the Modern British Isles, 1914–99* (Oxford: Blackwell).

Mason, Laura and Catherine Brown (2004) *Traditional Foods of Britain: An Inventory* (Totnes: Prospect Books).

McCormick, John (1997) *Acid Earth: The Global Threat of Acid Pollution* (London: Earthscan).

McCormick, John (2001) *Environmental Policy in the European Union* (Basingstoke: Palgrave (now Palgrave Macmillan)).

McCormick, John (2005) *Understanding the European Union*, 3rd edition (Basingstoke: Palgrave Macmillan).

McCormick, John (2007) *The European Superpower* (Basingstoke: Palgrave Macmillan).

McKay, Stephen and Karen Rowlingson (eds) (1999) *Social Security in Britain* (Basingstoke: Palgrave (now Palgrave Macmillan)).

Meehan, Elizabeth (1999) 'Citizenship and Identity', in Ian Holliday, Andrew Gamble and Geraint Parry (eds) *Fundamentals in British Politics* (Basingstoke: Macmillan (now Palgrave Macmillan)).

Middleton, Roger (2000) *The British Economy Since 1945* (Basingstoke: Macmillan (now Palgrave Macmillan)).

Modood, Tariq (2005) *Multicultural Politics: Racism, Ethnicity and Muslims in Britain* (Edinburgh: Edinburgh University Press).

Mohan, John (1999) *A United Kingdom? Economic, Social and Political Geographies* (London: Edward Arnold).

Moran, Michael (2005) *Politics and Governance in the UK* (Basingstoke: Palgrave Macmillan).

More, Charles (2000), *Understanding the Industrial Revolution* (London: Routledge).

Morgan, Kenneth O. (2001a) *The Oxford History of Britain*, revised edition (Oxford: Oxford University Press).

Morgan, Kenneth O. (2001b) *Britain Since 1945: The People's Peace*, 3rd edition (Oxford: Oxford University Press).

Morley, David and Kevin Robins (eds) (2001) *British Cultural Studies: Geography, Nationality and Identity* (New York: Oxford University Press).

Morrill, John (ed.) (1990) *Oliver Cromwell and the English Revolution* (Harlow: Longman).

Mount, Ferdinand (2004) *Mind the Gap: Class in Britain Now* (London: Short Books).

Mugglestone, Lynda (2003) *Talking Proper: The Rise of Accent as Social Symbol* (Oxford: Oxford University Press).

Murphy, Robert (ed.) (2001) *The British Cinema Book*, 2nd edition (London: British Film Institute).

Norton, Philip (2001) *The British Polity*, 4th edition (New York: Longman).

Norton, Philip (2005) *Parliament in British Politics* (Basingstoke: Palgrave Macmillan).

Nugent, Neill (2006) *The Government and Politics of the European Union*, 6th edition (Basingstoke: Palgrave Macmillan).

Obelkevich, James and Peter Catterall (1994) 'Understanding British Society', in James Obelkevich and Peter Catterall (eds) *Understanding Post-War British Society* (London: Routledge).

O'Neill, Michael (2004) *Devolution in British Politics* (Harlow: Longman).

Packer, Richard (2006) *The Politics of BSE* (Basingstoke: Palgrave Macmillan).

Pantazis, Christina, David Gordon and Ruth Levistas (eds) (2006) *Poverty and Social Exclusion in Britain: The Millennium Survey* (London: Policy Press).

Pattie, Charles, Patrick Seyd and Paul Whiteley (2004) *Citizenship in Britain: Values, Participation and Democracy* (Cambridge: Cambridge University Press).

Pierre, Jon and Gerry Stoker (2000) 'Towards Multi-Level Governance', in Patrick

Dunleavy, Andrew Gamble, Ian Holliday and Gillian Peele (eds) *Developments in British Politics 6* (Basingstoke: Palgrave (now Palgrave Macmillan)).

Pittock, Murray (2001) *Scottish Nationality* (Basingstoke: Palgrave (now Palgrave Macmillan)).

Polley, Martin (1998) *Moving the Goalposts: A History of Sport and Society since 1945* (London: Routledge).

Putnam, Robert (2000) *Bowling Alone: The Collapse and Revival of American Community* (New York: Simon & Schuster).

Rackham, Oliver (2004) *Trees and Woodland in the British Landscape* (London: Phoenix Press).

Rawcliffe, Peter (1998) *Environmental Pressure Groups in Transition* (Manchester: Manchester University Press).

Reiner, Robert (2000) *The Politics of the Police*, 3rd edition (Oxford: Oxford University Press).

Richards, Jeffrey (1997) *Films and British National Identity: From Dickens to Dad's Army* (Manchester: Manchester University Press).

Riddell, Peter (1989) *The Thatcher Decade* (Oxford: Basil Blackwell).

Riddell, Peter (2003) *Hug Them Close: Blair, Clinton and the 'Special Relationship'* (London: Politico's).

Robbins, Keith (2002) *The British Isles 1901–1951* (*Short Oxford History of the British Isles*) (Oxford: Oxford University Press).

Roberts, Clayton and David Roberts (2002) *A History of England, 1688 to the Present*, 4th edition (Englewood Cliffs, NJ: Prentice-Hall).

Roberts, Ken (2001) *Class in Modern Britain* (Basingstoke: Palgrave (now Palgrave Macmillan)).

Rootes, Christopher (2003) 'Britain', in Christopher Rootes (ed.) *Environmental Protest in Western Europe* (Oxford: Oxford University Press).

Rubinstein, W. D. (1998) *Britain's Century: A Political and Social History 1815–1905* (London: Edward Arnold).

Sanders, Andrew (2000) *The Short Oxford History of English Literature* (Oxford: Oxford University Press).

Sanders, David (1997) 'Voting and the Electorate', in Patrick Dunleavy, Andrew Gamble, Ian Holliday and Gillian Peele (eds) *Developments in British Politics 5* (Basingstoke: Macmillan (now Palgrave Macmillan)).

Savage, Stephen and Rob Atkinson (eds) (2001) *Public Policy Under Blair* (Basingstoke: Palgrave (now Palgrave Macmillan)).

Scammell, Margaret (2000) 'New Media, New Politics', in Patrick Dunleavy, Andrew Gamble, Ian Holliday and Gillian Peele (eds) *Developments in British Politics 6* (Basingstoke: Palgrave (now Palgrave Macmillan)).

Schama, Simon (2003) *A History of Britain, Vols 1–3* (London: BBC Books).

Shellard, Dominic (1999) *British Theatre since the War* (New Haven, CT: Yale University Press).

Simpson, Mark, Tracy Shildrick and Robert MacDonald (eds) (2006) *Drugs in Britain: Supply, Consumption and Control* (Basingstoke: Palgrave Macmillan).

Singer, Bennett (1999) *42 Up* (New York: New Press).

Sloan, Stanley R. (2005) *NATO, the European Union, and the Atlantic Community: The Transatlantic Bargain Reconsidered*, 2nd edition (Lanham, MD: Rowman & Littlefield).

Smith, Adam (1976) *An Inquiry into the Nature and Causes of the Wealth of Nations* (Oxford: Clarendon Press).

Smith, Martin J. (1999) *The Core Executive in Britain* (Basingstoke: Macmillan (now Palgrave Macmillan)).

Smith, Michael (2006) 'Britain, Europe and the World', in Patrick Dunleavy, Richard Heffernan, Philip Cowley and Colin Hay (eds) *Developments in British Politics 8* (Basingstoke: Palgrave Macmillan).

Soffe, Richard (ed.) (2003) *The Agricultural Notebook* (Oxford: Blackwell).

Soffe, Richard (ed.) (2005) *The Countryside Notebook* (Oxford: Blackwell).

Spear, Joanna (2000) 'Foreign and Defence Policy', in Patrick Dunleavy, Andrew Gamble, Ian Holliday and Gillian Peele (eds) *Developments in British Politics 6* (Basingstoke: Palgrave (now Palgrave Macmillan)).

Spencer, Colin (2002) *British Food: An Extraordinary Thousand Years of History* (London: Grub Street).

Stark, Steven D. (2006) *Meet The Beatles: A Cultural History of the Band that Shook Youth, Gender and the World* (New York: HarperCollins).

Street, Sarah (1997) *British National Cinema* (London: Routledge).

Talbot-Smith, Alison and Allyson M. Pollock (2006) *The New NHS: A Guide* (London: Routledge).

Tanner, Duncan (2002), 'Electing the Governors / the Governance of the Elect', in Keith Robbins (ed.) *The British Isles 1901–1951* (*The Short Oxford History of the British Isles*) (Oxford: Oxford University Press).

Taylor, Andrew (2005) *The NUM and British Politics* (Aldershot: Ashgate).

Temperton, Paul (2001) *The UK and the Euro* (London: John Wiley).

Thomas, Keith (1996) *Man and the Natural World: Changing Attitudes in England 1500–1800* (Oxford: Oxford University Press).

Thomas, Robert (1999) 'Law and Politics', in Ian Holliday, Andrew Gamble and Geraint Parry (eds) *Fundamentals in British Politics* (Basingstoke: Macmillan (now Palgrave Macmillan)).

Thompson, Edward (1966) *The Making of the English Working Class* (London: Random House).

Toghill, Peter (2004) *The Geology of Britain: An Introduction* (Marlborough: Airlife).

Turner, Arthur and D. A. Gowland (eds) (2000) *Britain and European Integration: Primary Sources Since 1945* (London: Routledge).

Turner, Graeme (2003) *British Cultural Studies: An Introduction*, 3rd edition (London: Routledge).

Walker, Alexander (2005) *Icons in the Fire: The Decline and Fall of Almost Everybody in the British Film Industry, 1984–2000* (London: Orion).

Walker, Alison, Chris Kershaw and Siân Nicholas (2006) *Crime in England and Wales 2005/06* (London: Home Office).

Wallace, Helen, William Wallace and Mark Pollack (eds) (2005) *Policy-Making in the European Union*, 5th edition (Oxford: Oxford University Press).

Wallace, Michael and J. Craig Jenkins (1995) 'The New Class, Postindustrialism and Neocorporatism: Three Images of Social Protest in the Western Democracies', in J. Craig Jenkins and Bert Klandermans (eds) *The Politics of Social Protest: Comparative Perceptions on States and Social Movements* (London: University College London Press).

Wallace, William and Tim Oliver (2005) 'A Bridge Too Far: The United Kingdom and the Transatlantic Relationship', in David M. Andrews (ed.) *The Atlantic Alliance Under Stress: US–European Relations After Iraq* (Cambridge: Cambridge University Press).

Watts, Duncan and Colin Pilkington (2005) *Britain in the European Union Today*, 3rd edition (Manchester: Manchester University Press).

Webster, Charles (2002) *The National Health Service: A Political History* (Oxford: Oxford University Press).

Weight, Richard (2003) *Patriots: National Identity in Britain 1940–2000* (London: Pan Books).

White, Brian (2001) *Understanding European Foreign Policy* (Basingstoke: Palgrave (now Palgrave Macmillan)).

Whiteley, Paul (2001) 'Turnout and Participation', in Pippa Norris (ed.) *Britain Votes 2001* (Oxford: Oxford University Press).

Winder, Robert (2004) *Bloody Foreigners: The Story of Immigration to Britain* (London: Little, Brown).

Woodhead, Chris (2002) *Class War: The State of British Education* (London: Little, Brown).

Woods, Michael (2005) *Contesting Rurality: Politics in the British Countryside* (Aldershot: Ashgate).

Worcester, Robert and Roger Mortimore (2001) *Explaining Labour's Second Landslide: Polls, Politics and Principles* (London: Politico's).

Young, Hugo (1990) *One of Us* (London: Pan Books).

Young, Hugo (1999) *This Blessed Plot: Britain and Europe from Churchill to Blair* (Basingstoke: Macmillan (now Palgrave Macmillan)).

Zurcher, Arnold J. (1958) *The Struggle to Unite Europe 1940–58* (New York: New York University Press).

Z/Yen Limited (2005) *The Competitive Position of London as a Global Financial Centre* (London: Z/Yen).

Index